The Early Church

The Christian Church to 325AD

Raymond
Banks

Colourpoint Educational

6 5 4 3 2

© Raymond Banks
2003

Designed by Colourpoint Books, Newtownards
Printed by The Universities Press (Belfast) Ltd

ISBN 1 904242 10 3

The author

Raymond Banks
Raymond Banks BD (Hons),
PGCE, is Head of Religious
Studies at Regent House
Grammar School,
Newtownards and has taught
Early Church History for ten
years.

Colourpoint Books
Colourpoint House
Jubilee Business Park
21 Jubilee Road
Newtownards
County Down
Northern Ireland
BT23 4YH
Tel: 028 9182 0505
Fax: 028 9182 1900
E-mail: info@colourpoint.co.uk
Web-site: www.colourpoint.co.uk

Cover picture: Origen. Christian writer and teacher. One
of the Greek Fathers of the Church. Engraving in Thevet's
Les Vrais Portraits et vies des hommes illustres.

All pictures are courtesy of Mary Evans Picture Library.

Contents

Author Preface

This text has been written specifically to assist teachers and students to meet the requirements of CCEA's* GCE Religious Studies AS and A2 courses on the Early Church. The first section of the book covers the AS course ('The Early Christian Church') and the remainder the A2 course ('The Development of the Christian Church in the Roman Empire to AD 325'). In each case the order of the chapters matches that of the topics listed in the relevant section of CCEA's Specification. This order, of course, is not prescriptive and teachers are therefore free to deal with the topics within each section in whatever order they choose. Several chapters include a section entitled 'The New Testament' which, while not specifically required by the Specification, is included to provide some idea of the beginnings from which later developments evolved.

The need for a working text for the classroom tailored specifically to the needs of these courses, both in their present form and previous life as the old A Level, has long been recognised by myself and others involved in the teaching and learning of them. No claim is made for originality. Rather, the book represents a collation of the work of many others before me, to whom I gladly acknowledge my debt, as well as my own understanding of the primary literature.

The abbreviation *ANE* will be found frequently in the following chapters and provides regular links to relevant primary sources collected in *A New Eusebius*, edited by J Stevenson and revised by WHC Frend (SPCK: London,1987). There is no substitute for familiarity with the early sources themselves, which students are advised to consult regularly.

Thanks are due to all at Colourpoint Books for their professional experience and expertise which have enabled a novice author to complete this book. Above all, I owe a special debt to my wife, Jennifer, whose word processing abilities saved me many hours of labour, and to my sons Christopher and Andrew for their patient acceptance of my preoccupation with finishing this project. To them I affectionately dedicate this book.

R Banks
October 2003

*Northern Ireland Council for the Curriculum, Examinations and Assessment.

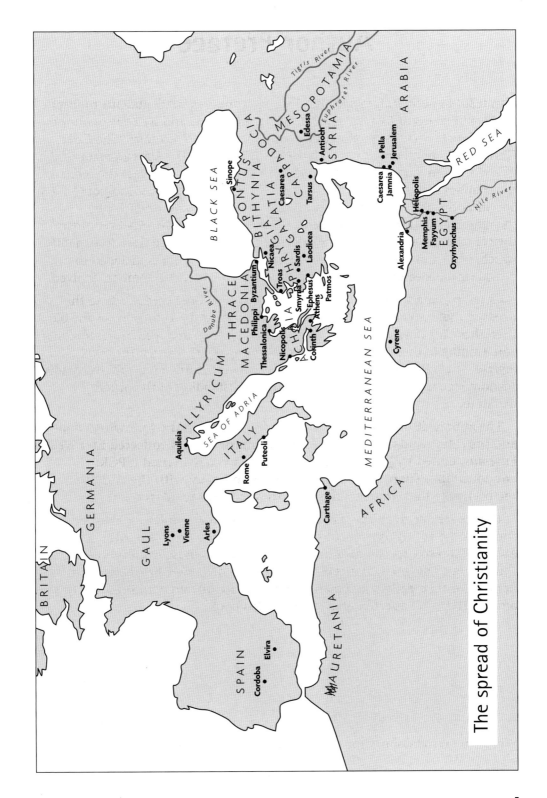

The spread of Christianity

Baptism

The doctrine and practice of baptism with particular reference to the writings of Justin, the Didache, Hippolytus, Tertullian and Cyprian.

(NICCEA Specification)

Definition

Christian baptism is the religious use of water as the sacrament or ceremony of initiation into the Christian Church. The 'doctrine' of baptism refers to teaching about the meaning and significance of baptism, how baptism is understood. The 'practice' of baptism refers to the administration of baptism, how baptism is performed.

Task

In your own words, explain the meaning of 'sacrament' and 'initiation'.

Objective

In this chapter we shall gain a knowledge and understanding of how the doctrine and practice of Christian baptism arose and developed in early Church history. We shall focus particularly on the Didache, Justin, Hippolytus, Tertullian and Cyprian.

BACKGROUND AND ORIGINS

BEFORE CHRISTIAN BAPTISM, WATER was used in various religious ceremonies, often in association with forgiveness, purity and life. The following have been suggested as possible backgrounds and contexts for the emergence of Christian baptism in the early Church:

(a) **The Old Testament** – Jewish priests were required to undergo ceremonial washings before performing their duties.

(b) **The Essenes** – these Jewish monks, who lived near the Dead Sea during the two centuries before Christ and in the first century of our era, practised daily ritual washings.

(c) **Jewish Proselyte Baptism** – Gentiles (non-Jews) who converted to Judaism were baptised, though it is not clear if this practice was in place before Christianity began.

(d) **John the Baptist** – at the beginning of the Gospels we read of John's baptising ministry in preparation for the coming of the Messiah. It is described as 'a baptism of repentance for the forgiveness of sins' (Mark 1: 4). The Gospels report that John baptised Jesus, who received the Holy Spirit on this occasion (Mark 1: 10).

(e) **Jesus** – according to John's Gospel, Jesus instructed his disciples to baptise during his ministry (3: 22; 4: 1, 2). Also, Matthew records that the resurrected Jesus instructed his apostles to make disciples of all nations, 'baptising them in the name of the Father and of the Son and of the Holy Spirit' (28: 19).

Early Christians may have taken over John the Baptist's practice of baptism. After the death and resurrection of Jesus it would have been given new meaning. Yet, whatever backgrounds may be found for the early Church's practice, Norbert Brox has stated: "... Christian baptism is something new, unprecedented, in the history of religion, though individual elements of the interpretation (like rebirth) also occur elsewhere."[1]

THE NEW TESTAMENT

According to the book of Acts, the first Christian baptism occurred on the Day of Pentecost, seven weeks after the death of Jesus. Peter tells concerned inquirers: "Repent and be baptised everyone of you in the name of Jesus Christ for the forgiveness of sins and you will receive the gift of the Holy

Read Acts 2: 38. Identify four ideas connected with baptism in this important baptismal text.

---

[1] Brox, Norbert *A History of the Early Church*, SCM: London, 1994, p94

Spirit." (Acts 2: 38).

Throughout the New Testament various religious concepts and spiritual benefits are associated with baptism, eg faith, union with Jesus' death and resurrection (only in Paul's writings), admission to the Church, salvation, commitment to God (Father, Son and Spirit). These are in addition to the baptismal associations noted above in Acts 2: 38.

In the New Testament we find that people were baptised as soon as they believed the Christian message, without going through a period of instruction beforehand. It has been argued that household baptisms, such as those in the book of Acts, may have included infants. Believers were immersed in water. The word 'baptise' is from the Greek, meaning 'dip, immerse', and in Paul's writings baptism symbolically represents dying and rising with Jesus. Baptism is 'in' or 'into' the name of Jesus (Acts) or the name of the Father and of the Son and of the Holy Spirit (Matthew). These phrases may be descriptions of the meaning of baptism, rather than words that were pronounced over the person being baptised. And it is possible that some confession or statement of faith was made by the person being baptised, eg 1 Peter 3: 21.

THE DIDACHE

The *Didache* is an early Christian book, usually included in the collection of early Christian writings known as the 'Apostolic Fathers'. It was written in the late first or early second century, possibly in Syria, and contains various instructions on baptism (see *A New Eusebius*, edited by J Stevenson and revised by WHC Frend, SPCK: London, 1987, excerpt 8 – hereafter *ANE*).

It seems that a period of preparation was required before the baptism. The moral teaching in the earlier part of the *Didache* had to be reviewed, and there was to be fasting by the one being baptised, the baptiser and 'any others who are able'.

As for the method or mode of baptism itself, immersion is preferred but pouring three times on the head is permitted. There is preference for running and cold water, though alternatives are also permitted. The baptism, as in Matthew, is in the threefold divine name, possibly spoken over the person being baptised. However, some believe that this 'trinitarian formula' was added to later copies of the *Didache* (and Matthew), which originally mentioned baptism in the name of Jesus only, as in the book of Acts. It has been suggested too that the practical instructions in the *Didache* reflect a time when baptism was becoming less an outdoor, missionary practice (immersion in cold, running water) and more an indoor practice (pouring, warm, 'other water').

In relation to the doctrine or understanding of baptism found in the *Didache* a number of points can be made. That baptism is to be performed in or into the threefold divine name would indicate that through baptism the person is committed to and belongs to the Father, the Son and the Holy Spirit. Also, the preference for 'living water' (usually translated 'running water') may be a reference to Jesus' use of these words for eternal life and the Holy Spirit (John 4: 10-13; 7: 37-39). Finally, it is stated that only the baptised may share in the Eucharist, which implies that baptism admits believers to full membership of the Church.

T a s k s

a. *Outline what the* Didache *has to say about the method of baptism.*

b. *What doctrine of baptism is found in the* Didache?

c. *The* Didache *has more baptismal regulations than the New Testament. Is this new emphasis on baptismal procedure a good development? Give reasons to support your answer.*

JUSTIN MARTYR

Justin was a Christian Apologist (see chapter on The Apologists). In his *First Apology*, written in Rome in the middle of the second century, he provides our earliest account of a baptismal service (*ANE* excerpt 39). We should not assume that he provides full details of the service nor that the account reflects baptismal practice in Rome alone.

Like the *Didache*, in Justin's account there is preparation for the baptism – a period of instruction, and prayer and fasting by the person to be baptised and by members of the church. The baptiser is said to pronounce the threefold divine name over the one being baptised, who makes a confession of his faith ('declared his assent'). The baptised are brought to the main congregation where prayers are offered. It has been suggested that in the prayers for the newly baptised we find a hint of Confirmation, that is, that prayer is made for the baptised that they might receive the Holy Spirit. However, this may be reading too much into the account. The baptised then exchange the kiss of fellowship with the other believers and receive their first Eucharist.

The doctrine of baptism in Justin's account is apparent in the following ways. Clearly, repentance, faith and commitment to Christian living are all required before baptism. Baptism in the threefold name provides forgiveness of sins, new birth and enlightenment. As with the *Didache*, baptism is the means of admission to full membership of the Church and participation in the Eucharist.

Tasks

a. Outline the practice and doctrine of baptism in Justin.

b. Why, do you think, would an outline of a baptismal service be included in an 'apology'?

HIPPOLYTUS

Hippolytus was a church leader in Rome in the early third century. In his book *Apostolic Tradition* there are instructions concerning baptism (*ANE* excerpt 121). It should be noted however that this book, in part or whole, may not actually have come from Hippolytus, and may have been written at a later time, possibly in the early fourth century.

Compared with the sources we have looked at so far, these baptismal instructions are clearly more detailed, and the service is more elaborate. We should note the following points:

- The period of preparation for baptism (the 'catechumenate') was normally three years long and involved teaching, prayer, examination and spiritual preparation.

- Those in occupations considered morally inconsistent with Christian standards could not be admitted to baptism.

- There is a preference for Easter baptisms, hinted at in the *Apostolic Tradition* and clear in Hippolytus' *Commentary on Daniel*. This may be the beginning of the recovery of Paul's idea of baptism as union with Jesus in his death and resurrection – hardly any writer before the fourth century mentions Paul's view of baptism.

- As the time drew near for the act of baptism the preparation became more intense, involving the performance of daily exorcisms. On the Thursday before the Easter Sunday baptism, the candidates bathe; on the Friday and Saturday they fast, and on the Saturday a final exorcism is performed by the bishop, followed by Bible reading and instruction.

- At dawn on the day of the baptism, Easter Sunday, prayer is said over the water. The water should be pure and flowing and will make direct contact with the naked bodies of the baptismal candidates.

- Children are baptised first and, if necessary, a family member can answer for them. Here, and in Tertullian, we have the first clear mention of infant baptism in our sources. Men are baptised next, followed by women whose hair must be loose and who must not wear any jewellery.

- The baptismal service included the rejection and exorcism of Satan and all evil spirits, the participation of three different types of church leader or official (a bishop, presbyters and deacons), the application of two different consecrated oils (exorcism and thanksgiving), and a triple interrogation followed by a triple response and a triple baptism, relating to the Father, the Son and the Holy Spirit.

- The newly baptised are brought to the church which they can now fully join.

- The bishop's hand is laid on them and he prays that they might receive God's Spirit or God's grace (depending on what text is read). The difference in these texts reflects different views about when the Spirit is received. In the third century, especially in the West, the gift of the Spirit was located not in baptism but in some later ceremony.

- The bishop then anoints the baptised with the holy oil of thanksgiving, this now being the second anointing after the baptism. This double post-baptismal anointing is found only in the Roman baptismal services.

- The newly baptised pray with the church, exchange the kiss of peace and share in their first Eucharist (as in the *Didache* and Justin).

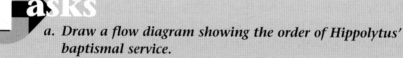

Tasks

a. *Draw a flow diagram showing the order of Hippolytus' baptismal service.*

b. *Identify the key words and acts which show Hippolytus' understanding of the meaning of baptism.*

TERTULLIAN

Tertullian lived in Carthage, North Africa, and wrote many Christian books around the beginning of the third century. While he does not provide an account of a baptismal service, he refers to baptism throughout his writings, especially in *On Baptism* (*ANE* excerpts 149-151).

It was his view that it would be appropriate for baptisms to be conducted at Passover (Easter), "for then was accomplished the Lord's passion, into which we were baptised", and after that Pentecost:

for during it our Lord's resurrection was several times made known among the disciples, and the grace of the Holy Spirit first given ... But every day is the

Lord's: any hour, any time is suitable for baptism.

(On Baptism, 19)

We have already noted the preference for Easter baptisms in Hippolytus, a contemporary of Tertullian, and the suggestion that this may reflect a recovery of Paul's distinctive view of baptism.

Preparation for baptism was required:

Those who are about to enter upon baptism must pray, with frequent prayers, fasts, kneelings, and all-night vigils, and with confession of all their past sins, that they might make a copy of John's baptism.

(On Baptism, 20)

While no specified period of time is given, there was probably a period of instruction ending with a final stage of intensive repentance, such as expressed in the passage just quoted.

The water too was prepared:

All waters, when God is called upon, acquire the sacramental power of sanctification; for immediately the Spirit comes down from heaven and stays upon the waters, sanctifying them by his own power; and they absorb the power of sanctifying ... Therefore when the waters have been as it were medicated by an angel's intervention, the spirit is in those waters physically washed, while the body in those same waters is spiritually cleansed.

(On Baptism, 4)

Tertullian sees the moving of the Spirit on the waters at the creation (Genesis 1: 2) as illustrative of baptism. The mention of an angel may refer to John 5: 4 (in some manuscripts). Tertullian appears to be the first writer to mention the idea of calling upon the Holy Spirit to come upon the water. It has been suggested that this new development was a result of a move from outdoor (rivers, lakes) to indoor (tanks, baths) baptism. While outdoor water was flowing and 'living', empowered by God's Spirit, indoor water was seen to lack this vitality. However, Tertullian states that because of the Spirit's presence "... it makes no difference whether a man be washed in sea, freshwater stream or spring, lake, or tub ..." (*On Baptism*, 4).

The bishop has the right to perform the baptism, but may delegate this right to presbyters and deacons. Even the laity (church members not holding office) may baptise, but women may not (*On Baptism*, 17).

As in Hippolytus there is a rejection of the devil just before the act of baptism:

When coming to the water we then and there, as also some time earlier in church under the bishop's control, affirm that we renounce the devil and his pomp and his angels.

(On the Crown, 3)

13

These words imply that the renunciation of the devil happened during preparation for baptism as well as immediately before the baptism itself. It may have been in the form of a declaration or in response to a question, as in Hippolytus' account.

Also like Hippolytus' account are the triple response and triple baptism, relating to the Father and the Son and the Holy Spirit. Tertullian writes, "We are three times immersed, making more extensive responses than those appointed by the Lord in the gospel." (*On the Crown*, 3), and "For not once only, but three times we are baptised into each of the three persons at each of the several names." (*Against Praxeas*, 26).

After the baptism, the candidates are anointed with oil: "... we come up from the washing and are anointed with consecrated oil." (*On Baptism*, 7). Tertullian links this with the anointing of Old Testament priests and the anointing of Jesus with the Spirit. The baptised also receive the sign of the cross to protect their souls from evil. This post-baptismal anointing reminds us of Hippolytus, as does the post-baptismal laying on of hands also mentioned in Tertullian: "Next the hand is laid upon us, inviting and welcoming the Holy Spirit through the act of blessing." (*On Baptism*, 8).

In Tertullian, the Spirit is not given through baptism, which rather makes the baptised ready for the later gift of the Spirit, by the washing away of sins. Yet, in *Against Marcion,* Tertullian states that the Spirit is attained through baptism. As in the other sources we have considered, the baptised are welcomed into the church and receive their first Eucharist: "Then we are made welcome and partake of a mixture of milk and honey. And for a week from that day we abstain from our daily washings." (*On the Crown*, 3).

Tertullian refers to infant baptism, but only to disapprove of it. He, along with Hippolytus, provides us with the first clear references to the practice. Tertullian argued for delaying baptism depending on the state and character of each person, especially in the case of infants: "... let them become Christians when they are able to know Christ. Why does the age of innocence rush to the forgiveness of sins?" (*On Baptism*, 18). This is influenced by Tertullian's view of the seriousness of post-baptismal sin, which led him to argue for the delay of baptism in the case of virgins and widows also. He also rejected baptisms performed by heretics. Concerning heretics he wrote, "... they and we have not the same God, or the same Christ, nor one baptism ..." (*On Baptism*, 15).

Tertullian stressed the importance of repentance and faith, of which baptism was the seal (*On Repentance*, 6). Baptism is effective because of the death and resurrection of Jesus (*On Baptism*, 11), providing forgiveness of sins, deliverance from death, rebirth, the Holy Spirit (all in *Against Marcion* 1.28) and, as we have already noted, admission to the Church and its Eucharist.

Tasks

a. *What did Tertullian say about the appropriate time for baptism?*

b. *Outline what Tertullian said about the preparation of (i) the baptismal candidates and (ii) the baptismal water.*

c. *Summarise Tertullian's views concerning who should administer baptism.*

d. *In Tertullian what happened before, during and after baptism?*

e. *Comment on the view that with Tertullian's reference to the Spirit giving power to the water, we come across for the first time an almost magical or mystical idea of baptism.*

f. *Was Tertullian right to object to the baptism of infants? Give reasons to support your answer.*

CYPRIAN

Cyprian was bishop of Carthage, North Africa, in the middle of the third century. His views on baptism are found in various letters/epistles that he wrote beginning around the time of the persecution by the emperor Decius (*ANE* excerpts 212-216).

Unlike Tertullian, who lived and wrote in the same area fifty years before, Cyprian approved of the baptism of infants:

If forgiveness of sins is given even to the worst offenders, and to those who have previously committed many sins against God, when they later believed, and if no one is excluded from baptism and grace, how much less should an infant be excluded, who being newly born has committed no sin, except that being physically born of Adam's line he has at his first birth contracted the disease of the ancient death? Indeed the infant's approach to receive forgiveness of sins is the easier from the very fact that the sins forgiven are another's, not his own.

(Epistle 64. 5)

In this letter Cyprian states that the crying of infants can be taken as their request to be baptised, and that there was no need to wait until the infant's eighth day for baptism, as was the case for circumcision.

He insisted too that baptism must be performed in the name of the three divine persons, and not in the name of Jesus only. While immersion was the proper mode of baptism, individuals could be sprinkled with water if this was necessary, for example, in the case of illness. Through baptism the baptised receive forgiveness of sins and rebirth, while the devil is driven out.

In Cyprian we find contradictory views on when the Spirit is received. On the one hand, "It is through baptism that the Holy Spirit is received ..." (Epistle 62. 8). And yet Cyprian also writes: "A man is not born by laying on of the hand, when he receives the Holy Spirit, but in baptism. Thus he is born first and then receives the Holy Spirit" (Epistle 74. 7). Cyprian then immediately compares this with Adam, who was made first and after had the breath of life breathed into him. Also, referring to how the Spirit came upon previously baptised believers through the laying on of apostolic hands (Acts 8), Cyprian states:

The same practice is followed among us now; those baptised in the church are brought to the officers of the church and by our prayer and laying on of the hand they acquire the Holy Spirit and are made perfect by the seal of the Lord.

(Epistle 73. 9)

Cyprian also applies Jesus' words about being born again of water and the Spirit (John 3: 5) to 'both sacraments', that is, to baptism and the laying on of hands which follows (Epistle 62. 1). The baptised person is also anointed, receiving the 'chrism', that he may be God's anointed and have Christ's grace (Epistle 64.5). And those who have been baptised and have received the Spirit "are admitted to drink the cup of the Lord." (Epistle 62. 8). Thus, as with our other sources, baptism brings a person into the full eucharistic fellowship of the Church.

Like Tertullian before him, Cyprian rejected heretical baptism, baptism performed by those outside the one true Church. There is one baptism and, "... that one baptism is in the catholic Church. And if there is one Church, there can be no baptism outside it." (Epistle 71. 1). Therefore, "Our assertion is that those who come to us from heresy are baptised by us, not re-baptised." (Epistle 71. 1). However, Stephen, the bishop of Rome, took a different view to Carthage on this matter and accepted heretical baptism as valid, as long as it had been properly administered. Cyprian stated that his position was no recent innovation, having been approved by a large number of bishops in Carthage some time before (AD215-17). Cyprian rejected the idea that the baptised's faith is all that matters, rather than that of the baptiser. The content of the faith that a person is being baptised into is important. If it is the faith of heretics and schismatics such as Marcion or Novatian, then the baptism is not valid or effective. The heretics do not have the Church, nor the Spirit, nor grace among them.

Tasks

a. Outline Cyprian's views on baptismal practice.

b. Summarise Cyprian's teaching concerning (i) infant baptism (ii) heretical baptism and (iii) the Spirit and baptism.

c. In your view, was Cyprian or Stephen right? What makes a baptism a valid or proper baptism? To what extent should this depend on the beliefs of the baptiser and the baptised, and on the method and form of administration?

What implications does this have for inter-Church relations?

THE DEVELOPMENT OF BAPTISM

The study of our sources in their historical order has shown that the doctrine and practice of baptism evolved during the history of the early Church. Beginning with relative simplicity in the earliest sources we can trace a tendency to ever increasing complexity, regulation and ceremonialism.

To be more specific, as Bridge and Phypers concluded:

Compared with the New Testament itself, accounts of baptism in the early church show three areas of development: the extent of baptismal preparation, the way the rite is administered, and the way the rite is understood.[1]

(*The Water that Divides, page 58*)

Baptismal preparation

In the New Testament there was little or no preparation and, according to the book of Acts, converts were baptised on the spot, as soon as they believed.

Then in the *Didache* and Justin, we read of an unspecified period of instruction, fasting and prayer which was not just for the baptismal candidates. By the time of Hippolytus we find that preparation for baptism has become formalised into the catechumenate – a long period, normally three years, of intensive moral, spiritual, and doctrinal probation.

---

[1] Bridge, Donald and Phypers, David *The Water that Divides*, Mentor/Christian Focus Publications: Fearn, 1998, p58

Some have regarded this gradual change as a necessary development. For instance Garret says:

> *Though the elaboration was a departure from apostolic simplicity, the increased length of the catechumenate and the greater thoroughness of instruction was a necessary development. In New Testament times the urgency of the expectation of the end of the age had led the early evangelists to baptise with only a minimum of preparation. Now the very length and complexity of Christian initiation helped to stress its overriding importance in the life of the Church, as did also the fact that it was presided over by the Bishop as chief pastor of the Church.[1]*

(Christian Worship, page 25)

It is argued that the rapid growth of the Church required careful baptismal preparation to ensure that conversion from paganism was genuine, before full admission to the Church was granted. However, others would favour the immediacy and simplicity of the apostolic practice recorded in the foundational and authoritative writings of the Church. When infant baptism eventually became the normal practice then, of course, pre-baptismal instruction ceased.

Baptismal administration

The baptismal service and the act of baptism became increasingly complex as well. In the New Testament, the *Didache*, and Justin, as far as we can tell, baptism is a relatively straightforward matter, although with the *Didache* we see the beginnings of the regulation of baptism. Baptism was performed in the threefold divine name on confession of one's faith. When we come to Hippolytus and Tertullian baptismal services are much more elaborate, involving exorcisms, renunciations of the devil, anointings, participation by various church officials, invocation of the Spirit upon the water, and laying on of the bishop's hand.

There is a growing formalism (concern with proper order), institutionalism (fixed organisation), clericalism (emphasis on church officials), and ritualism (focus on the sacramental ceremony). Some feel that these were positive developments because they underlined the importance and seriousness of baptism, and reflected the growing significance of Christianity in wider society. Others regard such trends as an unfortunate shift of emphasis, moving the focus from the personal faith and commitment of the baptised to external and mechanical rituals.

---

[1] Garret TS *Christian Worship*, OUP: London, 1963, p25

Baptismal understanding

In relation to the doctrine or theology of baptism, our sources reveal that from the beginning baptism has been associated with forgiveness of sins, rebirth (regeneration), and admission to full eucharistic fellowship in the Church. In the later sources we find that renunciation of the devil and exorcism are also related to baptism. With the progress of time and the growth of the Church, debate arose over infant and heretical baptism. Eventually doctrinal support was provided for the practice of infant baptism in Cyprian's connection of it with original sin from Adam. A growing belief that God's grace and salvation were mediated only through the one catholic or universal Church, and its ministers and sacraments, ensured the rejection of baptisms conducted by heretics. Our sources also show differences of opinion over whether the Spirit is given through baptism. From the third century on, as we have noted, the gift of the Spirit came to be connected with post-baptismal rites such as the laying on of the bishop's hand, especially when infant baptism became the normal practice.

Task

Draw a table showing the main similarities and differences in our sources relating to the doctrine and practice of baptism.

Practice Essay Title

Outline your knowledge and understanding of the development of the practice of baptism in the early Church. (30)

Assess the view that the early Church did not have a consistent understanding of baptism. (15)

AS level **The Eucharist**

The doctrine and practice of the Eucharist with particular reference to the writings of Justin, the Didache, Hippolytus, Tertullian and Cyprian.

(NICCEA Specification)

Definition

Eucharist (Greek for 'thanksgiving') became the usual term in the early Church for the sacrament or ceremony in which bread and wine are used to recall Jesus' death. The 'doctrine' of the Eucharist refers to teaching about the meaning and significance of the Eucharist, how the Eucharist is understood. The 'practice' of the Eucharist refers to the administration of the Eucharist, how the Eucharist is observed.

Objective

In this chapter we shall gain a knowledge and understanding of how the doctrine and practice of the Eucharist arose and developed in early Church history. We shall focus particularly on the Didache, Justin, Hippolytus, Tertullian and Cyprian.

THE NEW TESTAMENT

IN THE NEW TESTAMENT Paul uses the terms 'communion' (1 Cor 10: 16; King James Version), 'the Lord's table' (1 Cor 10: 21) and 'the Lord's Supper' (1 Cor 11: 20) to refer to what later became known as the Eucharist. In the book of Acts it is called 'the breaking of bread' (eg Acts 2: 42, 46; 20: 7), though it may be that this refers to a fellowship meal rather than the Eucharist. The Eucharist

An *Agape* or 'love feast' of the first Christians.

Jeanron, in Clavel, *Histoire des Religions*, Vol 2

has its origins in Jesus' Last Supper, of which the New Testament provides four accounts (Matthew 26: 26-29; Mark 14: 22-25; Luke 22: 15-20; 1 Cor 11: 23-26). In the first three Gospels Jesus' Last Supper is presented as a Jewish Passover meal when Jews recall their salvation from God's judgement by the blood of lambs and their deliverance from slavery in Egypt. Jesus gave new meaning to the Passover bread and cup by relating them to his body and blood, the sacrifice of which introduce the new covenant and the forgiveness of sins. He also instructed his disciples to take the bread and wine to remember him.

A 'sevenfold shape' has been identified in the accounts of the Last Supper and other meals in the New Testament, which reflects the pattern of formal Jewish meals generally: Jesus (1) took bread, (2) blessed/thanked God, (3) broke the bread, (4) distributed it; and after the meal (5) took a cup of wine, (6) blessed/thanked God, and (7) distributed it. It may be that the institution of the Eucharist in the words and acts of Jesus are recorded as a pattern for first century churches to follow, and that the accounts themselves reflect the eucharistic liturgies (forms of worship) of these churches.

It appears that at first the early Christians observed the Eucharist as part of a fellowship meal or 'love feast' (called the *agape*: Jude 12). Paul rebuked the Corinthian church for its abuse of this combined Eucharist and fellowship meal (1 Cor 11: 17-34). We have no details about the practical observance of the Eucharist in the New Testament, though there is a reference to one loaf symbolising the unity of the Church (1 Cor 10: 17), and it has been inferred from Acts 20: 7 that it was customary to observe the Eucharist each Sunday (but see also Acts 2: 46; assuming that these are references to the Eucharist). Also, since eucharistic services of the second and third centuries are all similar to the form of first century Jewish synagogue services, it may be that there was to some degree a set pattern of eucharistic service in earliest Church history.

As for the eucharistic elements themselves, there is debate whether the New Testament writers had a merely symbolic view of the bread and wine or a realistic view of the elements as in some sense the actual body and blood of Jesus. Finally, there is no evidence that the Eucharist was regarded as a sacrifice for sins.

Task

Compare the similarities and differences between the four New Testament accounts of the Eucharist (see the references above).

THE DIDACHE

The *Didache*, written in the late first or early second century, contains two passages relevant to our study (*Didache* 9-10; 14; *ANE* excerpt 8).

There is uncertainty about whether the first passage (*Didache* 9-10) concerns the Eucharist or the love feast or a combination of both. If it refers to the Eucharist, why is there no mention of the Last Supper or the death of Jesus? If it refers only to the love feast, would the unbaptised be excluded and would the food and drink be described as 'holy' and 'spiritual'? The order of the service, however, is clear enough. There is thanksgiving first for the cup (unusually; but see Luke 22: 17-20); then for the bread. The meal itself is next, followed by thanksgiving to the Father, prayer for the Church, and finally a request for the Lord's return (using an Aramaic expression that we find also in Paul: 1 Cor 16: 22). There is a notable emphasis on thanksgiving, a regular theme in the account. Emphasis is also placed on the unity and future hope of the Church. These themes and the Jewish flavour of the passage (eg David, Hosanna, Maranatha) point to the primitive or early nature of this account. If indeed the passage is about the Eucharist we note that it is specifically for the baptised alone. The author uses words of Jesus to support his point (Matthew 7: 6). Also, the bread and wine are 'holy' and 'spiritual'.

The second passage from the *Didache* is clearly about the Eucharist:

On the Lord's own day come together and break bread and give thanks, having first confessed your sins, so that your sacrifice may be pure. But let no one who has a dispute with a companion join with you until they are reconciled, so that your sacrifice may not be defiled. For this is the sacrifice spoken about by the Lord, 'In every place and at every time offer me a pure sacrifice, for I am a great king, says the Lord, and my name is wonderful among the nations.'

(Didache 14)

Here the Eucharist is to be on 'the Lord's own day', probably Sunday or possibly Easter. From the beginning Sunday ('the first day of the week'), the day of Jesus' resurrection, was an important day for Christian worship and fellowship (compare this passage with Acts 20: 7). We may note again the importance of thanksgiving. Confession of sin and reconciliation with other Christians is also required to ensure the purity of the sacrifice being offered to God (as in Matthew 5: 23, 24). The Eucharist is called a sacrifice more than once in this brief passage and, as was quite common in the early Church, is regarded as the fulfilment of Malachi 1: 11. For the Church to be accepted as a legitimate religion at this time it was essential for it to have sacrifices. However, the Eucharist was a sacrifice in the sense of a thank-offering, rather than an atonement for sin or an appeasement of God as in Judaism or paganism.

asks

> a. *Draw a table showing reasons for and against treating* Didache *9-10 as a passage about the Eucharist.*
>
> b. *Outline the doctrine and practice of the Eucharist in the* Didache.
>
> c. *Discuss the view that it is misleading for sources such as the* Didache *to refer to the Eucharist as a sacrifice.*

JUSTIN MARTYR

Justin was a Christian Apologist (see chapter on The Apologists). He wrote in Rome in the middle of the second century and in his *First Apology* we have two important passages about the Eucharist.

The first passage concerns the first Eucharist of the newly baptised (*Apology* 1. 65,66; *ANE* excerpt 39).

He also provides an account of the weekly Eucharist held each Sunday:

And on the day which is called the Sun's Day an assembly is held of all who live in town or country, and the memoirs of the apostles or the writings of the prophets are read, as long as time allows.When the reader has finished, the president in a discourse admonishes and exhorts us to imitate these good things. Then we all stand up together and offer prayers; and, as I said before, when we have finished praying, bread and wine mixed with water are brought, and the president similarly offers prayers and thanksgivings to the best of his ability, and the people express their assent with 'Amen'. Then follows the distribution of the things over which thanks have been offered and everyone partakes of them; and they are sent to those who are not present by the deacons.

(Apology 1. 67)

Justin then explains that a voluntary collection is taken which is distributed by the president to the needy. Justin also states that Christians assemble on Sunday because it was the first day of creation and the day of Jesus' resurrection when he appeared to his apostles and taught them the things which Justin is now passing on.

Here we have the earliest outline of a eucharistic service. Combining the two accounts above we get the following picture. The Sunday meeting included readings from the Gospels and the prophets, followed by a sermon given by 'the president' (or 'that one who was presiding'), who is someone other than the reader. The congregation stands for prayers and, in the account of the baptismal eucharist, greet each other with a kiss. Bread and a cup of wine mixed with water are brought to the president who gives praise and thanks for the elements ('to the best of his ability' and 'at some length') to the Father through the Son and the Holy Spirit. The congregation affirm their agreement by saying 'Amen'. Deacons distribute the elements to those present and later to absentees. A voluntary collection is taken and later distributed by the president to the needy.

The following points may be noted in Justin's references to the Eucharist:

a) Thanksgiving is important in both accounts (as in the New Testament and the *Didache*). Elsewhere he says, '... the bread of the eucharist' was 'handed down to us ... in order that we might give thanks to God ...' (*Dialogue* 41.1).

b) The Eucharist was only for baptised believers who lived in accordance with Christ's directions.

c) There is no mention of the love feast which we read about in the New Testament and which continued for several centuries. Rather, we read simply of the actions relating to the eucharistic bread and wine. Now that there is no meal separating the bread and the wine (as there was in the New Testament), the prayer of thanksgiving is said over the elements together.

d) The service itself (readings, preaching, prayers) seems to be a Christian form of Jewish services in the synagogue. A similar situation is found in the New Testament (eg Acts 20: 7-12; 1 Cor 14: 26).

e) There is a mixture of formality and informality. As well as a general order of service we find that the readings are 'as long as time allows' and that the president gives thanks 'to the best of his ability', rather than repeating set prayers.

f) There is an emphasis on the unity and fellowship of the Church. An assembly of 'all who live in town or country' is held in one place; 'all stand up together and offer prayers'; they greet each other with a kiss; at the end of the eucharistic prayer 'all the people present' respond with 'Amen'; everyone partakes of the elements, which are also brought to absentees; and there is a collection for the needy.

g) The Eucharist is regarded as a sacrifice, in fulfilment of Malachi 1: 11 (*Dialogue* 117.3; as in the *Didache*). But a little earlier Justin writes that 'prayers and thanksgivings made by worthy men are the only sacrifices that are perfect and well pleasing to God.' (*Dialogue*, 117. 2). Thus, as in the New Testament and the *Didache,* there is no suggestion that the Eucharist is a sacrifice for sins, but rather a thank offering to God.

h) The bread and wine are not 'ordinary' or 'common' food and drink – 'the food over which thanks has been given ... is the flesh and blood of that Jesus who was made flesh.' Depending on how Justin's words are translated, the elements become the flesh and blood of Jesus through prayer, as Jesus prayed at the institution of the Eucharist ('through the prayer of the word which we have from him'), or, through the activity of the Word (Jesus) upon the elements ('through the prayer of the Word who is from him' ie God the Father). Like Ignatius, bishop of Antioch, before him (early second century), Justin's realistic view of the eucharistic bread and wine may have been a useful weapon against Gnosticism's denial of Jesus' real humanity (see chapter on Heresy).

Tasks

a. Explain the setting of Justin's two main accounts of the Eucharist.

b. Describe the eucharistic service in Justin by combining these accounts.

c. Outline Justin's understanding of the significance of the Eucharist.

d. Is Justin's realistic understanding of the bread and wine as the body and blood of Jesus based on apostolic understanding of the Eucharist? Consider the possible relevance of the following New Testament references: Matthew 26: 26, 28, 29; John 6: 48-63; 1 Corinthians 10: 16; 11: 27-29.

HIPPOLYTUS

Hippolytus was a church leader in Rome in the early third century. In his book *Apostolic Tradition* there are two accounts of the Eucharist, one relating to the ordination of a bishop and another for the newly baptised. However, there are doubts about the origin, date and authorship of this book.

First, after the ordination of a bishop, the deacons present the bread and wine ('the offering') to him and he, along with all the presbyters, lays hands over the offering, and gives thanks:

Bishop: "The Lord be with you"

People: "And with your spirit."

Bishop: "Lift up your hearts."

People: "We lift them up to the Lord."

Bishop: "Let us give thanks to the Lord."

People: "It is right and proper."

Bishop: "We give thanks to you, O God, through your beloved child Jesus Christ, whom in the last times you sent as Saviour, Redeemer and Messenger of your will; who is your inseparable Word, through whom you made all things, and in whom you were well pleased. You sent him down from heaven into the womb of a virgin; and having been conceived he was made flesh and was shown to be your Son, born of the Holy Spirit and the virgin. Fulfiling your will and acquiring for you a holy people, he stretched out his hands as he suffered that he might free from suffering those who trust in you.

And when he was betrayed to voluntary suffering in order to destroy death, and break the chains of the devil, and tread down hell, and give light to the righteous, and fix a term, and reveal the resurrection, he took bread and gave thanks to you saying, 'Take, eat; this is my body, which will be broken for you.' In the same way also, the cup, saying, 'This is my blood, which is poured out for you; when you do this you make my remembrance.' Remembering therefore his death and resurrection, we offer to you the bread and the cup, giving thanks to you for counting us worthy to stand before you and minister to you. And we ask you to send your Holy Spirit upon the offering of your holy Church; that gathering them into one, you would grant to all who partake of the holy things that they may be filled with the Holy Spirit for the strengthening of faith in truth, in order that we may praise and glorify you through your child Jesus Christ, through whom be glory and honour to you, with the Holy Spirit, in your holy Church, both now and throughout all ages. Amen.

(Apostolic Tradition 4)

In the following passage from the *Apostolic Tradition* we read of the first Eucharist of the newly baptised:

Then the offering shall be presented by the deacons to the bishop; and he shall give thanks over the bread for the representation (which the Greeks call 'antitype') of the body of Christ; and over the cup mixed with wine for the antitype (which the Greeks call 'likeness') of the blood that was poured out for all who have believed in him; and over milk and honey mixed together in fulfilment of the promise which was made to the fathers, in which he said, 'A land flowing with milk and honey' ... and over water too, as an offering signifying the washing, that the inner man, the spiritual man, may receive as well as the body ... And when he breaks the bread, in distributing fragments to each, he shall say: The bread of Heaven in Christ Jesus. And he who receives shall answer: Amen.

And if there are not enough presbyters, the deacons too shall hold the cups, and stand by in good order and reverence: first the one who holds the water; second, the milk; third, the wine. And those who receive shall taste of each three times, he who gives it saying: In God the Father almighty. And he who receives shall say: Amen. And in the Lord Jesus Christ. Amen. And in the Holy Spirit and the holy Church. And he shall say: Amen: So shall it be done with each one.

When these things have been done, each one shall hasten to do good deeds and to please God and to conduct himself rightly, being zealous for the Church, putting into practice what he has learned and progressing in devotion.

(Apostolic Tradition 33)

Compared with our earlier sources these passages reveal a growing formality and complexity in eucharistic services, even if some of the details were added later, after Hippolytus' time.

In the account of the ordination Eucharist we have one of the earliest examples of a eucharistic prayer. Hippolytus stated that the bishop was not required to follow its exact wording, rather, each man should pray according to his own ability. Nevertheless, a general pattern is provided so that we have here a transition from earlier, more informal services to the increasingly fixed forms of later times. The prayer begins and continues with an emphasis on thanksgiving noted in earlier sources, the focus of the gratitude centring on the incarnation and redemptive sufferings of God's Son, with only a fleeting reference to creation. There then follows the words of institution from the Last Supper. Since the narrative of institution began to appear in eucharistic prayers from around the middle of the fourth century, it may be that this section was added to the text about this time. If it is original, we have a direct link with the Last Supper.

Then follows the *anamnesis* (commemoration) of Jesus' death and resurrection and the offering of the elements to God. As in the previous sources, the Eucharist is seen as a thank-offering rather than an atonement for sins. However, some have understood the words, 'when you do this you make my remembrance' to mean that the Eucharist was a reminder to God of Jesus' sacrifice on the communicant's behalf. We read also, for the first time in our sources, of the 'epiclesis' – 'calling upon' God to send his Holy Spirit upon the offering and that those who partake might be filled with the Spirit. This may be a later addition, though there is no reference to the Spirit consecrating or transforming the elements, as in later texts; rather the emphasis is on the reception of the Spirit by the Church in its eucharistic worship.

The bread and wine are 'holy'. Indeed, Hippolytus urged that care be taken lest the unbaptised or an animal should consume the body and blood of Christ. None of the elements should fall or be spilt (*Apostolic Tradition* 32). Though, in the account of the baptismal Eucharist above we can see that Hippolytus regarded the elements symbolically too, as antitypes and representations of Christ's body and blood.

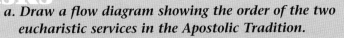

a. Draw a flow diagram showing the order of the two eucharistic services in the Apostolic Tradition.

b. Discuss the doctrine of the Eucharist found in the Apostolic Tradition.

TERTULLIAN

Tertullian (Carthage, North Africa, around the beginning of the third century) does not provide an account of a eucharistic service, but refers to the Eucharist in several of his writings (eg *ANE* excerpt 149).

Tertullian tells us little about the practical administration of the Eucharist. He writes: 'We take also, in meetings before daybreak, and only from the hand of the presidents, the sacrament of the Eucharist'. (*On the Crown*, 3). There may be evidence of a daily Eucharist in Tertullian's complaint against those who abuse the Eucharist by offering violence to the Lord's body 'every day' (*On Idolatry*, 7). However, it is likely that this expression should be taken rhetorically to mean 'repeatedly'. Also, Tertullian may refer to the practice of taking the eucharistic bread home for private consumption when he writes, "Your husband will not know what it is you taste secretly before you partake of food." (*To My Wife*, 2. 5; he also refers to the Lord's body being 'reserved' in *On Prayer*, 19).

In Tertullian's doctrine of the Eucharist we see that he had a 'realistic' understanding of the bread and wine – they were the body and blood of Jesus. So we read: 'The flesh feeds on the body and blood of Christ so that the soul may be fattened on God.' (*On the Resurrection of the Flesh*, 8). He also writes: '... his body is acknowledged as being in the bread: "This is my body."' (*On Prayer*, 6) and that Christians 'touch the Lord's body' with their hands in the Eucharist (*On Idolatry*, 7). Mention is made too of the care that is taken to prevent any of the bread and wine being dropped (*On the Crown*, 3). Yet, a symbolic view of the Eucharist is found in his *Against Marcion*. He explains 'This is my body' by adding, '... that is, the symbol of my body ... (4.40), and says that the bread 'represents' the Lord's body (1.14). However, in Tertullian's time it was generally understood that there was a close association between a symbol and what it symbolised. Also, 'represents' probably means 'makes present' as it does in other places in Tertullian. As well as a realistic view of the elements, we may note too that Tertullian had a sacrificial understanding of the Eucharist. In *On Prayer* (19) he refers to the Eucharist as a 'sacrifice' and the table as 'God's altar'.

Finally, in his *Apology* (39. 16-19) Tertullian describes a non-eucharistic love feast (*agape*; see above under New Testament).

CYPRIAN

The views of Cyprian (bishop of Carthage, North Africa, in the middle of the third century) on the Eucharist are found in various letters (epistles) that he wrote around the time of the persecution by the emperor Decius.

The following information regarding the practice of the Eucharist can be gleaned from Cyprian's letters. A possible reference to daily observance of the Eucharist may be found in Cyprian's statement concerning those who drank the cup of Christ's blood daily. Against the Aquarians who used water only in the eucharistic cup, Cyprian insisted on the use of both water and wine mixed together, since the Lord himself took a cup in which was mingled both wine and water. Without wine the Lord's example is not followed, nor is his blood signified; and the communicants are dissociated from Christ. Without water the blood of Christ is dissociated from the communicants. Both wine and water mixed unite Christ and the communicants. Deacons distribute the elements to the communicants, who must be baptised before they can partake. Cyprian appears to refer to the practice of infant communion when he relates that an infant who had been involved in idolatry instinctively refused the Eucharist, and vomited when a deacon forced her to partake. The importance of worthy participation of the Eucharist is underlined by Cyprian in his reference to Paul's teaching on the matter (1 Corinthians 11: 27). Cyprian also recounts stories of what happened to unworthy participants, eg the elements went on fire or became a cinder in the communicant's hands!

Cyprian's eucharistic realism is clear when he writes about approaching the holy table to touch the body and blood of the Lord, and when he states that communicants are fortified with Christ's body and blood. Cyprian also regarded the Eucharist as a sacrifice:

For if Jesus Christ, our Lord and God, is himself the high priest of God the Father, and has first offered himself as a sacrifice to the Father, and has commanded this to be done in remembrance of himself, then certainly that priest acts truly in Christ's place, when he imitates what Christ did, and he offers then a true and complete sacrifice to God the Father, if he begins to offer as he sees Christ himself has offered.

(Letter 63. 14)

A close comparison is made here between Christ's sacrifice and the priest's (ie the bishop's) actions in the Eucharist. This may mean that in the Eucharist Christ is sacrificed again to God. Indeed, a little later Cyprian writes: 'Since we make mention of his passion in all our sacrifices, for the passion is the Lord's sacrifice which we offer, we ought to do nothing other than he did [at the Last Supper].' (Letter 63: 17). However, Cyprian's words may be read less literally – as Christ offered himself as a sacrifice, so too does the bishop offer a sacrifice in memory of him. The context of Cyprian's words must be kept in mind – the cup must contain water and wine since, according to Cyprian, it did so at the Last Supper. Whatever view we take, it is clear that Cyprian at least provided the basis for the later understanding of the Eucharist as an atoning sacrifice which pardons sin and removes God's judgement.

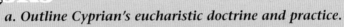

a. Outline Cyprian's eucharistic doctrine and practice.

b. Comment on the claim that Cyprian's accounts of what happened to unworthy communicants reveal a superstitious or magical view of the eucharistic elements.

THE DEVELOPMENT OF THE EUCHARIST

As with our investigation of baptism, the study of our sources in historical sequence has shown that the doctrine and practice of the Eucharist evolved in the direction of greater complexity during early Church history. The earliest sources reveal the emphases of the Jewish origins of the meal, with the stress being put on thanksgiving, commemoration and fellowship. Compared with these earlier sources there is a noticeable trend in later sources towards formalism and regulation (eg Hippolytus) and signs of development in the theological understanding of the Eucharist (eg Cyprian). However, in addition to the emphases of the earlier sources that we have just mentioned, we have seen that the early Fathers generally viewed the Eucharist sacramentally (God's blessing and grace were imparted to the communicant), realistically (the bread and wine were the actual body and blood of Christ), and sacrificially (the bread and wine are offered to God – Cyprian may imply that this was a repetition of Christ's atoning sacrifice). Initially there would have been local variation in approach and emphasis, in different regions under different bishops, before a more uniform practice and theology emerged.

In his book *The Lord's Supper*[1] William Barclay detects three 'movements' in the development of the Eucharist in Church history, the beginnings of which are apparent in the early centuries of the Church. Firstly, there was a movement from the house to the Church – what began as a family (Passover) or fellowship (love feast) meal in a private house eventually took on a new character in the more formal and liturgical surroundings of the Church building. Secondly, arising from this, there was a movement from a real meal to a symbolic meal. Thirdly, there was a movement 'from bare simplicity to elaborate splendour'. The simplicity of the earliest sources gave way to a growing liturgical complexity and formalism. Barclay finds the causes of this last development in the move from the private home to the Church building, an emphasis on the sacraments at the expense of preaching, the developing idea of the conversion of the elements into the Lord's body and blood, a change of emphasis from the language of devotion to the language of theology, and, a move from lay to exclusively priestly celebration of the Eucharist. The last development may be hinted at in Justin (see earlier) but is very clear as early as Ignatius, bishop of Antioch, in the early second century: 'Let that be regarded as a valid Eucharist which is celebrated by the bishop, or by one whom he appoints ...' (*To the Smyrnaeans* 8.1).

Many today, particularly in the Protestant Free Church tradition, would call for a return to the simplicity and directness of the eucharistic practice and theology of the New Testament and other early sources. The earliest Christians assembled on Sunday to hear the Scriptures read and to remember with thankfulness the sacrificial death of Jesus, through which their sins had been forgiven and through which they had become God's new covenant people. Later developments are regarded as harmful departures from the apostolic pattern, such as the requirement that an ordained minister must conduct or celebrate the service, that the table becomes an altar and that the elements are 'consecrated' or 'blessed' and offered to God as a sacrifice for sins. However, many, particularly in the Catholic tradition, regard later developments in eucharistic theology and practice as legitimate developments of the New Testament and that the tradition of the Church has been directed by the Spirit of Christ, providing a rich legacy of eucharistic understanding and worship.

Certainly the modern Church can learn something from the eucharistic doctrine and practice of the early centuries of Church history. As Eleanor Kreider has put it:

---

[1] Barclay, William *The Lord's Supper*, John Hunt: Alresford, 2000, p111-113

Outstanding features of these early Eucharists which could be provocative for us are the balance of clear forms with spontaneous or flexible expression, and the repeated rooting of worship in the story of Jesus and his teachings. But most important of all is the overall tone of thanksgiving.[1]

Task

Discuss the strengths and weaknesses of contemporary attitudes to the Eucharist noted above.

Practice Essay Titles

1. **Outline your knowledge and understanding of the origins and practice of the Eucharist in the early Church. (30)**

   Comment on the claim that the writings from this period shed light on the meaning of the Eucharist. (15)

2. **With particular reference to the writings of the period, outline your knowledge and understanding of the celebration of the Eucharist in the early Church. (30)**

   Comment on the claim that the celebration of the Eucharist was a social event as well as a religious act. Justify your answer. (15)

---

1 Kreider, Eleanor *Given for you,* IVP: Leicester, 1998, p45

AS level

Creeds

The emergence of early Christian Creeds

(CCEA Specification)

Definition

A Christian creed is a formal summary of Christian beliefs (from the Latin 'credo' – ' I believe'). Or, as JND Kelly puts it, a Christian creed is 'a fixed formula summarising the essential articles of [the Christian] religion and enjoying the sanction of ecclesiastical authority'.[1]

Task

Take some time to analyse and understand Kelly's definition (above).

Objective

In this chapter we shall gain a knowledge and understanding of how Christian creeds arose and developed in early Church history.

THE NEW TESTAMENT

IN THE NEW TESTAMENT, our earliest Christian sources, there are no fully developed creeds. However, the New Testament authors refer in various ways to a body of teaching that has been handed down from the apostles eg 'the faith once for all delivered to the saints' (Jude 3); 'the pattern of teaching' (Romans 6: 17); and 'the confession' (Hebrews 3: 1 etc). Paul records traditions relating to the Eucharist and the gospel which he has 'received' and 'passed on' (1

---

[1] Kelly, JND *Early Christian Creeds*, Longman: Harlow, 1972, p1

Corinthians 11: 23; 15: 3).

While developed creeds are absent from the New Testament, credal 'elements' or 'fragments' or 'formulae' (as they are often called) have been detected. The content of these primitive creeds focuses on Jesus, the founder and centre of the Church's faith. There are:

(a) **single-clause confessions** – eg 'Jesus is Lord' (1 Cor 12: 3; Rom 10: 9; for other examples see 1 John 4: 2, 15; 5: 1).

(b) **two-clause confessions** – which include reference to God the Father as well (eg see 1 Cor 8: 6; 1 Tim. 2: 5, 6; possibly based on the 'Shema': Deut. 6: 4-9).

(c) **three-clause confessions** – trinitarian passages including Father, Son and Spirit (eg see Matt 28: 19, the important baptismal text; and 2 Cor 13: 14, the benediction).

Some scholars (eg Oscar Cullmann) have suggested that this reflects a historical progression in three stages, but others (eg JND Kelly) argue that these three types of NT confession existed side by side from the beginning.

There are also fuller Christological confessions (eg Rom 1: 3, 4; 1 Cor 15: 3-5) and 'hymns' (eg Phil 2: 6-11) which refer to the acts of Jesus as well as his identity.

The content and structure of these early undeveloped creeds were influenced by the various needs and situations that they were designed to meet, such as: baptism (eg Matt 28: 19; 1 Peter 3: 21); liturgy (public worship eg 2 Cor. 13: 14; and the 'hymns' noted above); heresy (false teachings eg the 1 John references above); evangelism (Rom 6: 17; and the apostolic *kerygma*/proclamation identified by CH Dodd[1] in the sermons of Acts and Paul's letters); and exorcism (eg Mark 5: 7).

Research CH Dodd's presentation of the apostolic kerygma, especially in his book The Apostolic Preaching and its Developments.

THE APOSTOLIC FATHERS

In the non-New Testament writings of the late first and early/mid second century we find a similar situation to that of the New Testament – there are no formal creeds, but rather 'an abundance of quasi-credal scraps'[2]. However, the

---

[1] Dodd, CH *The Apostolic Preaching and its Developments,* Hodder & Stoughton: London, 1936

[2] Kelly, JND *Early Christian Creeds,* Longman: Harlow, 1972, p66

content and structure of these fragments form the basis of later, developed creeds. We find the following types of confession:

(a) **Catechetical** – semi-formal teaching, probably used in preparing people for baptism in Rome, is found in 'The Shepherd of Hermas': 'First of all, believe that God is one ...' (*Mand 1*; possibly a fragment of a larger trinitarian confession).

(b) **Baptismal** – in the *Didache* (7.1) instructions are given to baptise 'in the name of the Father and of the Son and of the Holy Spirit' (as in Matt 28: 19). This may reflect an interrogative creed (the baptised simply replied 'I believe' to questions about the Father, Son, and Spirit) which accompanied a triple immersion. Similarly, there is a trinitarian question in *1 Clement* (46. 5) which possibly reflects an interrogative, baptismal formula – 'Do we not have one God and one Christ and one Spirit of grace who was poured out upon us?'

(c) **Polemical** – in the letters of Ignatius, early second century bishop of Antioch, there are clearly creed-like passages with a polemical purpose (ie designed to attack). These were composed to oppose docetism (teaching which denied the real humanity of Jesus), for example:

Be deaf, therefore, when anyone speaks to you apart from Jesus Christ, who was of the family of David, who was the son of Mary; who really was born, who both ate and drank; who really was persecuted under Pontius Pilate, who really was crucified and died while those in heaven and on earth and under the earth looked on; who, moreover, really was raised from the dead ...

(To the Trallians, 9)

There is only one physician, who is both flesh and spirit, born and unborn, God in man, true life in death, both from Mary and from God, first subject to suffering and then beyond it, Jesus Christ our Lord.

(To the Ephesians, 7.2)

In the first excerpt the repetition of the word 'really' and the reference to Pontius Pilate underline the genuine humanity and historical reality of Jesus' life and suffering against docetic denials of these. The second excerpt reveals an antithetical (contrasting) credal pattern, highlighting the two natures (human and divine) and states (humiliation and exaltation) of Jesus. Since some of these Ignatian 'creeds' are hymn-like, it has been suggested that they were used eucharistically or in some other liturgical setting. It has been noted too that in addition to these Christological confessions, there are also two-clause (eg *To the Magnesians* 8. 2) and three-clause/trinitarian formulae (eg *To the Magnesians* 13.1).

Tasks

> *a. Outline, with examples, the main types of confession found in the Apostolic Fathers.*
>
> *b. Identify the key beliefs about Jesus in the Ignatian passages above.*

JUSTIN MARTYR

Justin the Apologist, writing in mid second century Rome, provides us with the earliest example of semi-formal, relatively fixed creeds. Most are trinitarian in structure, eg:

> *Thus we are not atheists, since we worship the creator of this universe ... and that we with good reason honour him who has taught us these things and was born for this purpose, Jesus Christ, who was crucified under Pontius Pilate, the governor of Judaea in the time of Tiberius Caesar, having learned that he is the Son of the true God and holding him in the second rank, and the prophetic Spirit third in order, we shall proceed to demonstrate.*

Apology 1. 13

While some of these creeds are quoted in a eucharistic context (eg *Apol.1.* 65), two examples are found in Justin's famous description of baptism:

> *For they received a washing in the name of the Father and Lord God of the universe, and of our Saviour Jesus Christ, and of the Holy Spirit ... Over him who has chosen to be reborn and has repented of his sins the name of the Father and Lord God of the universe is named, the official who leads the candidate to the water using this, and only this, description of God ... Moreover, it is in the name of Jesus Christ, who was crucified under Pontius Pilate, and in the name of the Holy Spirit, who through the prophets announced beforehand the things concerning Jesus, that the man who is enlightened is washed.*

Apology 1. 61

Justin specifically says that these words are spoken by the minister rather than the baptised, who probably responded to questions put by the minister.

The similar wording of these two examples suggests a certain degree of fixity of liturgical form, yet it is not clear if this reflects the liturgy of the church in Rome.

Justin also has many examples of single-clause Christological confessions, with a similar form and content – Jesus' virgin birth, humanity, crucifixion, death, resurrection, ascension and return. For example, the exorcism formula in his *Dialogue with Trypho*:

> For in the name of this very Son of God and first-born of all creation, who was born through the virgin, and became passible man, and was crucified under Pontius Pilate by your people, and died, and rose again from the dead, and ascended to heaven, every demon is exorcised, conquered and subdued.

Dialogue 85. 2

Justin is faithfully quoting the early *kerygma* with little evidence that his distinctive Logos theology is altering the content of these credal summaries. As well as exorcisms (as above) these creeds would have been useful in other contexts, eg the Eucharist, catechesis, teaching.

Tasks

a. Comment on the form, content and function of Justin's credal material.

b. Justin was the leading second century Apologist. In what ways were creeds apologetically useful?

THE RULE OF FAITH

In the late second and early third centuries, especially in the writings of Irenaeus (bishop of Lyons, Gaul) and Tertullian (Carthage, North Africa), we find summaries of Christian belief called 'the rule of faith' (Tertullian) or 'the canon of the truth' (Irenaeus), eg:

> For the Church, though dispersed throughout the whole world as far as the limits of the earth, has received from the apostles and their disciples this faith: in one God the Father almighty, who made the heaven and the earth and the seas and all things that are in them; and in one Christ Jesus, the Son of God, who became incarnate for our salvation; and in the Holy Spirit, who proclaimed through the prophets the dispensations and the advents, and the birth from a virgin, and the suffering, and the resurrection from the dead, and the incarnate ascension into heaven of the beloved Christ Jesus, our Lord, and his future manifestation from heaven in the glory of the Father, to sum up all things and to raise up all flesh of all humanity, so that he may make a just judgement among all, sending into eternal fire the spiritual forces of evil and the angels who transgressed and fell into rebellion, and the ungodly ... among men, but upon the righteous conferring life and immortality and securing for them eternal glory.

Irenaeus, Against Heresies 1. 10, 1 (ANE excerpt 93)

> *The rule of faith is ... that rule by which we believe that there is one, and only one, God, and he is the creator of the world, who by his Word coming down in the beginning brought all things into being out of nothing; and that this Word, called his Son, appeared in various ways to the patriarchs in the name of God, made his voice heard always in the prophets, and last of all entered into the virgin Mary by the Spirit and power of God his Father, was made flesh in her womb and was born from her as Jesus Christ, thereafter proclaimed a new law and a new promise of the kingdom of heaven, worked miracles, was nailed to the cross and rose again the third day, was taken up to heaven and sat down at the Father's right hand, and sent in his place the power of the Holy Spirit to guide believers, and will come again in glory to take the saints to the enjoyment of life eternal and of the heavenly promises and to condemn the wicked to eternal fire, both these being raised from the dead, with the restoration of their flesh.*

Tertullian, On the Prescription of Heretics 13 (ANE excerpt 143)

Both these examples of the rule are trinitarian in structure and are probably long expansions of three-clause, interrogative, baptismal creeds which are also found in these writers. While fixed in outline, the various examples of the rule, even within the same writer, vary in wording and detail. Often the claim is attached that the rule is both apostolic and universal (eg Irenaeus above), in opposition to Gnostic claims to secret apostolic traditions and in contrast to the wide diversity of Gnostic beliefs. The rule represents the second century Church's self-understanding as the historically legitimate and theologically consistent heir of the first century apostles, over against Gnosticism's rival claim.

At times the phrasing of the rule is affected by the individual writer's doctrinal emphases and particular polemical context eg Tertullian's emphasis on only one God (against Gnosticism's two gods), and Irenaeus' recapitulation theology ('to sum up all things'). The content and wording of the rule was shaped by the desire to attack Gnostic and Marcionite heresies. Thus there is an emphasis on the oneness and goodness of God, the goodness of creation, the historicity of the incarnation, the reality of Jesus' humanity, and the unity of the old and new covenants (bound together by prophecy and fulfilment).

Tasks

a. Comment on the structure and origin of the rule of faith.

b. What claim is often attached to the rule which reflects the Church's self-understanding?

c. What words and phrases from the two examples of the rule given above are clearly anti-heretical in design?

BAPTISMAL CREEDS

There is a close connection between baptism and creeds from earliest Church history. Indeed, it has been argued that preparation for and the act of baptism provide the source and root of all creeds in the early Church.

While there is no explicit baptismal creed or confession in the New Testament, there are hints that a confession of faith, probably interrogative in nature, accompanied baptism. Matthew presents Jesus as instructing his disciples to baptise 'in the name of the Father and of the Son and of the Holy Spirit.' (28: 19), while in Acts baptism is 'in the name of Jesus' (eg 2: 38). Paul's 'If you confess with your mouth, "Jesus is Lord" ...' (Romans 10: 9) may well be a baptismal confession, and Peter's description of baptism as a 'pledge' towards God (1 Peter 3: 21) may reflect something similar. The association of baptism and 'calling on his name' (Acts 22: 16) and several references to 'the confession' in Hebrews (3: 1; 4: 14; 10: 23) may reflect a baptismal setting. An early, though not original, variant of Acts 8: 37 puts a primitive 'declaratory' baptismal confession in the mouth of the Ethiopian eunuch: " I believe that Jesus Christ is the Son of God."

In the *Didache* and in Justin (see above for both) baptism was in the threefold name and the latter notes that it was the baptiser rather than the baptised who spoke. Tertullian (cAD160-220), in a number of places states that responses were made by the baptised to three questions (on the Father, Son, and Spirit) asked by the baptiser, for example:

In the presence of the congregation and under the hand of the president we solemnly swear that we renounce the devil and his pomp and his angels. Then we are three times immersed, making somewhat fuller responses than those appointed by the Lord in the Gospel.

On the Crown, 3

Most clearly of all we have interrogative baptismal confessions in the *Apostolic Tradition* (21; *ANE* excerpt 121) of the early third century, traditionally ascribed to Hippolytus of Rome:

The baptiser asks, *"Do you believe in God the Father almighty?"*

The baptised answers, *"I believe."* Then, after the first immersion:

The baptiser: *"Do you believe in Christ Jesus, the Son of God, who was born by the Holy Spirit from the virgin Mary, who was crucified under Pontius Pilate and died, and rose again on the third day living from the dead, and ascended into the heavens, and sat down on the right hand of the Father, and will come to judge the living and the dead?"*

The baptised: *"I believe."* Then, after the second immersion:

The baptiser: *"Do you believe in the Holy Spirit, in the holy Church, and the resurrection of the flesh?"*

The baptised: *"I believe."* Then there is the third immersion.

We may note too that Cyprian, bishop of Carthage, in the mid third century, also refers to a threefold baptismal interrogation to which the baptised affirmed their faith (Letter 69).

Thus, the early evidence for baptismal confessions points to two main conclusions: they were trinitarian and interrogative. Declaratory baptismal creeds, in which the baptised recite a creed rather than just replying to questions, appear clearly first in the fourth century (though brief, exceptional examples occur earlier eg Acts 8: 37). They probably originated in catechetical (pre-baptismal) instruction, of which they were useful summaries. Towards the end of the period of catechesis (final weeks of Lent) the bishop 'handed out' the creed (the 'tradition' of the creed) to those worthy to be baptised. They in turn would memorise the creed and 'give it back' or recite it (the 'rendering' or 'reddition' of the creed) on the eve of their baptism.

Task

Construct a flow diagram to show the development of baptismal creeds.

THE CREED OF NICAEA

The creed of Nicaea was issued by the Council of Nicaea in AD325. Before this, creeds were local (in source and authority), but in the fourth century a 'great revolution'[1] took place in the development of creeds, with the introduction of synodal and conciliar creeds (produced by synods and councils). The Council of Nicaea is regarded as the first ecumenical (universal) council of the Church, although in reality many areas were not represented. Thus in theory its creed would have been legally binding on the whole Church. In summoning the Council and urging the adoption of its creed the first Christian emperor, Constantine, was seeking for doctrinal and episcopal unity in the Church to ensure political unity in his empire. Until now creeds were primarily liturgical in general and baptismal in particular, but now a truly theological creed emerges with the express purpose of defining orthodoxy (correct belief) in distinction from heresy (specifically the Arian heresy). This creed would be a test of orthodoxy for the whole Church and especially for its bishops. As CH Turner noted, 'the old creeds were creeds for catechumens, the new creed was a creed for bishops.'[2]

---

[1] Kelly *Early Christian Creeds*, (*op cit*) p205

[2] Turner, CH – quoted in Kelly (*op cit*), p205

However, while the creed of Nicaea was the first substantial and ecumenical theological creed, similar creeds existed before this. A synod in Antioch in AD268 issued a statement of faith, which it regarded as catholic and apostolic, with the expectation that the heretic Paul of Samosata subscribe to it. An even clearer example is found in the doctrinal statement issued by a council in Antioch at the beginning of AD325. This creed, issued by 59 bishops, condemned Arianism and to some degree anticipated the creed of Nicaea.

The history of the development of the creed of Nicaea is unclear due to the sparsity and, sometimes, unreliability of the relevant sources. Not much weight is given to Eusebius of Caesarea's claim that it was basically his own church's (baptismal?) creed which he presented to the council and to which the emperor added the crucial term *homoousios* (see below). There are significant differences between the two creeds and Eusebius' real motive seems to have been to clear himself of any charge of implication in the Arian heresy (see *ANE* excerpt 291 for both creeds). It appears rather that the creed of Nicaea was based on earlier creeds from Jerusalem and Antioch, with specifically anti-Arian additions:

We believe in one God the Father almighty, maker of all things visible and invisible; and in one Lord Jesus Christ, the Son of God begotten of the Father, only begotten, that is, of the substance of the Father, God from God, light from light, true God from true God, begotten not made, of one substance with the Father, through whom all things were made, things on heaven and things on the earth; who for us men and our salvation came down and was made flesh, and became man, suffered, and rose on the third day, ascended into the heavens, will come to judge the living and the dead; and in the Holy Spirit.

But those who say, 'There was when he was not' and 'Before he was begotten he was not' and that 'He came into existence out of nothing' or who say that the Son of God is 'of another substance or essence' or is 'subject to alteration or change' – these the catholic and apostolic Church anathematises.

The traditional trinitarian structure of the creed is clearly apparent, with particular emphasis on the second clause due to the Arian controversy. Arius, a presbyter in Alexandria, Egypt, taught that the Son of God was not fully God; that he was a creature and therefore had not always existed; that he had no real knowledge of the only true God (the Father); and that he was capable of change and sin.

Four anti-Arian statements or interpolations have been added to the basic framework provided by earlier creeds. The Son is:

a) 'of the substance of the Father' (ie not created out of nothing, as Arius claimed);

b) 'true God from true God' (ie the Son is 'true God' as much as the Father);

c) 'begotten not made' (the Arians equated these terms);

d) 'of one substance with the Father' – the words 'of one substance' translate the Greek *homoousion* (accusative of *homoousios* = 'same essence/substance/being'). This was the most controversial term in the creed. Arians, and others, were not happy with it because it implied a material/physical view of God's being, the Father and the Son being separable parts of it. It tended to deny a real distinction between the Father and the Son (Sabellianism/modalism). The word had already been condemned by orthodox bishops at a synod in Antioch (AD268); and it was not a biblical term. Many anti-Arians found this last point to be a real problem but, as Athanasius of Alexandria noted, the Arians were seen to be twisting biblical words and thus a non-biblical term was needed which expressed biblical teaching and dealt with the crucial area of contention.

As well as these anti-Arian interpolations in the main body of the creed, the creed concludes with anti-Arian anathemas or condemnations, similar to those in the Antioch statement, early in AD325. They specifically condemned the following Arian slogans about the Son of God:

a) 'There was when he was not'

b) 'Before he was begotten he was not'

c) 'He came into existence out of nothing'

d) He is 'of another substance or essence'

e) He is 'subject to alteration or change'

The first two statements deny the Son's eternity; the third and fourth deny that he came from the Father's being. The final statement denies his immutability and infallibility. The creed finishes by stating that those who say these things 'the catholic and apostolic Church anathematises'. This has been viewed as a new stage in the institutional development of the Church, since it now has the right to totally unchurch the unorthodox. The creed of Nicaea, however, did not settle the Arian controversy. It was not until this creed was incorporated into the Constantinopolitan or Nicene Creed, issued by the Church's second ecumenical council (Council of Constantinople, AD381), that anti-Arian theology became dominant.

Tasks

a. Explain the political and theological factors that led to the production of the creed of Nicaea.

b. What similar creeds existed before it?

c. Discuss Eusebius of Caesarea's claims about the creed of Nicaea.

d. Comment on the structure of the creed.

e. Clearly show the anti-Arian elements of the creed.

f. Explain how the conclusion of the creed is significant.

g. "Christian creeds should use only biblical terminology." Evaluate this claim.

THE APOSTLES' CREED

This famous creed is widely accepted by Catholics and Protestants, and is respected by the Orthodox Church. Its title (the first occurrence of which appears in AD390) is due to an early legend (Rufinus mentions it in AD404) that the twelve apostles composed it, each providing a separate clause. This legend was generally believed until the sixteenth century when historical criticism revealed it to be unsound. There is no early evidence, for example from the New Testament, to support it. Nor does it neatly divide into twelve clauses or articles! However, it may be argued that while it is not apostolic in authorship, it is so in content.

Its origins have been traced back to the Old Roman Creed, a catechetical creed from the late second century. This creed was the ancestor and core of a variety of Western catechetical and baptismal creeds (eg in Spain, Gaul, North Africa), of which the Apostles' Creed is the final product – 'the mature flower of Western credal development'[1]. The Old Roman Creed is found in a commentary by Rufinus, the Aquileian priest, in AD404, and an earlier Greek form of it in an apology by Marcellus, bishop of Ancyra, Cappadocia, in AD340.

It has been suggested that the Apostles' Creed is an edited form of the Old Roman Creed, produced in Rome. However, in Western writers before the ninth century it is the Old Roman Creed that is apparent rather than the Apostles' Creed. And it seems certain that for several centuries following the sixth century, the Roman church used the Constantinopolitan Creed for

---

[1] Kelly *Early Christian Creeds* (*op cit*), p371

its baptismal creed. Rather, it appears that the developed Apostles' Creed has its origins in south Gaul – creeds practically identical with the Apostles' Creed begin to appear here from the fifth century onwards, and the Apostles' Creed itself probably originated in this general region in the late sixth or seventh century. It eventually became the sole baptismal creed of the Western Church and was the standard creed in Western Europe at around the beginning of the ninth century.

Below, the two creeds are displayed side by side for comparison.

THE OLD ROMAN CREED

I believe in God the Father
almighty;
and in Christ Jesus his only
Son, our Lord, who was born
from the Holy Spirit and the
virgin Mary, who under
Pontius Pilate was crucified
and buried, on the third day
rose again from the dead,
ascended to heaven, sits at
the right hand of the Father,
from where he will come to
judge the living and the dead;
and in the Holy Spirit, the
holy Church, the forgiveness
of sins, the resurrection of
the flesh.

THE APOSTLES' CREED

I believe in God the Father almighty,
creator of heaven and earth;
and in Jesus Christ his only
Son, our Lord, who was conceived
by the Holy Spirit, born from the
virgin Mary, suffered under
Pontius Pilate, was crucified, dead
and buried, descended to hell, on the
third day rose again from the dead,
ascended to heaven, sits at
the right hand of God the Father
almighty, from there he will come to
judge the living and the dead;
I believe in the Holy Spirit, the
holy catholic Church, the communion
of saints, the forgiveness of sins, the
resurrection of the flesh, and eternal life.
Amen.

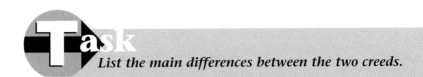

List the main differences between the two creeds.

Some comment may be made on several of the additions. There is no evidence that 'creator of heaven and earth' was added to combat Gnosticism. The phrase is absent from ancestors of the creed which existed when Gnosticism flourished. Rather, it seems to be simply a natural expansion. The word 'conceived' has been placed before the Holy Spirit to clarify the distinction between the roles of Mary and the Spirit. The addition 'descended to hell' is found in some sixth century Spanish creeds, but made its first credal appearance in AD359. The idea that Jesus was in the underworld between his death and resurrection is a very early Christian belief (eg Matt 12: 40; Acts 2: 27- 31; 1 Peter 3: 19; 4: 6). It was believed that he was preaching salvation to Old Testament saints or even liberating them. The words may have been added initially to underscore the reality of his death in order to combat docetism. The 'catholic' Church originally referred to the universal Church, and then after the mid second century it designated the Church as distinct from heretical and schismatic sects. 'The communion of saints' first appears in a late fourth century creed. The traditional interpretation of these words is 'fellowship with holy persons', living and dead. Another view is 'fellowship of holy persons', meaning simply the unity of God's people. A third view is 'participation in the eucharistic elements' (the meaning of the Greek equivalent of the creed's wording). The traditional view was dominant between the fifth and eighth centuries, reflecting increasing devotion to saints and martyrs. The eucharistic view came later perhaps because of the creed's lack of reference to the sacraments. The inclusion of 'eternal life' was necessary to indicate that there was more beyond 'the resurrection of the flesh'.

In addition to the traditional trinitarian structure of the Apostles' Creed we may note that it is in the first person singular ('I believe ...'), reflecting its baptismal history, which may be contrasted with the first person plural ('We believe ...') of ecumenical/conciliar creeds such as the creed of Nicaea.

Tasks

a. Comment on the title of the creed.

b. Explain the relationship between the Apostles' Creed and the Old Roman Creed.

c. List the one name, three titles, and eleven acts confessed concerning Jesus in the Apostles' Creed.

d. Is this creed a sufficient confession of faith to unite all churches?

FUNCTIONS OF CREEDS

It is clear from our study of the development of creeds in the early Church that they had different uses, met various needs and functioned in several settings in Church life. Occasions as varied as catechesis, baptism, teaching, liturgy and exorcism provided contexts for the use of creeds. We may note too the devotional or private use of creeds, such as the Lord's Prayer and the Apostles' Creed. In theological dialogue an individual might state his own position in the form of a personal creed, such as the bishop Heraclides in his dialogue with Origen in the early third century.

Using the information in this chapter, provide examples of the various functions of creeds listed above.

THE VALUE OF CREEDS

The usefulness of creeds has been appreciated throughout Church history right up to the present day. Even churches that are careful to safeguard their belief in the supreme authority and sole sufficiency of the Bible, often recognise the usefulness of subordinate or secondary confessions of faith as convenient and clear summaries of their particular understanding of biblical teaching.

Many of the uses that creeds were put to in the early Church are still relevant for the contemporary Church. Doctrinal clarity, especially in the quest for Church unity, is essential. Memorisation and recitation of creeds in church services can inspire and express worship, as well as educating and uniting worshippers. Creeds are also useful summaries of the Christian faith for the inquiring outsider. Not least, creeds provide a sense of historical continuity with the early Christian Church.

However, there may also be drawbacks in the use of creeds. Often they can be couched in formal, technical, abstract language which may please philosophically minded theologians, but which can be inaccessible and alienating for the average worshipper. Sometimes, because they were originally composed at a different time, dealing with unfamiliar issues, the language and themes of creeds can be outdated.

It can be argued that creeds are still useful and relevant, but there is a need for ongoing credal revision. Clear, understandable language, that takes account of newer developments in theology and inter-Church dialogue, and which seeks to address contemporary issues, is essential if creeds are to be meaningfully used in today's churches. The old faith can wear new clothes!

Task

What beliefs should form the core of contemporary Christian creeds and in what ways could the language of creeds be made more meaningful?

Practice Essay Titles

1. *Outline your knowledge and understanding of the development of Christian creeds in the early Church. (30)*

   Evaluate the claim that creeds were summaries of Christian faith. (15)

2. *Outline the content and explain the origin of the Apostles' Creed. (30)*

   Explore the claim that creeds are still important for Christians today. (15)

AS level **Monasticism**

The origins of monasticism

(CCEA Specification)

Definition

Monasticism, in its developed form, is communal withdrawal from society, especially material possessions and sexual relations, and dedication to God in prayer, fasting and meditation. The word 'monk' comes from the Greek 'monachos' meaning 'single, alone'.

Objective

In this chapter we shall gain a knowledge and understanding of the emergence and beginnings of monasticism in early Church history.

BACKGROUND

MONASTICISM, IN VARIOUS FORMS, existed in other religions before Christianity eg Buddhism, Jewish Essenes. Also, Greek philosophy's contempt for the body and material things generally, as well as its belief in the superiority of the soul or spirit or mind, had some influence on monastic attitudes. However, the Bible and the writings of some early Church Fathers were particularly important influences on the beginnings of Christian monasticism, as it developed in the fourth century.

In the Bible, not only does the Old Testament require abstinence from food, alcohol and sex in certain circumstances (eg Numbers 6), the New Testament too stresses self-denial and dedication of oneself to God. Desert monks would look back to the solitary ministry of John the Baptist in the desert, and to Jesus in the desert alone, fasting and battling with the devil. Also, Jesus' celibacy and homelessness (Luke 9: 58) were imitated by wandering monks. His teaching concerning self-denial (Luke 9: 23), giving up all of one's possessions (Luke 14:

33; 18: 22), hating one's life in this world (John 12: 25), and celibacy in this life and the next (Matt 19: 11, 12; Luke 20: 35, 36) also influenced those who later pursued a monastic lifestyle. Paul too wrote about mastering his body (1 Corinthians 9: 27) and the spiritual superiority of the celibate life (1 Corinthians 7: 1, 7, 8, 25-27, 32-35).

However, Jesus approved of marriage and regarded the call to a celibate life as a gift from God (Matt 19: 9-12). The New Testament in general approves of living in normal society, of marriage and ownership of property, and is opposed to a negative attitude to the body, food and marriage (eg Matt 5: 13-16; 1 Corinthians 5: 9-11; Colossians 2: 21-23; 1 Timothy 4: 3-4).

Second century Church Fathers and apocryphal writings (eg Ignatius, Hermas, Justin, Gospel of Thomas) commended virginity and celibacy. Origen, in third century Alexandria, had a wide influence on later monks – his self-castration due to a literal reading of Matthew 19: 12, enthusiasm for martyrdom and his representation of Christ's army as having a small number of spiritual, elite troops on the front line, inspired many to follow the monastic way of life. The development of monasticism can also be explained in part as a reaction to and protest against declining spirituality and moral standards in the Church, particularly after Christianity became the State religion in the fourth century and when a nominal Christianity developed in many cases. Now that persecution and martyrdom belonged to the past, monks became the new spiritual heroes.

Tasks

a. Outline the factors which contributed to the emergence of monasticism.

b. Discuss the claim that monasticism is a valid development of New Testament teaching.

TYPES

At first there were domestic or village ascetics (from the Greek *askesis*: training) who remained in their churches and communities while they practised self-denial, fasting and celibacy. For example, Pachomius, in early fourth century Egypt, lived such a life of asceticism before moving on to a monastic way of life. Domestic asceticism developed into various forms of monasticism. The variety of monastic lifestyles that evolved in Egypt are documented in the 'Sayings' of the desert elders which their disciples preserved. A similar diversity of types of monasticism is found in the *History of the Monks of Syria*, written by Theodoret, a fifth century bishop of Cyrrhus. While such variety does not permit a rigid or precise classification of types of monasticism, three broad trends or forms may be noted.

Eremites

Eremites, also called hermits (both words are from the Greek word for 'desert') or anchorites (from the Greek for 'withdrawn'), lived lives of individual and solitary asceticism. They often lived in huts or cells or caves, sometimes near villages and towns and sometimes in more desolate parts of the desert. The earliest monks that we know of in Palestine lived in caves in the desert near Jericho, not far from the site of Jesus' baptism. Individual asceticism took a variety of forms – dendrites lived in trees, stylites sat on the top of pillars, Adamites went naked.

Anthony (about AD251-AD356), the Egyptian monk, is often regarded as the father of hermits, the first real eremite and founder of monasticism. Certainly he was the most influential early monk, whose solitary asceticism became the model and inspiration for many later hermits in Egypt and beyond. Athanasius, bishop of Alexandria, wrote the *Life of Anthony* soon after his death. This work provides us with an idealised, romantic account of Anthony's life and was influenced to some extent by classical biographies of heroes and wise men. Along with a few surviving letters from Anthony himself, it is our main source for his life and became a very influential text in the development of monasticism generally.

In the late third century, Anthony gave away his sizeable inheritance (three hundred good acres) to his fellow-villagers. In his local church he had been reflecting on how the disciples had left all to follow Jesus and how the early believers in the book of Acts sold their possessions to help the needy. In church he heard Jesus' words to the rich young ruler being read, "If you would be perfect, go and sell what you have and give to the poor; and come, follow me and you will have treasure in heaven." (Matt 19: 21). He took this as God's word for himself, sold what he had and gave the money to the poor, keeping a little for his sister's welfare.

At first he became the pupil of an ascetic who lived nearby and stayed on the outskirts of the village. Most ascetics lived like this, near to settlements, earning a living through seasonal work and handcraft. Anthony lived for short spells in tombs (the residence of the dead and demons), not far into the desert. He also lived in an abandoned hilltop fort where his disciples would visit him with food every six months and seek his wisdom through a door which he kept shut. He had one vegetarian meal each day, eating bread, vegetables and olives, except when he was fasting. He slept on a mat or cloak, wore a garment of goat skin with the hair side against his body and never washed. But not only did he spend time in the 'Outer Mountain' in the near desert, he also sought greater solitude in the far desert, on the 'Inner Mountain'.

Anthony, like the early monks in general, saw the desert as the haunt and home of the devil and his demons (eg Luke 4: 1-13; 11: 24). He went into enemy territory to do battle with Satan, to wage a spiritual warfare (the imagery of Ephesians 6: 11-17 is reflected at least five times in Athanasius' biography), and to discern and defeat demonic forces. Anthony's temptations were portrayed as assaults of the devil who sought to remind him of his past wealth, the pleasures of food, the comforts of life, as well as the hardships of asceticism. The devil came in the form of a seductive woman and the demons were coming through the four walls of his dwelling in the likeness of ferocious animals. Such were the psychological effects of his intense solitude.

By prayer, the sign of the cross, calling upon the name of Christ and the recitation of the Scriptures, the evil spirits were conquered. Salvation, made possible by Christ's incarnation and resurrection, became actual through self-denial and the 'resurrection of the mind' from bodily passions.

Anthony's isolation was not absolute, however. After nearly twenty years of solitude in the fort on the Outer Mountain, many came and forced open the doors of his dwelling. He came out, initiated in the mysteries and filled with God's Spirit, to teach his eager listeners, heal the sick and exorcise demons. Even though he said that a monk out of his cell is like a fish out of water, he went to Alexandria on two occasions. During the Great Persecution, under the emperor Diocletian in the early fourth century, he counselled and comforted those undergoing persecution – and secretly hoped to be arrested himself! Then in the late 330s he visited the city again to support Athanasius in his fight against Arianism. At the end of his life he was cared for by two of his disciples on the Inner Mountain, where he died at the age of 105.

Tasks

> *a. Describe the lifestyle of eremites.*
>
> *b. Outline the life of Anthony.*
>
> *c. Research the life of early stylites such as Simon and Alypius.*

Semi-Eremites

Semi-eremitical ascetics represented the transition from the almost absolute solitude of the eremites/anchorites to the communal life of traditional monasticism. They were individuals who lived near a spiritual leader and would periodically leave their isolation to meet together for worship and fellowship. But they lacked the authority structure and community rule or discipline of communal monasticism.

The Egyptian **Ammonius** (died mid fourth century), for instance, directed around six hundred semi-eremites in northern Egypt at the time of the Council of Nicaea (AD325). Monks lived at Nitria and Scetis in partial isolation, near elders. The teachings of these elders have been preserved in writings known as the 'apophthegmata' or 'Sayings'.

Chariton, from Asia Minor, developed semi-eremitism in the Judaean desert in the early fourth century. The term for such a settlement was a 'laura' (or 'lavra'), which typically included a central area for Sunday worship and common meals, with individual cells at some distance being occupied by the monks during the week. The word 'laura' is Greek for 'lane' and the term may have been used because the cells or dwellings were often situated along the ridge of a canyon.

A similar kind of semi-eremitic monasticism was established in Gaul (France) by **Martin of Tours** (AD316-AD397), a hermit who attracted a number of disciples. He became bishop of Tours in northern Gaul in AD371, where a settlement developed around him. He founded a similar settlement at Marmoutier, also in northern Gaul. His biographer, Sulpitius Severus (about AD360-430), tells us that the purpose of such settlements was to battle with demons, to erect churches and monasteries on former pagan shrines, to evangelise the pagans and to raise the dead.

Cenobites

Cenobites (from the Greek for 'common life') were monks who lived together in organised communities with an authority structure and a rule of life. The Egyptian **Pachomius** (about AD292-AD346) is normally considered to be the originator of communal monasticism. He was converted in the army through the kindness of Christians who assisted him while in prison. He began his monastic life living in a deserted pagan temple, before sharing a cell with an elderly hermit called Palamon. He then established his first monastery on the Nile at Tabennisi, which had as many as thirteen hundred members. Initially things did not go smoothly – there was opposition from his eremitic brother and some monks exploited his desire to teach by patient example rather than moral rules. Eventually he saw the need for common regulations and the renunciation of private property. He named his community *Koinonia* (Greek for 'community', 'fellowship'), after the communal lifestyle of the early Jerusalem church (Acts 2: 42-45). Both male and female communities were formed. Pachomius' sister, Mary, became leader of one of the female communities.

Pachomius oversaw eight or nine male communes, whose organisation and discipline reflected in part his military background. Admission was not easy. An aspiring monk would have to prove his seriousness by waiting outside for many days, learning many passages of the Bible including some twenty Psalms and the native Coptic language (if necessary), as well as parting with his money. The monasteries themselves were enclosed by walls and contained from thirty to forty houses in a community, with each house holding about forty monks. An abbot (father) was in charge of each monastery and Pachomius himself was the abbot-general. To the ascetic disciplines of celibacy and poverty was now added the need for obedience. Each house had a different trade (eg carpentry, farming) and the monks travelled to market by boat on the Nile. They wore simple clothes, slept on hard beds, rather than on the floor, and received corporal punishment only for serious offences.

While each monk had his own cell, they gathered in the houses twice daily for worship, including prayers and Bible readings and meals, when conversation was discouraged. On Saturdays and Sundays they were taught by the abbot and partook of the Eucharist. Pachomius' cenobitic form of monasticism became quite popular, with more than seven thousand adhering to it in Egypt at the time of his death in AD346. And Pachomius' monastic 'Rule' became influential beyond his own country. Athanasius, for instance, brought it with him to his exile in Germany (AD340-AD346).

Indeed, monastic communities soon developed outside Egypt. In Palestine they were linked to biblical sites such as Jerusalem, Bethlehem and the Judaean desert. They often provided practical help to visiting pilgrims. In the late fourth century there were Greek communities in Jerusalem and Bethlehem, with male and female members. A learned community was established by Latin Christians (the female Melania and Rufinus) on the Mount of Olives.

Basil of Caesarea (about AD329-AD379) played an important role in the development of cenobitism. He lived as a hermit in the hills near his home in Cappadocia, eastern Asia Minor. He then set about organising communal monasticism in Asia Minor and beyond, of a type that in various ways was an improvement on Pachomian cenobitism. He drew up a rule for monasteries which included a probationary period for new monks, to identify those not suitable for monastic life. Also, monasteries were to be located near urban settlements so that they might be of service to the wider community. Monks provided hospital care, education and engaged in various kinds of social relief work. Further, the severity of Pachomian communities was rejected in favour of an emphasis on brotherly love and fellowship. Communities were to be pastorally manageable, having thirty to forty members each. Communal prayer was important and Basil is responsible for establishing the seven times of prayer in the monastic day. This is based on Psalm 119: 64, "Seven times a day I praise you". Monks were encouraged also to engage in study and scholarship. Of crucial importance too was bishop

Basil's requirement that monasteries be overseen by local bishops to ensure good relationships with the institutional church.

In Gaul, **Honoratus** (died about AD430) founded a monastery composed of former eremites on the island of Lérins, off the south coast and produced a written rule in the early fifth century. Nearby, **John Cassian** (AD360-AD435) established communities, male and female, at Marseilles. His 'Institutes' was an important work which, along with other of his writings, favoured Egyptian monastic ideas. Western monasticism generally was influenced by these communities in the south of Gaul.

Augustine (AD354-AD430), bishop of Hippo in North Africa, was influenced by monasticism in Italy. Due to his influence, male and female communities were established in North Africa. His *Praeceptum* ('Instruction'), written in the late fourth century, became an important monastic rule in the Middle Ages and stressed the priority of brotherly love.

Tasks

a. Describe semi-eremitism and the work of one semi-eremite.

b. Define cenobitism and outline the life of Pachomius.

c. Draw a table showing the main types of early monasticism, outlining their characteristics and giving examples of each.

RELATIONSHIPS WITH THE CHURCH

Developing monasticism had an uneasy relationship with the institutional Church and its bishops. Monks were often separate from the Church and its sacraments, critical of its clergy and insubordinate to their leadership. For their part, the bishops were often suspicious of or opposed to the separatist, individualistic and elitist attitude of many monks, particularly the excesses of some individual ascetics. For instance, Jerome (about AD345-AD419) complained about the drunkenness and violence of certain monks. Monasticism was not established initially by Church leaders and its early founders, Anthony and Pachomius, were not clergy. Monasticism itself was becoming more institutionalised and was perceived as an increasing threat and rival to the Church, not least financially. A mid fourth century council at Gangra in northern Asia Minor sought to deal with the unacceptable excesses of asceticism such as the rejection of worship in church services, Sunday fasting, spiritual elitism and contempt for married Christians.

However, bishops sometimes found the support of monks useful in opposing heresy and defeating paganism. Monks could even be organised into private armies. Schnoudi, abbot of the White Monastery, led such an army of monks in rural Egypt who destroyed pagan temples and attacked Christians that they regarded as heretics. At the Council of Ephesus (AD431) he threw a book at Nestorius, patriarch of Constantinople, because of his perceived heretical views!

Yet, while Pachomius and others wanted to keep the monastery and the Church separate, fourth century bishops like Eustathius and Basil tried to reconcile the two. Eustathius, bishop of Sebaste in Armenia, sought to make monastic communities more useful to the Church and society by, for instance, the provision of a hospice in Sebaste. Basil, bishop of Caesarea, also tried to create a more harmonius relationship between monastery and Church. In his commentary 'Asceticon' he endeavoured to promote a distinct yet not separatist role for monasteries, a place for instruction by bishops and a less sharp distinction between the Christian and the monastic callings. Like bishop Augustine after them, these bishops sympathised with monasticism and sought to integrate it into the life of the wider Church.

The Council of Chalcedon (AD451) introduced legislation in order to standardise and regulate monasticism and more clearly define its relation to the Church. Only with the permission of the bishop could monasteries be built and indeed monks were to be subject to the bishop. While monks were to be given due respect, they were not to interfere with matters of Church or State. Monks could not go to war nor could they or the monasteries be secularised in any way.

Tasks

> *a. Describe the uneasy relationship that developed between monasticism and the Church.*
>
> *b. Outline the attempts to integrate the two.*

ATTITUDES TO MONASTICISM

Christian attitudes to monasticism have varied over the years and still do. It can be argued that its emphasis on spirituality and self-discipline as opposed to materialism and self-indulgence, its legacy of hospitality and charitable work, as well as its careful transcription and transmission of the Bible in former days, all represent important Christian values and a positive contribution to the Church.

However, others have found fault with a perceived neglect of certain strands of New Testament teaching such as the importance of a Christian presence and influence in society rather than detachment from it. The dangers of an introspective individualism, a possible denial of the goodness of the body and sexuality and the perceived creation of a superior class of Christian, have also been noted by those unsympathetic towards the monastic lifestyle.

Indeed, even at its beginnings monasticism was opposed by fourth century writers such as the former monk Jovinian who regarded virginity as no greater than marriage and fasting no greater than eating, in God's eyes. Around the same time Vigilantius characterised monasticism as moral cowardice. He argued that those who kept their possessions could help the poor and that Christians who remain in society can convert the pagans. Jerome wrote against both these early critics of monasticism.

Whatever view one takes of monasticism, there is no doubt that the foundations for its enduring legacy were laid, as we have seen, in the early centuries of the Church's life.

Task

Outline the strengths and weaknesses of the monastic lifestyle.

Practice Essay Title

Outline your knowledge and understanding of the beginnings of monasticism in the early Church. (30)

Explore the claim that monasticism was an inevitable development in early Christianity. (15)

AS level

Spread of Christianity

The spread of Christianity

(CCEA Specification)

Objective

In this chapter we shall gain a knowledge and understanding of the numerical, geographical and social expansion of Christianity and of the factors which contributed to its growth in early Church history.

NUMERICAL GROWTH

IN THE ABSENCE OF firm historical evidence, various suggestions have been made about the size of the Church and its proportion of the general population during its first three hundred years.

A recent attempt at quantifying the rate and ratio of early Church growth has been made by the sociologist Rodney Stark[1]. Estimating a total population of 60 million in the Roman empire he has presented the following outline (Table 1) of the Church's numerical increase and percentage of the general population, assuming a growth rate of 40% each decade. Stark observes that the Mormon church grew on average at about 43% per decade in the twentieth century and argues for a similar rate of expansion for early Christianity.

Stark's numerical scheme is not without its problems. On the one hand, it has been noted that it finds some support from the limited knowledge we already have. In the mid third century, Rome's population was about 700,000 of whom, according to Stark's scheme, around 14,000 were Christians. This fits well with the information reported by Eusebius, the fourth century church historian, concerning the Roman church – about AD250 the church had some 155 clergy and 1500 widows and others in need. However, Stark's uniform and

---

[1] Stark, Rodney *The Rise of Christianity*, Princeton University Press, 1996

Table 1   Christian Expansion (AD40–350)

Year	Number of Christians	% of Population (60 million)
40	1,000	0.0017
50	1,400	0.0023
100	7,530	0.0126
150	40,496	0.07
200	217,795	0.36
250	1,171,356	1.9
300	6,299,832	10.5
350	33,882,008	56.5

consistent growth rate does not account for the variables of real life. Growth was uneven throughout the Empire (as the geographical section overleaf will indicate) and fluctuated due to factors such as persecution, plagues and war. Further, it has been pointed out that a fairly slight change of Stark's number of Christians in AD40 (from 1,000 to 2,000) would result in an unlikely 12.6 million (not 6.3 million) Christians in AD300.

Paul McKechnie in *The First Christian Centuries*[1] believes that at the end of the first century the Church was much bigger than Stark estimates. Unlike some other historians of early Christianity, McKechnie is not sceptical about the numbers of early Christians reported in the New Testament book of Acts. Less than seven weeks after Jesus' death there were about 120 believers in Jerusalem (1: 15), then a little later about 3000 on the day of Pentecost (2: 41), the number growing to about 5,000 (4: 4) and finally 'many thousands' of Jewish converts in the early 60's of the first century (21: 20). Further, Suetonius reports (*Claudius* 25. 4) that the emperor Claudius expelled certain Jews (probably Christians) from Rome in AD49 because of the trouble they were causing, most likely by their preaching. Thus, not only had Christianity arrived in Rome by this early date, but was also sizeable enough to cause a social disturbance requiring imperial action. In about AD115 the Roman historian Tacitus wrote about the 'vast numbers' in Rome convicted as Christians during

---

[1] McKechnie, Paul *The First Christian Centuries*, Apollos/IVP: Leicester, 2001, p57, 58

Nero's persecution in AD64 (*Annals* 15. 44). The Roman official Pliny in AD112 informed his emperor Trajan of the existence of many Christians of all ages, every rank and both sexes in Bithynia, Asia Minor (modern northern Turkey) and of their rural, as well as urban, influence (*Epistle* 10. 96)

Hard data on the numerical growth of Christianity in its early period is unavailable and Stark's profile provides only a very general framework for the perceived growth of the early Church. When we turn to consider the geographical and social expansion of early Christianity, we are on somewhat firmer ground.

Task

Outline the difficulties involved in attempting to quantify the growth of early Christianity, with particular reference to Rodney Stark's scheme.

GEOGRAPHICAL EXPANSION

Christianity began in the city where its founder was crucified – Jerusalem. Our earliest Church history, the New Testament book of Acts, records in its opening chapters the progress of the Jerusalem church under the leadership of the apostles Peter and John. We are told that some 120 Christians (1: 15) grew to about 3,000 on the day of Pentecost seven weeks after Jesus' death (2: 41) and 5,000 some time after (4: 4). Later, James is the leader of the Jerusalem church and it is reported that many thousands of Jews have become Christians (21: 17-20). While some regard these numbers as unreliable, others accept them as plausible. Jewish persecution of the Jerusalem church resulted in the dispersal of its members throughout the province of Judaea and neighbouring Samaria, according to Acts (8: 1). Naturally the earliest Christianity in Palestine was of a Jewish character. However, after the First Jewish Revolt (AD66-AD74) imperial policy promoted Gentile elements in the region. And after the Second Jewish Revolt (AD132-AD135) Jewish Christians were removed from Palestine and Gentile Christianity developed thereafter.

From its beginnings in Palestine, Christianity spread out in three main directions: north-west, south-west and east.

North-West

Antioch in Syria, where followers of Jesus were first called 'Christians' (Acts 11: 26), heard the Christian message from members of the Jerusalem church who had been displaced by the persecution at the time of Stephen's death (Acts

11: 19). Both Jewish and Gentile residents of the city became Christians (Acts 11: 19–21). Antioch was the base for Paul's missionary journeys westwards through Asia Minor (modern Turkey) and Greece (Acts 13: 1–3; 14: 26–28; 15: 35, 36; 18: 18–23). In the early second century the church's bishop, Ignatius, was taken from here to martyrdom in Rome. From Antioch the Christian message spread into the neighbouring towns and countryside and indeed eastwards to Armenia, Mesopotamia and Persia. By the end of the fourth century, half of Antioch's half a million residents were reported to be Christian.

Paul both planted and wrote to Christian churches in **Asia Minor** (modern Turkey). The book of Acts reports his missionary travels in this region (Acts 13 and 14 in particular) and the New Testament contains letters written to young churches there (Galatians, Ephesians, Colossians and the letters in the first three chapters of Revelation; note also 1 and 2 Timothy and 1 Peter). Indeed before Paul, some from this part of the Empire may have been among the converts on the day of Pentecost (Acts 2: 9, 10, 41). At the end of the first century there were churches in forty-two cities of the Roman Empire and the majority of them were in Asia Minor. Early in the second century, Ignatius, bishop of Antioch, wrote letters to five churches in the region (Ephesus, Magnesia, Tralles, Philadelphia and Smyrna) and one to Polycarp, bishop of Smyrna. Further, around the same time, Pliny's letter to the emperor Trajan, gives us an insight into the rapid expansion of Christianity in rural Bithynia, north-west Asia Minor. He mentions that there are many Christians, old and young, male and female, of every class, in town and country. Such was the impact of Christianity that pagan temples were being neglected. However, the urban Greek-speakers of Asia Minor were more responsive to the Christian message than the Greekless rural peoples. In the sixth century the emperor Justinian sought to remove remaining paganism in these inland areas.

For **Macedonia and Achaia** (Greece), we have information in the New Testament about Paul's pioneering missionary activity (Acts 16: 9–18: 18; 20: 1–6) and letters to young churches in the region (1 and 2 Corinthians, Philippians, 1 and 2 Thessalonians). We have also the Roman church's letter to the Corinthian church (*1 Clement*) at the end of the first century and Polycarp's letter to the Philippian church near the beginning of the next. Thereafter, the picture is unclear.

Visitors from **Rome** were present on the day of Pentecost and may have brought the Christian message back to the capital of the Empire a matter of weeks after Jesus' death and resurrection (Acts 2: 10, 41). The emperor Claudius expelled Jews from Rome in AD49, including Christians whose message seems to have led to disturbances in the city (Acts 18: 1, 2; Suetonius – *Claudius* 25. 4). Certainly there is a well established church there in about AD57, to which Paul wrote his famous letter. Also, the Roman historian Tacitus, in AD115, wrote of 'vast numbers' of Christians in the city who were persecuted by the emperor

Nero in AD64 (*Annals* 15. 44). In AD96 the Roman church, as we have seen, corresponded with the Corinthian church (*1 Clement*). Early in the second century, Ignatius, bishop of Antioch, writes to the Roman church urging that they do not try to prevent his impending martyrdom in their city.

The Roman church grew as Christians from elsewhere came to the city and swelled its numbers. In AD166 Bishop Soter reports that there are more Christians than Jews in the city. In the mid third century we have specific details about the size of the Roman church from bishop Cornelius (cited by Eusebius) – forty-six presbyters, seven deacons, seven sub-deacons, forty-two acolytes, fifty-two exorcists, readers and door-keepers and over 1500 widows and needy persons. This may have represented some 14,000 Christians out of a population of around 700,000. However, the Church historian Adolf von Harnack reckoned that it reflects over twice this number of Christians. In Italy as a whole at this time, there were one hundred dioceses, ie areas governed by bishops. The prestige and authority of the Roman church and its successive bishops developed, of course, into the medieval papacy and its supremacy in the western church.

Christianity may have been first brought to **Gaul** (France) by Paul's companion Crescens, who is said to have gone to 'Gaul', as ancient commentators and some manuscripts interpret 2 Timothy 4: 10. Tradition connects him with the churches of Vienne and Mayence. Irenaeus was bishop of Lyons in the late second century in the south of Gaul where Christianity made most progress. As well as combating Gnosticism in the area, Irenaeus used Celtic to evangelise the rural areas, as well as Greek for the townspeople. In AD177 Christians in Lyons and nearby Vienne were tortured and martyred during the reign of Marcus Aurelius. However, the church in Gaul grew and in the early fourth century, Arles, Vaison, Autun, Rouen, Paris, Bordeaux, Trier and Rheims all had episcopal oversight.

Spain was in Paul's sights as he looked for new mission fields. He told the Roman church that he had spread the gospel from Jerusalem all the way round to Illyricum (modern Albania) and was planning to go to Spain (Romans 15: 19, 24). In the late second century Irenaeus (Lyons) and Tertullian (Carthage) are aware of a Christian presence in Spain and in the mid third century, Cyprian (Carthage) knew of churches in several of its main cities. Near the end of the third century, the region had almost sixty churches. In the first decade of the fourth century, thirty-six dioceses were represented at the Council of Elvira, the canons of which reveal limited Christian influence in the region.

As for **Britain**, Tertullian (in early third century Carthage) and Origen (later that century in Alexandria) believed that there were Christians there in their time. It may be that St Alban was martyred there during the Great Persecution (early fourth century) – pilgrims were visiting his shrine by the early fifth century. And we know that three British bishops, from York, London and Colchester or Lincoln, were at the Council of Arles (AD314) in southern Gaul. Archaeology has uncovered evidence of fourth century British Christianity – a chapel in a villa in Kent and Christian silver at a fort near Peterborough. Pelagius is the earliest Christian writer from Britain (early fifth century) and Patrick began his mission to Ireland in about AD432. In Britain it appears that the Christian faith took hold among the urban Romano-British, rather than the more primitive Celts.

In bullet point form, make brief notes on the main areas to which Christianity spread north-westerly from Palestine.

South–West

To the south-west of Palestine, **Egypt** and especially the port of Alexandria, became an important centre and missionary base of early Christianity. Egyptians were present in Jerusalem on the day of Pentecost (Acts 2: 10) and if they were among the many Christian converts on that day (Acts 2: 41), then they would have taken the Christian message back to their homeland. The book of Acts also tells us about an Alexandrian Jewish Christian called Apollos (18: 24), a convert from among the city's large Jewish population. Firm evidence about the origins of the Alexandrian church is lacking, despite the early tradition (eg Clement of Alexandria, late second century) that it was founded by Mark, the presumed author of the New Testament Gospel that now bears his name. There is evidence, however, of Christian expansion in the second century, especially among the Greek speaking urban dwellers rather than the Coptic peasants. The famous catechetical school founded by Pantaenus and headed in turn by Clement (about AD150-AD215) and the very influential Origen (about AD185-AD254), sought to combine Christian orthodoxy and Greek philosophy, while rejecting Gnosticism. In the mid third century the Bible was translated into local dialects (Coptic) and later that century Egypt was becoming the home of early Christian monasticism under such monastic pioneers as Anthony and Pachomius. At the end of the third century there were around one hundred dioceses.

Christianity spread further west to **Cyrene**, home of Simon who carried Jesus' cross and whose sons were known to the original readers of Mark's Gospel (probably in Rome – Mark 15: 21; Romans 16: 13). Some from this region were present on the day of Pentecost and, as we have noted in other cases, may have brought the Christian message home from Jerusalem (Acts 2: 10, 41). Also in the book of Acts, we are told that Cyrenians were among those who first brought the gospel to Gentiles (11: 19, 20). By the early fifth century there were six dioceses in the region.

Further west again, **North Africa** (modern Tunis and Algeria) became one of the leading provinces of early Christianity. The Christian message came from Rome across the Mediterranean and from Egypt in the east. However, Henry Chadwick notes that Carthage had trade links with eastern Mediterranean countries and that the first missionaries may have come from there[1]. With the martyrdom in Carthage of twelve Christians from nearby Scilli in AD180, we have the earliest indication of Christianity in the region. Here we find the beginnings of Latin speaking Christianity, particularly with the influential writings of Tertullian (about AD160–AD220) and Cyprian (about AD200–AD258). Tertullian could write of the Church's growth in the following terms:

We are but of yesterday and we have filled everything you have – cities, islands, forts, towns, assembly halls, even military camps, tribes, town councils, the palace, senate and forum. We have left you nothing but the temples.

(Apology, 37)

He is aware of churches not only in the north of the region in and around Carthage but also further afield in what is now south Tunisia and Algeria. In the mid third century there were about eighty bishops. Indeed the region had a higher concentration of bishops than elsewhere in the West where they were found only in the cities rather than in town and village too. By the end of the third century there were over one hundred, mostly urban, churches and local Christian writings reveal that there was most success among the Romanised upper classes.

East

Among the Pentecost pilgrims in Jerusalem were Parthians, Medes, Elamites and residents of Mesopotamia (Acts 2: 9), some of whom may have been among the many Christian converts on that day (Acts 2: 41). Christianity may well have spread to the lands east of Palestine by means of these returning pilgrims, and also from Antioch in Syria which became an important missionary base for the eastwards expansion of the Church. Certainly, by the end of the second century the Christian faith had taken hold in Persia (modern Iraq and Iran), centred in the Syriac speaking cities of Nisibis and Edessa. And by AD235 the Persian empire had some twenty bishops and eighteen dioceses. Probably from Edessa and Syria, Christianity spread northwards to Armenia – Tertullian knew of Christians there in the early third century. And in neighbouring Georgia there were Christian

---

[1] Chadwick Henry *The Early Church*, Penguin: London, 1993, p65

converts in the second and third centuries. By the early third century Syriac Christianity had spread as far east as what is now southern India, if we can rely on the 'Acts of Judas Thomas'.

This outline of the geographical spread of early Christianity shows that the Church had most success north-west of Palestine through Syria, Asia Minor, Rome and south Gaul; south-west to Egypt and North Africa, and eastwards through the Persian empire. However, it was not an even expansion and was most successful in urban areas where there was a sizeable Jewish population.

Tasks

a. *In bullet point form, make brief notes on the main areas to which Christianity spread south-westerly and eastwards from Palestine.*

b. *On a map, indicate the main areas to which Christianity spread from Palestine in the first three centuries.*

SOCIAL SPREAD

From the start, in theory at least, Christianity cut across social boundaries. Its socially inclusive message disregarded economic inequalities. While Jesus was presented as the champion of the materially poor and the socially marginalised (especially in Luke's Gospel), he also attracted some wealthier followers (eg Joseph of Arimathea – Matthew 27: 57). The classic egalitarian New Testament text is Galatians 3: 28: "There is neither Jew nor Greek, slave nor free, male nor female, for you are all one in Christ Jesus". In Christ there is a religious equality which overrides racial, social and gender distinctions.

However, it is clear from the beginning that the new faith was accepted mostly among those of a lower social status. Paul reminded the Corinthian church that such was their social background at the time of their conversion – 'not many' of them were wise or influential or of noble birth, rather God had chosen the foolish, the weak and the lowly (1 Corinthians 1: 26–29). James similarly referred to God's choice of the poor when social favouritism reared its head in the Church (James 2: 9).

The fact is that until the conversion of the emperor Constantine in the early fourth century Christianity spread mostly among the lower and middle classes.

By and large early Christian writings appear to be addressed to non-elites such as merchants and craftsmen. In the late second century Celsus, a pagan opponent of Christianity, made the somewhat exaggerated observation that the

Church's converts were merely women, children, slaves and fools.

However, there is early evidence that Christianity made some impact on the upper end of the social scale. Around the same time as Celsus, the Christian Apologist Tatian provided a counter-balance to the pagan's charge by writing, "Not only do the rich among us pursue our philosophy, but the poor enjoy instruction gratuitously." (*Address to the Greeks*, 32). At times, as in the book of Acts (17: 4, 12), the upper classes were evangelised through converted wives.

Before Constantine we know of at least ten Roman aristocrats in Christian churches[1]. During the Decian and Valerian persecutions of the mid third century senators and equestrians were among those who suffered for their faith. And surviving early Christian literature is testimony to the fact that there was a sizeable number of Christians in the top 2% of society. Also, social levels were not unalterable castes. Some Christians were upwardly mobile slaves who gained their freedom and entered the imperial civil service.

Indeed, there are various pieces of evidence which reveal the presence of Christians in imperial and government circles. As early as the sixties of the first century there were Christians in 'Caesar's household' (Philippians 4: 22). The third century Roman historian Dio Cassius reports that the emperor Domitian (reigned AD81-AD96) persecuted prominent Romans for atheism and Jewish sympathies, in what is probably a reference to Christians. Titus Flavius Clemens, consul in AD95, was executed and his wife Flavia Domitilla was exiled. In the fourth century they were regarded as Christian martyrs. In the *Martyrdom of Justin* (Justin was martyred in Rome in about AD165) we read that Euelpistus, one of his followers, was an imperial slave. Also, Callistus bishop of Rome was once the slave of Carpophorus, a Christian in the household of the emperor Commodus (AD180–AD192). Around this time too Irenaeus and Tertullian are aware of Christians in the royal palace.

Certainly, after Constantine and the establishment of Christianity as the official religion of the empire, many social elites joined the Church. Christian sermons from the fourth and fifth centuries reflect a largely upper class audience. In the view of such preachers and writers it was the middle classes (eg landowners, merchants, craftsmen) who were the 'poor'. Rural peasants were often passed by and only attended the urban churches on special holy days. Thus, before and after Constantine the social constitution of the Church was markedly different. What initially was a largely low to middle class Jewish community eventually became the preserve of predominantly upper class Gentiles. In earlier days the Church was a persecuted minority whom the general public was at least suspicious of and often hostile to. It seemed

---

[1] Barnes, TD 'Statistic and the Conversion of the Roman Aristocracy' in the *Journal of Roman Studies* 85 [1995]

inconceivable then that one day Christianity would become the imperial religion, to which allegiance was advisable.

Tasks

a. Compare and contrast the social constitution of the Church before and after Constantine.

b. What evidence is there of Christian influence on the upper classes?

c. Research the martyrdom of the noble-woman Perpetua and the slave-girl Felicitas (early third century Carthage) as a powerful symbol of the social equality of early Christianity.

CONTRIBUTORY FACTORS

From the perspective of Christian faith the spread of Christianity will be seen as the fulfilment of the promise attributed to Jesus in Matthew's gospel, "... I will build my church ..." (16: 18). But Christian faith accepts that divine providence often works through very human and historical means. In this section we shall consider the various factors that contributed to the rapid growth of Christianity from some one hundred and twenty Jewish believers in Jerusalem in about AD30 (Acts 1: 15) to its status as the official imperial religion with an estimated 30 million Gentile adherents in the fourth century.

We may note firstly that there were factors which facilitated the expansion of the Church which were not directly related to Christianity itself. For instance, there appears to have been a growing dissatisfaction with traditional religions and philosophies. Roman religion was creedless and therefore lacked definition. It had endless deities, variously favoured by different emperors. Many turned to Eastern mystery religions but they too were diverse, sometimes perverse and often fatalistic. Greek philosophy generally stressed the transitory and insubstantial character of the material world and yearned for immortality, but provided no certain answers.

The Church grew also because there was no consistent Roman policy for suppressing or exterminating Christianity. Before the Decian persecution (AD250–AD251), hostility was generally local, sporadic, populist and unplanned. The Roman governor Pliny's uncertainty about how to deal with Christianity in early second century Bithynia and the emperor Trajan's ambiguous reply to his request for advice (see next chapter) is one example of an official vagueness concerning the new faith which allowed it space to grow.

The *Pax Romana* (Roman peace) also provided conditions which were favourable to the spread of early Christianity. In the third century Origen reflected that God had prepared the nations for the gospel by bringing them under a sole ruler – the Roman emperor. A measure of political stability coupled with empire-wide security facilitated relatively safe travel on land and sea. Rome had also provided a network of easily passable roads along which the Christian message could be taken throughout the Empire.

The existence of a common tongue, the Greek language, greatly reduced linguistic difficulties in the communication of the gospel. Alexander the Great's conquests ensured that a 'common' Greek was spoken over a wide area before Rome's rise to power. However, since rural areas were largely resistant to the new language early Christianity became a mostly urban faith.

In addition to these factors external to Christianity there were, of course, Christian reasons for the growth of the Church. The Gospels record the Church's mandate for making disciples of 'all nations' in what has been called the Great Commission of Jesus (eg Matthew 28: 18–20). However, the motivational force of this was somewhat weakened by an early belief that the twelve apostles had already evangelised the world. The New Testament writings also present an exclusive gospel in the sense that only through Jesus Christ could the world be saved (John 14: 6; Acts 4: 12; 1 Timothy 2: 5). In the early days a belief in the imminent return of Jesus and the end of the world, found for example in the New Testament and the *Shepherd of Hermas*, created a sense of evangelistic urgency.

So, in an informal and spontaneous way Christians spread their faith through a network of daily personal relationships, business trips and casual encounters. In the second century Justin was converted through a conversation with an old man in Ephesus. In the next century it was a conversation with a church leader that led to Cyprian's conversion. Celsus observed how ordinary Christians took every opportunity to spread their faith.

There were of course many full-time missionaries who, like Paul and his companions in the book of Acts, took the gospel throughout the Empire, planting churches in the cities which would serve as missionary centres to the surrounding countryside. Public preaching in the open air, while common enough in Paul's day, is rarely mentioned in the second and third centuries, probably due to the growing threat of popular persecution. We know too that Christians entered into debate with unbelievers to win them over – Justin's *Dialogue* with the rabbi Trypho is but one example. Justin even held classes for inquirers, and in the third century there was a famous 'Catechetical School' in Alexandria headed by Clement and then Origen. And the presence of 'God-fearers' (Gentile converts to Judaism) in many of the Empire's cities provided, as in the book of Acts, a bridge for Christian mission into the Gentile world. Here were people who shared a common understanding of God and morality with the early Christians. We have evidence too of some missionary-minded bishops such as Irenaeus of Lyons who in the late second century evangelised the rural Celts in their native tongue.

It is clear also that early Christian preachers and writers made an effort to relate the gospel to diverse cultures by adapting the presentation of the message to the various thought forms of their audiences. Paul demonstrated this flexibility (eg 1 Corinthians 9: 19–23), as can be seen from a comparison of his different approaches to Jews and Gentiles as reported in Acts (eg compare 13: 16–41 with 17: 22–31). A similar process is discernible in the writings of second century Christian Apologists such as Justin and in the Alexandrian Fathers (Clement and Origen) who sought to communicate the gospel in the language of Greek philosophy. Indeed, early Christian literature in general was an important means of spreading the Christian message. The translation of the Greek New Testament into other languages made the faith accessible to an even wider audience. By the start of the third century Latin, Syriac and Coptic versions were available.

As for the message itself, in contrast to the traditional religions and philosophies mentioned above, the Christian message proved attractive to many. Instead of a confusing array of deities it presented one universal God. In place of ill defined mythologies it made clear statements about a historical person and historical events (the death, resurrection and return of Jesus of Nazareth). It affirmed the goodness of creation and the body, offered forgiveness of sins, release from guilt, power over demons and death and eternal life. Ordinary people in particular were impressed by the charismatic power, such as exorcisms and healings, that accompanied and authenticated the message, though such phenomena do not seem to have been prominent after apostolic times (Romans 15: 18, 19; Hebrews 2: 3, 4). The social inclusiveness of the gospel was also a factor in its universal appeal, as we noted in the previous section.

Further, Christian behaviour as well as Christian beliefs contributed to the success of early Christianity. Christian morality, particularly in relation to sexual and marital matters, provided an attractive alternative to much pagan immorality. Also, in the view of Henry Chadwick, it was the practical charity of early Christians that was the most powerful factor in the growth of the Church[1]. Adolf von Harnack has identified ten forms of Christian charity in the early Church, such as the care of the poor, widows, orphans, prisoners and hospitality to strangers[2]. We have already seen that in the mid third century the Roman church cared for more than 1500 widows and needy persons. Tertullian could quote the pagan observation, 'See how these Christians love one another.' And not only one another. When the emperor Julian (AD361–AD363) tried to revive Roman religion he found that Christian charity disposed the people in the

---

[1] Chadwick, Henry *The Early Church*, Penguin: London, 1993, p56

[2] von Harnack, Adolf, acc. to Neill, S, *A History of Christian Missions*, Penguin: London 1986, p37

Church's favour. He acknowledged that Christianity had advanced through its care of strangers and its concern for the proper burial of the dead. And he admitted that Christian charity extended to the pagan poor as well as to its own.

The dignified courage of Christians in the face of persecution and martyrdom was another factor in early Church growth, winning the sympathetic respect of many and the conversion of not a few to the Christian faith. While the emperor Marcus Aurelius (AD161–AD180) was opposed to Christianity, he acknowledged the bravery of its martyrs. The martyrdom of Perpetua, Felicitas and others in Carthage (AD202/AD203) resulted in the conversion of some spectators including a soldier involved in the execution of a church leader. Tertullian wrote to the governor Scapula some ten years after Perpetua's martyrdom and told him that those who see the noble patience of the martyrs are moved to examine the matter and often become disciples themselves. Indeed, in his *Apology* he wrote,

> *Your cruelty does not profit you, however exquisite. Instead it tempts people to our sect. As often as you mow us down, the more we grow in number. The blood of the Christians is the seed [of the Church] … The very stubbornness you criticise teaches for us. For who on seeing it is not excited to enquire what lies behind it? Who, having enquired, does not embrace our faith?*

(Apology, 50)

The conversion of the emperor Constantine (AD306–337) in the early fourth century ensured peace, protection and privilege for the Church. Galerius, the Eastern emperor (AD305–311) and Constantine in the West enacted the edicts of toleration (AD311 and 313) and Theodosius I established Christianity as the Empire's religion. The triumph of the Church was sealed.

Task

Rank the factors contributing to the spread of early Christianity in what you consider to be their order of importance.

Practice Essay Title

Outline the available evidence for the geographical and social expansion of early Christianity. (30)

Explore the claim that the Church would have grown even apart from Constantine's conversion. (15)

AS level **Persecution**

The causes and course of persecution in the first two centuries (Nero, Domitian, Trajan and Marcus Aurelius).

(CCEA Specification)

Definition

Religious persecution is the unfair and often violent treatment of a person or persons because of their religious identity or beliefs.

Objective

In this chapter we shall gain a knowledge and understanding of the causes and course of the persecution of the Church in its first two centuries during the reigns of the Roman emperors Nero, Domitian, Trajan and Marcus Aurelius.

THE CAUSES OF PERSECUTION

CHRISTIAN BELIEFS AND PRACTICES and their religious, political and social consequences often provoked popular hostility and imperial repression. Sources from the first two centuries of Church history show that the reasons behind the persecution of Christians included religious, political and social factors which were so inter-related and inter-dependent that it would be historically misleading to separate them out as isolated causes.

Christianity's Jewish origins ensured that it was a monotheistic religion; that is, that it affirmed the existence of one God. The worship of any other gods or beings was regarded as idolatry. Thus, the traditional gods of the Roman empire

Christians of Gaul in the arena at Lyons.
Engraved by E Luminais in Charles Seignobos, *Scenes et Episodes de l'Histoire Nationale* (1891)

and the belief that the emperors were divine and should be honoured as such, were rejected. From the second century on, therefore, Christians were referred to as 'atheists' because of their rejection of Rome's gods. For example, at the martyrdom of Polycarp, bishop of Smyrna, in the mid second century, he was urged to say to the Christians: 'Away with the atheists', but instead he said this to the Roman crowd (*The Martyrdom of Polycarp* 9.2; *ANE* p25). Christian rejection of the traditional gods also explains, for example, the Roman governor Pliny's requirement that alleged Christians recite a prayer to the gods to refute the allegation (about 112 in Bithynia: *Epistle* 10.96.5; *ANE* p18). The recent origin of Christianity prevented it from being granted the status of *religio licita* (legal religion) apparently enjoyed by its parent religion, Judaism. While it too rejected Rome's gods and imperial cult, it was an ancient and national religion which Rome had the good political sense not to confront. For the Romans, ancestral custom (*mos maiorum*) was an important legal principle which favoured the antiquity of Judaism but not the novelty of Christianity.

However, it is important to understand the social and political effects of Christianity's rejection of the gods. Christians' refusal to engage in what they regarded as idolatry resulted in social withdrawal and separatism. Roman religion touched so many social activities and institutions that Christians were perceived as anti-social. The Roman historian Tacitus, writing in the early second century about Nero's persecution of Christians in Rome (AD64), refers to Christians' perceived 'hatred of the human race' (*Annals* 15. 44; *ANE* p2). Social, political, economic, as well as specifically religious functions, were associated with pagan temples and shrines. Markets were often located in temple courts and membership of social clubs and trade guilds involved devotion to pagan gods. The religious festivals of the pagan calendar were social events in which the public participated. Thus, to avoid compromising their monotheism, Christians became exclusive and this strained relationships with pagan family and friends. From the earliest days, this separatism and pagan disapproval of it were problems for the Church (eg 1 Corinthians 8-10; 1 Peter 2: 11, 12; 4: 2-4: but note 1 Corinthians 5: 9-11). Sometimes, Christian rejection of pagan idolatry and religion had adverse economic effects which provoked further hostility since people's livelihoods were affected. In addition to New Testament evidence for this (Acts 16: 19-21; 19: 23-41), we have Pliny's reference to deserted pagan temples and a reduction in the trade of sacrificial victims (*Epistle* 10. 96.10; *ANE* p19). Pagan religious festivals, with their fairs and games, were an important source of income and Christianity was not helping profits.

Apart from the implicit criticism of the common people's religion, there was a threat to the *pax deorum* (the peace of the gods). The favour and prosperity of the gods were ensured by the religious devotion and rites of the people. In this contractual understanding of religion, the favour of the gods was ensured when the people kept their part of the bargain. Thus, when adversities, such as natural disasters or military defeats, occurred the Christians were blamed for angering the gods. Tertullian, in the late second century, complained that if the Tiber in Rome threatened to flood, or if the Nile in Egypt failed to irrigate the crops, or if there were famine or plague, the public would cry; 'The Christians to the lion!' and then mockingly asked, 'What, all of them to one lion?' (*Apology*, 40.2; *ANE* p158).

Christianity's 'atheism' also had political implications. In a culture where political and religious life were integrated, atheism could be read as treason. To reject Rome's gods was to reject Rome's authority. This was particularly acute when political loyalty was demonstrated through religious means, namely through the 'imperial cult' in which divine honour was given to the emperor. Remains of temples erected for this cult have survived, such as the Temple of Augustus and Roma at Pisidian Antioch (modern southern Turkey). Coins from the second half of the first century describe the emperors Tiberius and Caligula as sons of the 'divine Augustus'. A coin issued by Tiberius honoured the 'Divine Father Augustus' and Tacitus (*Annals* 4.36) mentions a town (Cyzicus) accused in Tiberius' reign of failing to observe the cult of the divine Augustus. Emperor worship is particularly associated with the emperor Domitian (AD81-96). His temple at Laodicea, his statue at Pergamum and the establishment of the imperial cult at Ephesus during his reign, show that he institutionalised the popular deification of the emperor. It may be that the New Testament book of Revelation reflects the imperial cult in Asia Minor under Domitian. The seven churches addressed in its first three chapters were all in imperial cult centres (note also the worship of the beast in chapter 13 and 14: 9-12). Pliny required not only prayer to the gods, but also offerings to the emperor's statue. Christian refusal to worship Rome's gods or to accord divine honours to its emperors, or to join its army because of the similar religious compromises involved, all gave the impression of political disloyalty. Arguments against Christian involvement in the military were presented by Tertullian in his *On the Crown*. When the private and secret nature of Christian meetings, which excluded the unbaptised from the Eucharist, is added to this, the general perception of the Church as a potentially subversive organisation is understandable. Rome's nervousness about 'clubs' (*collegia*) and their potential for destabilising Rome's law and order, is seen in Pliny's reference to Trajan's banning of such associations.

Further, in addition to the social and political effects of Christian rejection of the gods, it is clear from early sources that pagans associated Christianity with certain morally objectionable practices. Tacitus, in the passage referred to above, wrote that Christians were a class 'hated for their abominations.' In the second and third centuries, pagans linked Christianity with cannibalism, incest, infanticide, ritual murder, magical rites and orgies, among other things. In late second century Athens, the Christian Apologist Athenagoras stated that Christians were accused of three things – atheism, Thyestean feasts and Oedipodean intercourse (*Plea for the Christians*, 3. See *ANE* p66, 67). We have already seen that the first charge was due to their rejection of the traditional gods, and due also to the absence of idols, images or shrines in early Christianity. Thyestes unknowingly ate the flesh of his two sons and Oedipus unknowingly married his own mother and so the other two charges were cannibalism and incest. We find the same allegations made at that time against the martyrs of Lyons and Vienne (*ANE* p36). It may be that these popular rumours were due to misunderstandings or misrepresentations of Christian language and practices. Thus it may have been wrongly inferred from eucharistic language (eating Christ's flesh and drinking his blood) that Christians were engaging in cannibalism. The charge of incest may have arisen from the Christian emphasis on brotherly love and Christian 'brothers and sisters' greeting each other with a kiss.

The allegation of infanticide is referred to, for example, by Tertullian who caustically says that Christians should be tortured to discover the number of butchered babies they had eaten as well as how many incestuous acts they had performed in the dark (*Apology* 2.5). The claim of infant cannibalism and sacrifice may have been due to Christian rejection of abortion and infant exposure, which pagans may have viewed as motivated by a desire for a supply of infants.

There appears to have been also a popular belief that Christians were involved in secretive magical rites. The Roman historian Suetonius (early second century) referred to Christianity as a 'wicked superstition' (*Life of Nero*, 16.2; *ANE* p3) and the Latin word translated 'wicked' (*maleficus*) means 'magician'. As we have seen, Tacitus, a contemporary of Suetonius, wrote that many Christians in the Neronian persecution were convicted of 'hatred of the human race'. This was a charge often made against magicians, the penalty being death by burning. Practices such as tongue-speaking, exorcisms, prayer 'in the name of Jesus' and the sign of the cross were similar to magical rites and incantations.

All these popular perceptions of Christianity and others (including the belief that Christians and Jews worshipped a donkey's head eg Tertullian's *Apology* 16) resulted in general pagan hostility to Christians. However, it has been suggested that pagan slanders against Christianity were not due, as is often assumed, to popular misunderstanding of early Christian terminology and liturgy. Sociological theory suggests that the rumours were due to stereotypical generalisations. There is evidence that such charges were made against any group or indeed nation who were regarded as anti-social, simply because it was assumed that anti-social people engaged in such activities. The allegations were deviance labels with no foundation in reality. Indeed, Christians themselves made similar charges against heretical (especially Gnostic) groups eg Irenaeus (*Against Heresies*, 1.25; 2.31) and Hippolytus (*Refutation of All Heresies*, 7.32). Thus, Christians were not considered to be anti-social because they practised such things, but rather, because they were anti-social it was assumed that they practised such things[1].

---

[1] See de Vos, Craig *The Early Christian World* Vol 2 Ed Philip Esler, Routledge: London, 2000, ch 33

THE COURSE OF PERSECUTION

Nero

The early Christians generally regarded the emperor Nero (reigned AD54-AD68) as the first Roman persecutor of the Church. Thus, Tertullian in the 190s calls the persecution of Christians the *institutum Neronianum*, a practice begun by Nero (*To the Nations* 1.7.8-9). In the fourth century the Church historian Eusebius (*ANE* p5) and the Christian writer Sulpicius Severus (*Chronicle* 2.29) were of the same view.

Nero's persecution of Christians in Rome is associated with the fire of Rome in July AD64, which lasted a week and left thousands homeless. Our earliest and most substantial source is provided by the Roman historian Tacitus in his *Annals* (15.44; *ANE* p2-3), composed about AD115 (some fifty years after the event), in the closing years of his life. Tacitus says that despite Nero's efforts the suspicion that the fire had been ordered could not be quashed. It is known that Nero had ambitious building plans for which he may have wanted to make some room in the city. While Tacitus does not explicitly attribute the fire to Nero, other early Roman writers did (Pliny the Elder, Suetonius, Dio Cassius). To get rid of the rumour that the fire was politically authorised, Tacitus says that Nero blamed the Christians in Rome. The word Tacitus used for Nero's action (*subdidit* – 'set up'), suggests that Tacitus believes that the Christians were scapegoats to deflect the suspicion from Nero. Not until the late fourth century do we find another source which links the Christians with the fire of Rome (Sulpicius Severus, *Chronicle* 2.29).

However, this was a clever move from Nero's perspective. After all, the early Christians proclaimed that the world in general and Rome in particular would be destroyed by fire (2 Peter 3: 10-12; Revelation 18: 8-10; 19: 3 where Rome is called Babylon). But, WHC Frend regards it as possible that Nero blamed the Jews (whom he says were suspected throughout the empire of arsonist tendencies) for the fire and that they in turn blamed the rival Christian synagogue[1]. Yet, it has also been argued that Christians did indeed start the fire to fulfill their apocalyptic prophecies, as agents of divine judgement on those who had executed the founder of their sect and who had occupied their holy land. Jewish Christians, on

---

[1] Frend, WHC *The Early Church*, SCM: London, 2003, p31 (First edition, 1965)

this view, dispossessed, disgruntled, living in the slums of Rome, were guilty and Nero was right to blame them. Certainly when Tacitus said that all who 'confessed' were arrested, it is possible that they admitted arson, though it is usually assumed that it was a confession of Christianity.

What does come through clearly in Tacitus' account is the general public resentment towards Christianity, which Tacitus himself shared. We have already considered his description of Christians as a class of people detested for their abominations – probably a reference to common pagan slanders against Christians. He also refers to the Roman execution of Christianity's founder and uses various terms of contempt, directly or indirectly, for the sect – deadly superstition, evil, sordid and shameful, criminals deserving of the most exemplary punishment. As for the Christians' perceived hatred of the human race, we have noted above a possible reference to their practice of magical rites, as well as their generally perceived anti-social lifestyle.

As for the course of the actual persecution itself, Tacitus tells us that firstly, those who confessed (probably to being Christians rather than to starting the fire) were arrested. On the basis of their evidence, an immense multitude was convicted, indicating something of the numerical strength of the Roman church at the time. They were convicted not so much for arson, as for hatred of the human race. The death penalty was administered in such a way as to entertain and amuse the public as well as to mock and humiliate the victims – covered with the hides of beasts, torn to death by dogs, crucified like their founder and set on fire as was fitting for alleged arsonists, to illuminate the darkness of night when the light of day had passed. Tacitus underlines Nero's perverse delight in the cruel spectacle. He had opened up his grounds for the display, putting on an exhibition in the circus, probably the Circus of Gaius and Nero near Vatican Hill. Like a showman, he mixed with the public, dressed as a charioteer, or drove about in his chariot. Abominable though the Christians were in the eyes of the public, Tacitus reports that the manner of the persecution evoked a feeling of pity, since it seemed to be for the gratification of an individual's cruelty, rather than for the good of the public. No doubt, however, it proved to be a powerful deterrent to any would-be agitators.

About the same time as Tacitus was writing his Annals, another Roman historian, Suetonius, made mention of punishment inflicted on Christians during Nero's reign, when he refers to many abuses that he severely punished and repressed. We have noted above a possible reference to the perceived magical rites of Christians in his description of Christianity as a new and wicked superstition. While Suetonius blames the fire of Rome on Nero he does not link this to his persecution of Christians.

In the fourth century, Eusebius reports the tradition that the apostles Paul and Peter were martyred during Nero's reign, Paul being beheaded and Peter crucified.

To support this tradition he quotes Gaius, an early third century Roman writer, and Dionysius the late second century bishop of Corinth (*ANE* p5). In the late first century the author of *1 Clement* had made reference to their recent martyrdom (*ANE* p4). However, Sulpicius Severus placed their martyrdom somewhat later than the persecution connected with the fire of Rome (*Chronicle* 29.3). It is possible, indeed, that Peter's first letter in the New Testament, written in Rome (5: 13, described as Babylon), reflects the Neronian persecution, with its reference to the persecution of Christians and in particular the 'fiery trial that they were enduring (1: 7; 4: 12). However, the letter is addressed to Christians in Asia Minor and there is no evidence that Nero's persecution extended beyond Rome.

There is disagreement over the impact of Nero's persecution of Christians. Some feel that it represents the beginning of Christianity's status as an illegal religion (*religio illicita*) and that this situation remained until the end of the Great Persecution (AD312). Sulpicius Severus states that after Nero's persecution, laws and edicts were enacted which prohibited Christianity (*Chronicle* 29.3). Such decrees, it has been argued, would not have survived since they would have been abolished by the Senate after his death, (in accordance with *damnatio memoriae* – condemnation of memory). However, others regard the persecution as having been local to Rome and brief in duration – a local solution to a local problem. Throughout the Empire provincial magistrates already had powers to deal with potentially subversive groups. The historical reality probably lies somewhere between these two views. While no empire-wide decree against Christians was issued, to some degree at the least an imperial precedent had been set.

Tasks

a. What are the main sources for our knowledge of the Neronian persecution?

b. Provide a summary of Tacitus' account, noting its perception of Christianity.

c. Outline the different views concerning the cause of the fire of Rome.

d. Discuss the significance and impact of the Neronian persecution.

e. Research Nero's life to discover why the rumour about the fire of Rome was politically difficult for him, and to find out how characteristic his cruelty was.

Domitian

Domitian (AD81-AD96) was regarded as the second persecutor of the Church by Melito, bishop of Sardis (Asia Minor) in the second century (cited by Eusebius, *Ecclesiastical History* (*Hist Eccl*) 4. 26). And for Eusebius himself, Domitian was Nero's successor in terms of hostility to God (*Hist Eccl* 3.17). However, while early sources are clear about Domitian's harsh treatment of the Jews and those with Jewish sympathies it is not certain that this specifically included Christians.

The Roman historian Dio Cassius, writing in AD225 in Bithynia, reports that in the last year of his reign Domitian acted against many charged with 'atheism' who also followed Jewish customs (*Epitome* 67.14; *ANE* p6). He specifically mentions the consul Flavius Clemens, the emperor's cousin, and his wife Flavia Domitilla, who was also a relative of the emperor. Clemens was executed and Domitilla was exiled. Suetonius described Clemens as a man of disgraceful idleness (*Life of Domitian* 15) and this is sometimes understood as a reference to his social withdrawal due to his Jewish or, possibly, Christian faith. Dio Cassius also records that a certain Glabrio was executed by Domitian on the same charges but primarily because of his gladiatorial ability which had aroused the emperor's jealousy. According to Suetonius (*Life of Vespasian* 10), this Acilius Glabrio had already been exiled.

The charges of atheism and Jewish customs were appropriate for Christians. Certainly Domitilla, the emperor's niece, was considered to be a Christian by later writers. The association of her name with a Christian cemetery outside Rome may indicate that she was viewed as a member of the Church from the mid second century. Eusebius was clear that she was a Christian and states that her exile was due to her witness to Christ (*Hist Eccl* 3. 18. 4). Eusebius, dependent on the second century writer Hegesippus, also reports that the grandsons of Jesus' brother Jude were brought before Domitian who dismissed them with contempt (*Hist Eccl* 3. 19, 20). Glabrio was possibly a Christian also since his name is linked with the catacombs of Priscilla.

One possible source of conflict with the Church would have been Domitian's enthusiasm for the imperial cult. While it existed before Domitian it was encouraged during his reign (see page 74). Suetonius tells us that Domitian used the title 'Our Master and our God' as a self-reference and that it became a customary form of address in correspondence and conversation (*Life of Domitian* 13). We have already considered the possibility that the book of Revelation reflects Domitianic persecution of Christians because of their refusal to accord him divine honours. Eusebius cited Irenaeus, the late second century bishop of Lyons, as one who identified the beast of Revelation 13: 18 with Domitian (*Hist Eccl* 3. 18. 2, 3).

Nevertheless, it remains not completely certain that Domitian persecuted

Christians. Dio Cassius was writing from a province, Bithynia, with a strong Christian presence, yet he does not specifically identify the named victims of Domitian as Christians. Also, the early Christian letter, *1 Clement,* was written around the same time as Domitian's apparent persecution. While it refers in its opening sentence to the sudden and repeated calamities that have befallen the Roman church (*ANE* p7), it provides no details. In fact, the author's comparison of the Christian Church with the Roman army (*1 Clement* 47) seems unlikely if Domitian were acting against them. Further, Pliny was a lawyer in Rome at the time and yet informs Trajan seventeen years later that he had never taken part in the trial of Christians (*Epistle* 10. 96.1; *ANE* p18).

Outline the evidence for and against the assumption that Domitian persecuted Christians.

Trajan

During the reign of the emperor Trajan (AD98-AD117) the lawyer Pliny the Younger (to be distinguished from his uncle, Pliny the Elder) was sent by the emperor to Bithynia (modern northern Turkey) in about AD112 to correct corrupt and incompetent local government. In his travels he came across Christians in Amastris at the eastern end of the province. Pliny was unsure what to do with the Christians and wrote to the emperor who in turn replied (*Epistle* 10. 96, 97; *ANE* pp18-21). This correspondence provides us with valuable insights not only into the Roman treatment of early Christians but also into Church life and growth in early second century Bithynia.

Pliny's letter begins with an admission of his uncertainty about how to deal with Christians since he had no personal experience of investigating them. He is unsure if the name of Christian in itself is punishable or just the crimes associated with it. Here there is clearly a reference to the popular pagan anti-Christian slanders that we considered earlier. Such rumoured crimes had become synonymous with the name Christian and second century Apologists such as Justin and Tertullian protested that Christians were being punished for being Christian rather than for any proven crimes. Pliny was also uncertain about whether any allowances should be made for age or condition. And what about Christians who recant or former Christians? This uncertainty in a Roman lawyer about the legal status of Christianity, despite its perceived criminality, implies that there was no clear imperial policy on the matter.

After indicating his uncertainties Pliny then informs the emperor of the procedures he has followed thus far. Those accused before him as Christians were asked if this was so and if they answered affirmatively they were asked twice more with threats of punishment, since Roman law required that unverified confessions be repeated. If they persisted in their confession then Pliny sentenced them to death, reckoning that their stubbornness alone deserved punishment. No doubt their refusal to comply with a Roman governor appeared to support suspicions of sedition. Roman citizens of 'similar madness', however were to be sent to Rome.

But Pliny had to deal with another group. When it became known that Christianity was a punishable offence many new charges were brought, including an anonymous paper containing many names. Undoubtedly, many of these charges were spurious, made by people with an axe to grind. Pliny's response was to release those who denied that they were or ever had been Christians. Before release, however, they had to prove their claims by repeating a prayer to the gods at Pliny's dictation, by showing reverence to the emperor's statue with incense and wine, together with the image of the gods, and by cursing Christ. This, Pliny had heard, genuine Christians can't be forced to do (compare 1 Corinthians 12: 3). Others named by the informer said that they had been Christians, some of them three or more years previously and a few twenty years before, but had since disowned the faith. These also proved their claims by worshipping the emperor's statue and the images of the gods, and by cursing Christ.

The information that these former Christians gave to Pliny provides us with an insight into the worship and fellowship of the church in this area. In effect, Pliny was told that Christians were not politically dangerous nor morally perverse. They met before dawn on a set day which was probably Sunday, called 'the first day of the week' in the New Testament, the day of Jesus' resurrection and of Christian fellowship (eg Luke 24: 1-3; Acts 20: 7). To Christ they offered divine worship, reciting by turns a set form of words, which may mean that they sang a hymn, possibly an antiphonal or responsorial psalm (compare Ephesians 5: 19, 20; and the 'hymn' to the divine Christ in Philippians 2: 6-11). Pliny heard too that the Christians bound themselves by an oath but not for the purpose of committing crime. The oath (*sacramentum*) may have been viewed by the Romans as politically subversive and not in the Christian sense of *sacramentum*, referring to sacred rites and pledges. Rather, Christians pledged themselves to avoid immorality and injustice. After this early morning meeting the Christians would depart and then re-assemble to take food, but ordinary and harmless food. Thus, the pagan rumours of cannibalism were groundless.

We probably have a reference here to the *agape* or non-eucharistic fellowship meal observed by early believers (see chapter on the Eucharist). However, Pliny had issued an edict, in accordance with Trajan's instructions, forbidding clubs (*collegia*). Such secret societies could become centres of political or social agitation, and in other correspondence between Pliny and Trajan it appears that they did not have a good reputation in Bithynia and may have contributed to the poor administrative situation in the region (*Epistles* 32, 33, 92, 93). In the recent past, Trajan had prevented Nicomedia's 150 firemen from forming such a society (*Epistle* 10: 33). Not fully satisfied with the information of the former Christians, Pliny decided to get to the truth by torturing two maid-servants 'called deaconesses' (*ministrae*, equivalent of Greek *diakonoi*; compare Romans 16: 1 and probably 1 Timothy 3: 11). This is the final reference to female deacons until the fourth century. From the torture of these two unfortunate women Pliny discovered only what he considered to be a depraved and extravagant superstition, rather than a conspiracy, and postponed his investigation to consult the emperor.

Pliny concludes his letter with some comments about the growth and impact of Christianity in the region. Many of all ages and classes, and of both genders, urban and rural, had been affected by the contagion of the superstition. Pagan temples had been almost deserted, religious rites had been neglected and there were few buyers of sacrificial victims. Even if we allow for some exaggeration on Pliny's part, clearly the Church had expanded noticeably and was impacting social and economic life in the province. Pliny, however, informs the emperor that his actions have reversed this trend. The economic recovery and stability, that he was sent to produce, was on course.

Trajan's brief reply commends Pliny for the procedure he has followed. He then says that no general rule or set procedure can be laid down. In other words, in the early second century, there was no single imperial policy regarding Christianity and this appears to have been the general situation in the first two centuries. Trajan advises that while Christians are not to be sought out they are to be punished if convicted. Those who disown Christianity and prove it by worshipping the gods should be pardoned. Unsigned papers should be ignored since they set a bad precedent and are unworthy of imperial time. Tertullian's criticism of this policy at the other end of the century is well known – it is confused because it implies that they are both innocent ('don't seek them out') and guilty ('punish them if convicted'; *Apology* 2. 8). However, J Stevenson regards Trajan's attitude as a sensible and pragmatic decision, avoiding groundless accusations on the one hand, but retaining sanctions if necessary on the other[1] (*ANE* p21). And Sherwin-White sees administrative genius in Trajan's advice[2]. What is apparent is that Christians were punished merely for being Christians and apostates were free to go. There was no clear, universal, imperial policy regarding Christianity.

Also during Trajan's reign Ignatius, bishop of Antioch (Syria), was arrested and taken to Rome to be martyred (about AD107-AD110), possibly as part of a quota of victims for the Roman circus. He wrote to the Roman church, informing them

---

[1] Stevenson J, (Revised by Frend, WHC) *A New Eusebius*, SPCK: London 1987, p21

[2] Sherwin-White, AN *The Letters of Pliny: A Historical and Social Commentary*, Clarendon: Oxford 1966 p711

of the harsh treatment he was enduring at the hands of his military escort ('ten leopards') and urging them not to seek to prevent his martyrdom. He was looking forward with enthusiasm to facing the wild beasts, whom he would provoke to devour him quickly. Indeed, Ignatius welcomed a violent death that he might become a true disciple and attain to Jesus Christ (*To the Romans*, 5; *ANE* p12-13). Ignatius' enthusiasm for martyrdom was an important influence on the development of a martyr cult in the early Church (for more details on Ignatius and martyrdom, see the next chapter). Ignatius' letters demonstrate that Roman persecution of Christianity was not a constant threat for the churches that he wrote to, which were mostly in Asia Minor.

Tasks

a. *Outline the circumstances of Pliny's visit to Bithynia.*

b. *In bullet point form, summarise the main contents of Pliny's letter.*

c. *What can we learn from the Pliny-Trajan correspondence about (i) imperial policy towards Christianity, (ii) early Christian worship, (iii) the growth of the Church?*

d. *Discuss Tertullian's view of Trajan's policy towards the Church.*

Marcus Aurelius

Marcus Aurelius (reigned AD161-AD180) had been tutored by Marcus Cornelius Fronto, an opponent of Christianity, who in the first decade of the emperor's reign had delivered an anti-Christian speech containing the popular accusations of infanticide and incest (Minucius Felix, *Octavius* 9.6; 31.2). The emperor himself was a keen student of the Stoic philosophy and was, therefore, ideologically opposed to Christianity and criticised, for instance, Christians' eager readiness to die for their faith (*Meditations* 11.3).

During his reign, there were at least three notable incidents of persecution against Christians – the martyrdoms of Justin and his companions (Rome, AD165), of Lyons and Vienne (Gaul, AD177) and of Scilli (Carthage, AD180). The martyrdom of Polycarp, bishop of Smyrna, along with others, is placed within the reign of Marcus Aurelius by Eusebius and by some modern scholars[1]. However, many others[2] accept the earlier date of AD155/6, as indicated in *ANE*

---

[1] eg WHC Frend *The Early Church*, SCM: London, 2003, p59

[2] eg H Chadwick *The Early Church*, Penguin: London, 1993, p30

p23. Detailed discussion of the uncertainty of the date of Polycarp's martyrdom is not possible here (see *ANE* p29[1]), but it is assumed that the earlier date is the most likely. For details of and comment on the martyrdom of Polycarp see *ANE* pp23-30 (pp96-97 of this book).

Justin (AD100-AD165), originally from Palestine, studied various philosophies before he was converted and established a Christian school in Rome. It seems that he was betrayed to the authorities by a rival teacher, belonging to the Cynics, who bore a grudge against him. His martyrdom (which has given him the name Justin Martyr) and that of six of his pupils in Rome in AD165 is recorded in *Acta Martyrum*. The account of the martyrdom of Justin and his companions is apparently based on an official account of the proceedings (*ANE* p373). However, the edition in Stevenson (*ANE* pp32-34) may have come from as late as the early fourth century since it states, apparently anachronistically, that decrees were issued against Christians to compel them to worship the gods (see *ANE* p34 note).

Along with his six companions, Justin was brought before the prefect of Rome, the aged Junius Rusticus. They were ordered to obey the gods and the authorities. Justin was asked about his teachings and the whereabouts of their meeting-place, and replied that he lodged near certain baths; however the text is corrupt and the location unknown. He also stated, surprisingly, that he was unaware of any other Christian meeting-place in Rome. The seven of them, including a servant in Caesar's household, freely confessed that they were Christians, some of them attributing this to their Christian parents. When asked if he thought he would ascend to heaven after being flogged and beheaded, Justin replied that he did not think so but knew so. Rusticus tried to persuade them to sacrifice to the gods but Justin said that they knew that they would stand before a more terrible Judge. For this refusal to sacrifice to the gods and to obey the emperor's command they were flogged and beheaded. Their bodies were recovered by other Christians and laid in a convenient place, the location of which is unknown. This account reveals the strong faith and religious loyalty of early Christians and also underlines the close link between religion and politics in Roman society. Rejection of Rome's gods is rejection of Rome's authority.

The martyrs of Lyons and Vienne were put to death in the amphitheatre at Lyons, Gaul (southern France) in AD177. A contemporary account of the martyrdoms, in a letter from the churches in Lyons and Vienne to the Christians in Asia and Phrygia, has been preserved by Eusebius (*Ecclesiastical History*, 5.1. 3-63; *ANE* pp34-44).

The letter begins by outlining popular hostility to Christians in the region.

---

[1] Also Holmes, Michael *The Apostolic Fathers*, Baker Books: Grand Rapids, 1999, p223

Christians were socially excluded, verbally insulted and physically attacked. After being questioned in the market-place by the city leaders in the presence of the mob they confessed and were imprisoned until the governor arrived. A young Christian, Vettius Epagathus, requested that he be allowed to defend the Christians against the charges of the mob. However, the governor only wanted to know if he were a Christian and for that had him executed. Over a number of days Christians were imprisoned, placed in stocks in the noisiest and darkest part of the jail, and were brought out daily to watch the torture and execution of their fellow believers. Pagan slaves who worked in Christian households, urged on by the soldiers and fearing torture themselves, falsely accused Christians of cannibalism and incest. The rumours spread and even pagan friends of Christians became hostile.

A number of martyrs, whose torture and execution was greeted by the watching crowds, are singled out for special mention in the letter. For instance, Sanctus, a deacon from the church at Vienne, would respond to every question he was asked only with the words, 'I am a Christian'. He endured a variety of tortures, including the application of hot metal plates to the tenderest parts of his body and attacks by wild beasts, until finally he died in an iron chair suspended above a fire, along with the recently baptised Maturus. Blandina the slave girl is especially noted for her courage and inspiration of others in the face of a host of extreme tortures including suspension on a stake, attacks by wild beasts, flogging, the hot iron chair and, having been put in a basket, she was gored by a bull before she was finally put to death. Accompanying her was a fifteen year old boy called Ponticus who was encouraged by his sister to endure the tortures before he died refusing to swear by the gods. At the other end of life was Pothinus, bishop of Lyons, who though in his nineties suffered terrible beatings to avenge the gods and died two days later in prison. The letter mentions that some martyrs pardoned those who were not martyrs, a practice that was to cause difficulties in the Decian persecution of the next century.

When the governor realised that some of his prisoners were Roman citizens he then sought the emperor's advice. Attalus was such a person and was well known to the crowd, who called for his blood. He was led around the amphitheatre preceded by a placard on which was written: 'This is Attalus the Christian' as the crowd mocked him. Marcus Aurelius' reply to the governor's letter instructed that confessed Christians should be tortured to death but that those who denied the faith should be released (similar to Trajan's instructions to Pliny). Before this the governor had imprisoned even those who denied the faith because of the alleged crimes associated with it. The governor then decided to make a spectacle of the Christians at a local national festival, probably the annual feast of the Three Gauls on 1 August. Roman citizens were beheaded and the others were sent to the wild beasts. The corpses were guarded to prevent their Christian burial. Finally their bodies were burned and the ashes swept into the Rhone in an attempt to prevent their future resurrection.

According to later lists, nearly fifty Christians lost their lives in this persecution inspired by popular hostility and fed by unfounded rumours of crime and immorality. Indeed, it appears that the high point of popular resentment against Christians was reached during the reign of Marcus Aurelius. The gods had been offended and needed to be avenged, probably to ensure local agricultural prosperity. There was suspicion too that the local nobility were behind the popular attacks for economic reasons. The emperor had ruled that at a tenth of the normal cost, local criminals could be used as gladiators in the local annual games. The governor was in full sympathy with the local mob and seems to have been harsher than Pliny, who released those who denied that they were Christians and proved it. But, like Pliny, he sought his emperor's advice who, like Trajan, ordered the release of those who denied the faith and the punishment of those who confessed it.

Finally, during Marcus Aurelius' reign twelve Christians (seven men and five women) from Scilli in North Africa were beheaded in the provincial capital Carthage in AD180. Our source for their trial and martyrdom is the *Acta Martyrum* which we discussed above (*ANE* pp44, 45). This account provides us with the earliest evidence of Christianity in Roman North Africa. The trial was conducted by the governor Vigellius Saturninus whom the contemporary Carthaginian Tertullian regarded as the first governor to persecute Christians in the region (*To Scapula* 3).

The Christians were told that they might gain the emperor's tolerance if they changed their minds. The Christians' spokesman Speratus, however, declared their moral innocence and respect for the emperor. The governor urged them to swear by the genius (ie fortune, guiding spirit) of the emperor and to pray for his safety. Speratus stated that he did not recognise the empire of the present age but that he did pay taxes because he did recognise his Lord, the King of Kings and Emperor of all nations. The Christians confessed their faith and declined the offer of a thirty day referral of their cases. Speratus had with him tangible evidence of his faith in a case which he said, when asked, contained the Books and also the letters of a righteous man called Paul. The twelve were sentenced to die by the sword because of their confession that they lived according to the religious rites of the Christians and for their stubbornness – reminding us of Pliny – in refusing the opportunity to return to Roman religion. They all gave thanks to God and one, named Nartzalus, said that on that day they would be martyrs in heaven.

Failure to comply with Roman religion and its reverence for the emperor was regarded as political treachery. Speratus' comments about not recognising the empire of this age must have appeared particularly seditious. Note too the desire of the authorities to avoid taking punitive action, if possible. Early Christians from their perspective, however, would pay their taxes and respect the emperor but not engage in what they regarded to be idolatrous actions.

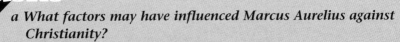

Tasks

a What factors may have influenced Marcus Aurelius against Christianity?

b. Research Stoicism to discover why Marcus Aurelius found Christianity to be intellectually objectionable.

c. Provide brief accounts of the main incidents of persecution during his reign, noting the sources in each case.

d. Compare the attitude of the Roman governor to the Christians in Lyons and Vienne with that of other governors noted in this chapter.

Practice Essay Titles

1. Outline your knowledge and understanding of the persecution of Christians in the first two centuries. (30)

   Discuss the claim that the persecution of early Christians was due to a complex of factors. (15)

2. Briefly describe the contents of the Pliny-Trajan correspondence, discussing its value for our understanding of early Christianity. (30)

   Comment on the view that Tertullian was right to find fault with Trajan's policy towards Christianity. (15)

AS level

Apostolic Fathers

The Apostolic Fathers with particular reference to the writings of Ignatius of Antioch.

(CCEA Specification)

Definition

Since the seventeenth century the name 'Apostolic Fathers' has been used to refer to a collection of early Christian writings from the late first to the mid second century. These are the earliest Christian writings outside the New Testament. It is important to note that the name and the collection are late even though the individual writings themselves were composed in early Church history.

Objective

In this chapter we shall gain a knowledge and understanding of the early Christian writings listed below, traditionally known as the Apostolic Fathers, paying particular attention to the writings of Ignatius of Antioch.

The Letters of Ignatius

The Letter of Polycarp

The Martyrdom of Polycarp

1 Clement

2 Clement

The Didache

The Letter of Barnabas

The Shepherd of Hermas

The Letter to Diognetus

The Fragments of Papias

The collection itself is artificial and arbitrary, as is clear from the fact that there has been uncertainty over what books should be included in the list. While the term was used as early as the sixth century, by Severus, patriarch of Antioch, its modern use goes back to William Wake, an archbishop of Canterbury, who in 1693 published a collection of early Christian writings which he attributed to the 'Apostolical Fathers'. He so-called them because he believed that they came from the contemporaries of the apostles and that their authors were taught either by Christ himself or his apostles. Wake included in his collection the letters of Barnabas, Clement, Ignatius and Polycarp, together with the Martyrdoms of Ignatius and Polycarp. Before this, in 1672, the French scholar JB Cotelier published the same works (apart from the *Martyrdom of Ignatius* which was a late fiction) which he regarded as having been written by 'holy Fathers who flourished in apostolic times.' In 1765 another French scholar, A Gallandi, added to the collection the *Letter to Diognetus, the Fragments of Papias* and the *Apology of Quadratus*. Finally, the latest addition to the collection was the *Didache*, discovered in 1873 and published ten years later.

Thus we can see that the boundaries of the collection are uncertain due to the fact that both the name 'Apostolic Fathers' and the collection of writings to which it refers are a matter of late tradition rather than historical necessity. We shall see indeed that within this arbitrary collection, there is quite a literary and theological diversity. One would expect this from a group of Christian writings whose main unifying factor is that they are the earliest Christian writings we possess outside of the New Testament, which may or may not have links with the first century apostles. However, the great value of these individual writings is the historical and theological insights which they provide into earliest Christianity outside the New Testament. Convenient English translations of and introductions to the collection include *Early Christian Writings* (Penguin Classics, Maxwell Staniforth and Andrew Louth 1968/1987; which, however, does not include Hermas, Papias and Quadratus) and *The Apostolic Fathers* (Baker Books, Michael Holmes, 1999; which also includes the Greek texts).

Tasks

a. Explain the origins of the name 'Apostolic Fathers'.

b. Why is it an arbitrary collection of early Christian writings?

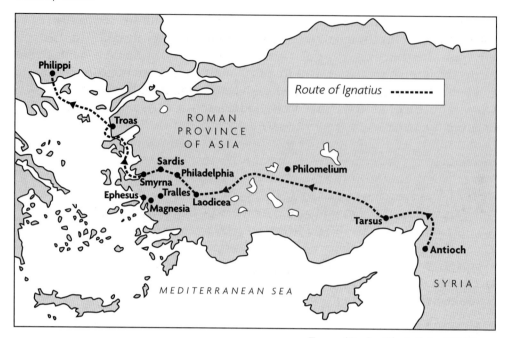

From 'Early Christiain Writings

THE LETTERS OF IGNATIUS

Ignatius (around AD35-AD110), who also introduces himself in each of his letters by the name Theophorus ('God-bearer'), was bishop of Antioch in Syria. Here he was arrested and brought under guard by ten Roman soldiers (the 'ten leopards' of Romans 5. 1) to Rome to be thrown to wild beasts. The circumstances of his arrest are unknown, though it has been suggested that divisions within his own church (Phld 10. 1; Smyrn 11. 2; Pol 7. 1) had brought the Christians and their leader, in particular, to the attention of the local authorities. It may be that he was brought to Rome, along with others, as part of a quota of victims which the provinces had to supply for the Roman amphitheatre. According to Eusebius, his martyrdom occurred during the reign of Trajan (AD98-AD117) in about AD107/8. Many, however, would place it later in Trajan's reign and some even locate it in Hadrian's time (AD117-AD138).

On his way to Rome, he was met by representatives of various churches to which he then wrote letters (see map above). In Smyrna he met the local bishop, Polycarp, and wrote to the churches of Ephesus, Magnesia and Tralles, whose delegates he had met, and also to the church in Rome where he was heading. In Troas he wrote to the churches of Philadelphia and Smyrna, whose delegates he had met also, and to Smyrna's bishop, Polycarp. Thus, Ignatius wrote letters to six churches, five of which were in Asia Minor, and one individual, Polycarp. At Philippi he was welcomed by the church (Pol Phil, 1. 1) and then, presumably, was taken on to martyrdom in Rome. It seems that Polycarp later collected Ignatius' letters and sent them, for instance, to the church in Philippi, at their request, telling them that they would benefit greatly from them since they had to do with faith, endurance and edification (Pol Phil 13. 2; *ANE* p16, 17). The letters have a complicated manuscript history and exist in three forms (long, middle, short), the so-called 'middle recension' preserving the original letters.

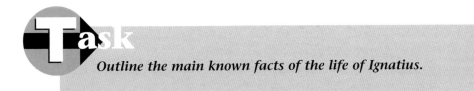

Task

Outline the main known facts of the life of Ignatius.

According to Michael Holmes, three main concerns appear to have been on Ignatius' mind as he wrote his letters en route to Rome[1].

Heresy

Ignatius was concerned that heretics (false teachers) were disrupting and deceiving the churches. The heretics were of two kinds – Judaizers and docetists. Though, it is possible that Ignatius was writing against one heresy which contained both Judaizing and docetic elements.

The Judaizers were Gentile Christians, probably former converts to Judaism, who believed that Old Testament requirements, such as the observance of the Sabbath, should still be followed. In the church at Philadelphia there was a group of Christians in disagreement with the bishop, because they believed that the Old Testament had supreme authority in relation to the gospel. Ignatius himself, having been allowed to spend an hour with the church, had heard them say that if they did not find a particular teaching in 'the archives' (probably the Old Testament) they would not believe it in the gospel. For Ignatius, 'the archives' were Jesus, his death and resurrection and the faith that came by means of him (Phld 8. 2). Ignatius loved the Old Testament prophets because they waited for and believed in Christ. Then he added: "But if anyone explains Judaism to you, do not listen to him. For it is better to hear about Christianity from a circumcised man than about Judaism from an uncircumcised man." (6. 1)

The church at Magnesia was also under threat from Judaizing Christians. Ignatius warned the church not to be deceived by strange teachings and ancient myths: "For if we are still living according to Judaism, we admit that

---

[1] Holmes, Michael *The Apostolic Fathers*, Baker Books: Grand Rapids, 1999, p129

we have not received grace." (Magn 8. 1; *ANE* p13, 14)). Even the Old Testament prophets, argued Ignatius, lived in accordance with Christ and were his disciples in the Spirit. Some Christians had lived in ancient practices but no longer kept the Jewish Sabbath, living now in accordance with the Christian Lord's Day. The old, bad leaven, which had become stale and sour, should be thrown out and the new leaven, Jesus Christ, should be received. "It is absurd to profess Jesus Christ and to follow Judaism. For Christianity did not believe in Judaism, but Judaism in Christianity ..." (Magn 10. 3; *ANE* p14).

Docetists (from the Greek for 'appearance') taught that Jesus only 'appeared' or 'seemed' to be human, to have a body, to have been born, to have suffered, died and risen again. In reality, he had no human nature or body since God would not unite himself with flesh. That he appeared to be human was merely an accommodation to human weakness. From Ignatius' letters, it is clear that three churches he wrote to were threatened by docetism – Ephesus, Tralles and Smyrna.

In creed-like statements, Ignatius insisted on the reality of Jesus' incarnation and humanity as essential for salvation. Writing to the Ephesians, he contrasted Jesus' two natures (human and divine) and his two states (humiliation and exaltation):

There is only one physician, who is both flesh and spirit, born and unborn, God in man, true life in death, both from Mary and from God, first subject to suffering and then beyond it, Jesus Christ our Lord.

(7. 2; ANE p13)

To the Trallians he stressed the actual humanity of Jesus by repeatedly using the adverb 'really/truly':

Be deaf, therefore, when anyone speaks to you apart from Jesus Christ, who was of the family of David, who was the son of Mary; who really was born, who both ate and drank; who really was persecuted under Pontius Pilate, who really was crucified and died while those in heaven and on earth and under the earth looked on; who, moreover, really was raised from the dead ...

(9. 1, 2; ANE p14, 15)

For the church at Smyrna, Ignatius drew out the implications of docetism. Denying the humanity of Jesus, docetists were also unconcerned about the human, physical needs of others such as widows, orphans, prisoners or the hungry and thirsty. Also, they denied the reality of Jesus' flesh and blood in the Eucharist and abstained from it. Further, they were robbing Ignatius' personal suffering and impending martyrdom of any meaning since he would be no longer sharing in the suffering of Jesus (6. 2; 4. 2).

Outline the heresy/heresies reflected in the Ignatian letters, and Ignatius' response to them.

Unity

Ignatius' solution to the divisive threats posed to the churches by the heretics was to insist on the authority of each church's bishop as the focus of unity. With Ignatius we have the first appearance of what has been called 'monarchical episcopacy' or 'monepiscopacy' – each church has one bishop (Greek for bishop/overseer is *episkopos*) in charge, assisted by presbyters (elders) and deacons. This threefold ministry seems to be a development of the twofold ministry found in other early Christian writings such as the New Testament and the *Didache* where a church has bishops, who are also called presbyters/elders, and deacons. While the threefold ministry existed in the churches in Asia Minor, including Ignatius' own church in Antioch, there is no indication of it in Ignatius' letter to the Roman church, nor in *1 Clement* or the *Shepherd of Hermas* which are also connected with Rome. Nor is there in Polycarp's letter to the church in Philippi, Greece. Thus, the threefold ministry with its emphasis on a single authoritative bishop was not universal. Indeed, some feel that Ignatius' repeated insistence on it in his letters is evidence that it is a new practice, while others disagree, arguing that Ignatius' insistence is due to the urgent threat to the unity of the churches (see pp140-142).

Thus, Ignatius urges the churches to submit to the bishop and the presbyters and to respect the deacons:

Make every effort to do everything in divine harmony, the bishop presiding in the place of God, and the presbyters in the place of the council of the apostles and the deacons, who are most dear to me, having been entrusted with the service of Jesus Christ ...

(Magn 6. 1)

Similarly, he writes to the Trallians:

Similarly, let all respect the deacons as Jesus Christ, just as the bishop also, who is a type of the Father, and the presbyters as the council of God and as the band of the apostles. Apart from these no assembly can be called a church. (3. 1)

The bishop in particular is the focus of authority and unity, apart from whom no church exists and no ministry of the church is valid:

Flee from divisions as the beginning of evils. Follow the bishop, all of you, as

Jesus Christ followed the Father, and follow the presbytery as you would the apostles; and respect the deacons as you would a commandment from God. Let no-one do anything relating to the church without the bishop. The only valid Eucharist is the one under the bishop's authority or whomever he authorises. Where the bishop appears there let the people be; just as wherever Jesus Christ is, there is the universal [Greek: katholikos] Church. It is not permissible either to baptise or to conduct a love feast without the bishop. But whatever he approves is also pleasing to God, so that everything you do may be sound and valid.

(Smyrn 8; ANE p15; see also Magn 7)

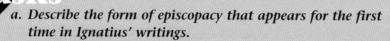

Tasks

a. Describe the form of episcopacy that appears for the first time in Ignatius' writings.

b. Explain why Ignatius insisted on the importance of the bishop in church life.

Martyrdom

Ignatius looked forward to his impending martyrdom in Rome with enthusiasm and urged the Roman church not to intervene in order to prevent it.

I am writing to all the churches and assuring everyone that I willingly die for God, unless you hinder me. I urge you not to be unseasonably kind to me. Allow me to be food for the wild beasts through whom I can reach God. I am God's wheat, ground by the teeth of the wild beasts, that I may be found to be pure bread. Rather, incite the wild beasts, that they may become my tomb and leave nothing of my body so that I will not be a burden to anyone when I have fallen asleep. Then I will truly be a disciple of Jesus Christ when the world will not see my body. Pray to the Lord for me that through these instruments I may be found a sacrifice to God.

(Rom 4. 1, 2; see also Rom 5, ANE p12, 13; and Rom 7. 2)

While some have regarded Ignatius as having a neurotic obsession with martyrdom (compare also "I passionately yearn to die", Rom 7. 2), Michael Holmes draws our attention to three factors which shaped Ignatius' thinking. Firstly, there was a desire to imitate Christ's suffering and by this to become his true disciple (Rom 5. 3; 6. 2). Also, his enthusiasm for martyrdom may have been an attempt to embolden himself because of an underlying fear of failure (Rom 3. 2; 7. 2). His release, by the intervention of the Roman church or otherwise, could be viewed as apostasy. Finally, the divisions in his own church in Antioch might imply that he was failing as a bishop. His martyrdom might improve the situation in his church and his own reputation[1]. Certainly Ignatius' attitude to martyrdom had an important influence on the development of a martyr cult in the early Church.

Discuss the view that Ignatius had an unchristian attitude to martyrdom.

Apart from these three main concerns in the Ignatian letters, other themes are of interest too. For instance, Ignatius' self-understanding is revealed in a number of places. While he refers to himself as 'the bishop of Syria' (Rom 2. 2), he is aware that he is not an apostle like Peter and Paul (Rom 4. 4). Yet, like a prophet, he claimed to speak by inspiration of the Spirit on occasion (Phld 7; *ANE* p16). We have seen also the importance of Ignatius for tracing the development of creeds in the early Church (page 36).

Of interest too is Ignatius' sacramental theology. Indeed, Ignatius provides the first use of the word 'Eucharist' for the communion service (Phld 4), which he sees as the focus of church unity. He writes of 'one altar' (Magn 7. 2) and of the bread as 'the medicine of immortality' and the 'antidote' of death (Eph 20. 2). And Jesus 'was baptised so that by his suffering he might cleanse the water' of baptism (Eph 18. 2).

The Ignatian letters also give us some insight into the development of the canon of the New Testament ie those Christian writings which came to be regarded as authoritative Scripture by the Church. We have seen already (under Heresy) that he accepted the Old Testament as authoritative, referring to its writings as 'the archives' (Phld 8), though some regard this as a reference to early gospel writings in distinction from later corrupted gospels. His reference to 'the gospel' and 'the apostles' alongside 'the prophets' (Phld 5), may be evidence of authoritative New Testament writings in addition to the Old Testament. Ignatius was certainly aware of at least oral traditions underlying Matthew (Pol 2. 2), Luke (Smyrn 3. 2), John (Phld 7. 1) and possibly even these Gospels themselves. Also, Ignatius may have known of a collection of Paul's letters (Eph 12. 2) and certainly had a knowledge of Romans, 1 Corinthians,

---

[1] Holmes, Michael *The Apostolic Fathers*, Baker Books: Grand Rapids, 1999, pp130, 131

Ephesians and Colossians and probably 2 Corinthians, Galatians, Philippians and the Pastoral letters (1 and 2 Timothy and Titus).

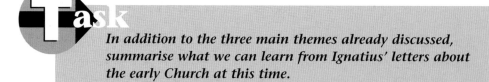

In addition to the three main themes already discussed, summarise what we can learn from Ignatius' letters about the early Church at this time.

POLYCARP

Polycarp (about AD69/AD70 – AD155/AD160) was bishop of Smyrna (western Asia Minor) and a recipient of a letter from his friend Ignatius. He wrote a letter to the church in Philippi (Macedonia) and we also have an account of his martyrdom. Both these documents are normally included in the collection known as the Apostolic Fathers.

Polycarp's letter to the Philippians seems to have been written a short time after Ignatius' martyrdom (about AD110; Pol Phil 1. 1; 9. 1; 13. 2) in reply to a letter from them seeking instruction about 'righteousness' (3.1). Most of the letter is an explanation of and an exhortation to Christian righteousness, the essence of which is faith, hope and love (3. 1-3). Polycarp explains what this means for various groups within the church (4-6; men, wives, children, youth, widows, deacons and presbyters). There is a warning to avoid heretics who reject the humanity of Jesus, future resurrection and judgement (6. 3-7. 2). Before the letter concludes, Polycarp deals with the matter of Valens, a former presbyter of the Philippian church, who strayed through a love of money. The church is urged to restore Valens and his wife (11. 1-4). Polycarp's pastoral concern in the letter was to maintain the church in correct belief and behaviour. In the letter, Polycarp reveals knowledge of Matthew, Luke, Acts, Romans, 1 and 2 Corinthians, Galatians, Ephesians, Philippians, 1 and 2 Timothy, 1 John and 1 Peter, as well as several Old Testament writings and 1 Clement. Though he does not quote the New Testament writings as 'Scripture' (apart from possibly Ephesians – 12. 1), he does regard them as authoritative.

'The Martyrdom of Polycarp' is a letter from Polycarp's church at Smyrna to the church at Philomelium (see map, page 90), providing an account of Polycarp's martyrdom in Smyrna at the age of eighty-six. It is the earliest account of a Christian martyrdom outside the New Testament writings and became the model for later martyrological literature. The letter seems to have been written by a witness of the martyrdom shortly after the event in the middle of the second century. There is, however, uncertainty as to the date of

Polycarp's martyrdom (see page 83). The letter begins with an account of earlier Christian martyrs (2-3) and of Quintus the coward who, after initially volunteering for martyrdom, sacrificed to Caesar (4). Most of the letter is about Polycarp's pursuit and arrest (5-8), trial before the proconsul (9-12), horrible death by fire and dagger (13-17) and burial (18). After the conclusion (19-20), there are a number of appendices (21-22).

The letter aims to counteract improper views of martyrs and martyrdom – the former are not to be worshipped (eg 17. 2, 3) and the latter is not to be sought (4). Yet, martyrdom is honourable (2. 12) and Polycarp's bones were preserved as relics with which to celebrate 'the birthday of his martyrdom' (18. 3). Polycarp's martyrdom is paralleled with that of Jesus, whom he imitates (eg 1. 2; 19: 1). His courage in the Lord Christ versus Lord Caesar contest (10. 1) inspired others to stand firm: "Eighty-six years I have served him and he has done me no wrong. How can I blaspheme my King who saved me?" (9. 3).

Tasks

a. *Outline the background and contents of Polycarp's letter to the Philippians.*

b. *What insight does 'The Martyrdom of Polycarp' give us into early Christian attitudes to martyrdom?*

CLEMENT

Clement was a late first century Christian leader in Rome to whom two writings in the Apostolic Fathers have been traditionally attributed. *1 Clement* is a long letter from the church in Rome to the church in Corinth, Greece (see its opening words), probably written about AD95-AD97. While the letter does not identify its author, most manuscripts and early tradition recorded by Eusebius attribute it to Clement. The Roman church had heard of division in the Corinthian church and that younger men had removed its presbyters from office (3. 3; 44. 6; 47. 6, 7). In addition to the letter, which appealed for a removal of jealousy and strife (3-6) and for order, harmony (eg 63. 2) and respect for leadership (44), the Roman church sent mediators (63. 3, 4; 65. 1) to restore peace in the church.

The letter gives us an insight into Church leadership and perceptions of the Roman Empire at this time. While Irenaeus in the late second century regarded Clement as the third bishop of Rome after Peter, there does not appear to have been monarchical episcopacy in Rome at this time. Rather, the terms 'bishop' and 'presbyter' appear to be synonymous and leadership was provided by a group of such men (44. 1-6). In *1 Clement* we have the first appearance of the laity (people) as distinct from the leaders (40) and of apostolic succession – the idea that bishops and deacons are successors of the apostles of Christ (42-44; see *ANE* pp7-9). As for attitudes to the empire, 1 Clement has a much more positive view of the Roman authorities (eg 37; 60. 4-61) than is found in the New Testament book of Revelation, written around the same time, in which Rome is a prostitute, drunk with the blood of the saints, reflecting the views of Christians in Asia Minor.

2 Clement is neither a letter nor a writing of Clement. It is rather a sermon based on Isaiah 54: 1. (2: 1 – 'Rejoice, O barren woman, who does not bear; break forth and shout, you who have no labour pains; for many are the children of the deserted woman, more than she who has a husband.'). It is the earliest surviving complete Christian sermon. The anonymous author, apparently an elder (17. 3), writing to a mainly Gentile readership (1.6. 3.1), which may be subject to Gnostic influence (10. 2-5; 1. 1; 9. 1-5), appeals for repentance (eg 5. 1; 8. 1; 13. 1), purity of life and brotherly love (eg 4), in the face of persecution (eg 4. 4; 5). The origin and date of the work is unknown. Rome, Corinth and Egypt have all been suggested, as have dates ranging from the late first to late second century.

In relation to the New Testament canon, Clement probably reflects awareness of a collection of Paul's letters including Roman, 1 Corinthians, Galatians, Ephesians, Philippians, 1 Timothy and Titus. He also knows Hebrews and possibly Acts and James or 1 Peter. He knew of sayings similar to those in our New Testament Gospels but evidence of direct dependence on them is lacking. *1 Clement* itself was regarded as 'Scripture' by some early Fathers eg Clement of Alexandria. *2 Clement* reveals knowledge of Matthew, Luke, 1 Corinthians and Ephesians and possible awareness of Hebrews, James and 1 Peter. It also contains the earliest example of a New Testament passage being cited as 'Scripture' (2. 4 quoting Mark 2: 17/Matthew 9: 13).

Tasks

a. Outline the background and contents of 1 and 2 Clement.

b. What can be learned about the early Church from these writings?

THE DIDACHE

The *Didache* (Greek for 'teaching') was known in ancient times as 'The Teaching of the Lord to the Gentiles by the Twelve Apostles', though no scholar would argue for its apostolic authorship now. It is an anonymous work which has been dated variously from the mid first century to the early third century. Although additions and alterations were made over time, in its final form most of it dates probably from the mid second century. As to the unknown place of its origin, Syria or Egypt have been most often suggested. A manual of moral instruction and church order, it has three main parts – an ethical section, a church practice section and an apocalyptic section.

The ethical section (1. 1-6. 2) appears to consist of teaching given to those preparing for baptism (7. 1). It focuses on the Two Ways – the 'way of life' (1. 2-4. 14) involves obedience to God's commands, opening with the two great love commands and the 'golden rule', while the 'way of death' (5. 1, 2) describes evil persons and practices. The section on church order and practice (6. 3-15. 4) provides instructions concerning food (6. 3), baptism (7. 1-4), fasting (7. 4-8.1; on days other than 'the hypocrites' ie the Jews), prayer (8. 2, 3; Matthew's 'Lord's Prayer' is to be prayed three times a day), the Eucharist (9. 1-10. 7), apostles and prophets (10. 7-13. 7; *ANE* p10-12; these travelling teachers should normally not receive hospitality for more than a day or two, nor ask for money or food), the Lord's Day (14; *ANE* p12; which may also refer to the Eucharist) and bishops and deacons (15. 1, 2; *ANE* p12; twofold structure, unlike Ignatius. These resident ministers are to be honoured as much as the travelling teachers). The letter closes with an apocalyptic section (16) similar to that of the New Testament Synoptic Gospels (ie the first three gospels, eg Mark 13) and refers to the coming of false prophets, lawlessness, persecution, the antichrist, tribulation, the return of Jesus and resurrection.

As well as providing us with a picture of the various aspects of early Church life mentioned above, especially the sacraments and church leaders, the *Didache* reveals awareness of New Testament Gospel traditions (especially in Matthew) and probably alludes to 1 Corinthians, Romans and 1 Thessalonians.

Tasks

a Discuss the origins and outline the contents of the Didache.

b. Comment on the significance of this writing for the study of early Church history.

THE LETTER OF BARNABAS

Dating from the late first or early second century, this writing was composed after the destruction of the Jerusalem temple in AD70 (16. 3-5) but before the rebuilding of the city by Hadrian (AD132-5). It argues that Christians are the proper heirs of God's covenant with Israel by using an allegorical (see below) method of interpreting the Jewish Scriptures, the Old Testament. While some early Fathers (eg Clement of Alexandria, Jerome) believed it was written by Barnabas, the apostolic companion of Paul (Acts 14: 14), the letter is anonymous and probably had no connection with its supposed author. Most scholars believe that it originated in Alexandria, Egypt, because of its allegorical interpretation of the Old Testament and because Clement of Alexandria is the first to refer to it.

While the work begins and ends like a letter (1. 1-8; 21. 1-19) it reads more like an essay which seeks to prove a point. It divides into two main sections – 'knowledge' (*gnosis*) which the author has received (ie traditional teaching; 1. 5-17. 2) and 'another knowledge and teaching' (18. 1), which is a version of the Two Ways noted above in the *Didache* (Barn 18. 1-20. 2). The first main section deals with various issues – 'the righteous requirements of the Lord' (2. 1-3. 6), preparation for the coming judgement (4. 1-14), the Lord's suffering (5. 1-8. 7), the true circumcision (9. 1-9), the correct understanding of the laws of Moses (10. 1-12), baptism and the cross foreshadowed in the Old Testament (11. 1-12.11), the Covenant and its people (13. 1-14.9), the Sabbath and the eighth day (15. 1-9) and the true temple (16. 1-10). The second main section is, as mentioned above, very similar to the Two Ways contained in the *Didache*.

In a context of expected imminent judgement, and conflict between the Christian Church and the Judaism from which it was emerging, this writing seeks to show that Christians are the true heirs and subjects of Israel's covenant and Scriptures (eg 4. 8; 6. 19; 13. 6; 14. 4, 5). Israel lost the covenant through idolatry (4. 8; 16. 1, 2) and misunderstood Moses by interpreting his laws literally rather than spiritually (10. 2, 9, 12). Thus, Israel's Scriptures should be interpreted allegorically ie looking for the symbolic, spiritual meaning hidden behind the plain, literal sense of the texts. This was a method of biblical interpretation used by both Jews and Christians in Alexandria in particular. The first main section of *Barnabas* applies this method to many parts of the Old Testament to show that their only meaning is a Christian meaning. To give just one example, the tree planted by streams of living water in Psalm 1 (which in this passage is a picture of the blessed man who meditates on the law of the Lord) is regarded by the author of *Barnabas* as a reference to both baptism and the cross of Christ (11. 6-8). As far as the New Testament writings are concerned, the only possible quotation is 'many called but few chosen' (4. 14; compare Matt 22. 14).

Tasks

a. Outline the background and contents of the Letter of Barnabas.

b. Explain what the allegorical method of biblical interpretation is and why 'Barnabas' used it.

THE SHEPHERD OF HERMAS

The *Shepherd of Hermas* was a popular work in the early Church; indeed, some Fathers treated it as Scripture. According to a late second century list of early Christian writings (the Muratorian canon), Hermas was the brother of Pius, bishop of Rome (about AD140-AD154). It is a Jewish Christian work which reflects Christianity in mid second century Rome and makes use of analogies from Roman culture. It consists of five Visions, twelve Mandates and ten Parables (or Similitudes). However, the book falls into two main sections: Visions 1-4, followed by the Mandates and Parables to which Vision 5 is an introduction.

The first section (Visions 1-4) is a Jewish Christian apocalypse whose contents may be outlined as follows:

Vision 1 – Hermas yearns for a woman whom he has observed bathing. He is challenged about his sin and that of his family by an old woman who symbolises the Church.

Vision 2 – The old woman gives him a book containing divine revelation of which he is given an interpretation after prayer and fasting. There is forgiveness for Christians if they urgently repent, and for the heathen until the last day (*ANE* pp50-53; p126 of this book).

Vision 3 – Continuing the theme of repentance, the Church is pictured as a tower, its diverse members as the various stones of which it is made and the apostles and other leaders as its foundation.

Vision 4 – Hermas sees a huge beast which foreshadows the coming great tribulation.

Vision 5 – Now the shepherd (rather than the old woman) is the mediator of revelation, and instructs Hermas to write down the Mandates and Parables that follow.

The twelve Mandates are commandments which are developed by lists of virtues, eg faith, repentance, self-control, and vices, eg evil desire, doublemindedness. The ten Parables are allegorical analogies making use of

Ta**sk**

Assess the value of Papias for an understanding of early Church history.

THE VALUE OF THE APOSTOLIC FATHERS

The Apostolic Fathers have been criticised for various reasons – poor style of writing, departing from superior apostolic teaching and spirituality into moralism and legalism, and institutionalising and formalising the faith. However, such criticisms often stem from an idealised view of New Testament Christianity or of the later Church. The writings should be appreciated for what they are: an arbitrary collection of the earliest Christian writings outside the New Testament which provide us with important insights into the diverse life and thought of early Christianity in an important period of transition, as it was emerging from its Jewish roots and branching out into wider pagan society. These writings bridge the gap between the first century apostles and the second century Apologists and provide us with information on various aspects of Church life at this time, such as heresy, leadership, persecution, sacraments, creeds, the evolution of a New Testament canon, Old Testament interpretation, apologetics and ethics.

Ta**sk**

Using the list of topics in the previous sentence, show how the writings of the Apostolic Fathers give us a varied picture of the early Church at this time.

Pra**ctice Essay Titles**

1. *Outline the collection of early Christian writings known as the Apostolic Fathers. (30)*

   Evaluate the claim that these writings provide us with an invaluable picture of early Church life. (15)

2. *Summarise the main themes of the letters of Ignatius of Antioch. (30)*

   Assess the view that his writings are not representative of the early Church at this time. (15)

AS level

Apologists

Second century Apologists as exemplified in the life and writings of Justin Martyr

(CCEA Specification)

Definition

The second century Apologists (from the Greek 'apologia' meaning 'defence' eg Acts 22: 1; 1 Peter 3: 15) were early Christian writers who defended Christianity against attack and misrepresentation, and who also positively commended their faith to Greeks, Romans and Jews by means of a variety of arguments.

Objective

In this chapter we shall gain a knowledge and understanding of the second century Christian Apologists, with particular reference to the life and writings of Justin Martyr.

IN THE SECOND CENTURY Christianity was beginning to make its presence felt in the wider world of the Roman Empire (see chapter 5) and its teachings and practices provoked the hostility of pagans as well as Jews.

In chapter 6 on persecution, we considered the causes of opposition to early Christianity which put it on the defensive – its rejection of polytheism, its recent origins, its social separatism, its perceived disloyalty and danger to the Empire and its alleged immorality eg cannibalism, incest, infanticide, ritual murder, magical rites and orgies. In addition to political oppression and popular hostility, there was an increasing philosophical opposition to the growing Church in the second century, represented in writers such as Lucian of Samosata, Fronto (the tutor of Marcus Aurelius) and, in particular, Celsus (*ANE* pp128-137).

More than the Apostolic Fathers before them, the Apologists were conscious of belonging to a Church that was emerging from its Jewish origins to become a predominantly Gentile faith. In the process it was clarifying its relationships to Jewish religion, Greek philosophy and Roman authority. The apologies, then, had an important social function in that they reflect the Church's self-definition as it established boundaries between itself, Judaism and paganism. This cultural role of the apologies as expressions of the early Church's increasing awareness of its distinct social identity is more significant than attempts to classify them into a superficially common literary type[1].

Christian Apologists drew from the example of earlier Jewish and pagan apologetic work such as Philo's *Embassy*, Josephus' *Against Apion* and Plato's *Apology of Socrates*. While there was apologetic Christian literature before (eg Matthew and Luke-Acts in the New Testament) and after (eg Tertullian's *Apology* and Clement of Alexandria's *Exhortation to the Greeks*), the collection of writers usually referred to as the second century Apologists include Justin Martyr, who was the most important writer in this group, Tatian, Athenagoras, Theophilus of Antioch and Aristides. As well as the surviving works of these writers, there are fragments of the writings of other second century Apologists – Melito of Sardis, Quadratus and Apollinaris of Hierapolis. However, the writings of Aristo of Pella and Miltiades have not survived. Another work which should be listed with the second century Apologists is the *Letter to Diognetus*, which, however, is traditionally included with the Apostolic Fathers. As with the collection of writings known as the 'Apostolic Fathers', so with the 'Apologists' – the category is a late invention by Church historians about which there is no universal certainty.

Tasks

a. *Outline the context and role of the second century Apologists. It would be useful to review the causes of persecution in chapter six.*

b. *Name the writers who are traditionally classified as the second century Apologists and comment on the legitimacy of the classification.*

c. *Research the attack on Christianity made by the second century intellectual Celsus, most of which has been preserved by the Christian writer Origen; ANE: pp131-136 and Index.*

---

[1] See *Apologetics in the Roman Empire – Pagans, Jews and Christians*, edited by M Edwards, M Goodman, S Price, C Rowland; 1999, OUP: Oxford, particularly the introductory chapter.

1. JUSTIN MARTYR

Life

Justin, who lived about AD100-AD165, was born of wealthy parents in Flavia Neapolis (modern Nablus, Palestine). In his *Dialogue* (Dial 2), he gives an account of his pre-Christian studies in four different Greek philosophies. After studying under a Stoic who showed no interest in theology, an Aristotelian who was self-important and eager for payment, and a follower of Pythagoras who expected Justin to study music, astronomy and geometry before philosophy, he eventually made most progress under a Platonist. Then he was converted to Christianity after a conversation with an old man by the sea, probably at Ephesus, who refuted his Platonism and told him to consider how Old Testament prophecies were fulfilled in Jesus Christ (Dial 3). Justin also appears to have been impressed by the courage of Christian martyrs, which he himself had witnessed (2 Apol 12.1).

He then regarded Christianity to be the only safe and profitable philosophy (Dial 8), the fulfilment of all that was good in Greek philosophy, especially Platonism. He lived and taught in Rome where he founded a Christian philosophical school which included Tatian amongst its students. Justin's 'surname' is a traditional addition due to his martyrdom in Rome in the AD160's during the reign of Marcus Aurelius. The account of his martyrdom and that of his companions (see pp83, 84 and *ANE* pp32-34) reveals his refusal to compromise his faith and his assurance of heaven.

In bullet point form, outline the main details of Justin's life.

Writings

Three genuine writings of Justin have survived: *First Apology*, *Second Apology*, and *Dialogue with Trypho the Jew*. Various other writings were wrongly attributed to Justin from about the fourth century onwards. However, in addition to the three certainly authentic writings, some probably genuine fragments of other writings of Justin have been preserved by Irenaeus (*Against Heresies*, 4. 6.2; 5. 26.3; where reference is made to a book Justin wrote against Marcion, a second century heretic); by Tatian (*Address to the Greeks*, 18); by Methodius (*On the Resurrection*, 2. 18.9 – preserved in Photius 'Bibl' 234); and by John of Damascus (*Sacra Parallela*, containing extracts from a work by Justin entitled *Concerning the*

Resurrection). Justin himself refers to a treatise which he wrote against various heresies (1 Apol 26. 8). His writing is not always logically arranged or coherently structured. Frequent digressions and loose ends make analysis difficult. Thus, the following outlines of his writings are an attempt to discern order in disorder.

First Apology

Justin's *First Apology*, which contains sixty-eight chapters and an appended letter by Hadrian (the previous emperor), is an 'open letter' addressed to the emperor Antoninus Pius (reigned AD138-AD161), his two sons, the Senate and the Roman people, in the mid second century. The appeal is being made, says Justin, on behalf of people of all nations who are unfairly hated and abused, including himself. It is a plea, therefore, to the Roman authorities and literate Romans generally, for the fair and just treatment of imperial citizens and of Christians in particular.

The contents of the *First Apology* may be broadly outlined as follows:

1. An Appeal for Justice in the Treatment of Christians (2-12)

- charges against Christians should be verified before conviction (2, 3)
- Christians are unfairly punished, merely for their name (4)
- Christians are not atheists – they worship the true God and not demons ie false gods (5, 6)
- Christians should not be punished merely for being Christians, but for wrongdoing (7)
- the confession of Christianity is no concern to others when crimes are not proven (8)
- the folly of idolatry, and the service of God (9, 10)
- Christian belief in a future judgement and kingdom with God make Christians good citizens in the present (11, 12)

2. A Presentation and Defence of Christianity (13-67)

- Christians reasonably worship 'a crucified man' in second place after God (13)
- Christians reject sexual immorality, magic, materialism and racism (14)
- Christ's teaching – moral (Sermon on the Mount) and civil ('Give to Caesar ...') (15-17)
- arguments for immortality and resurrection of the body (18, 19)
- similarities between pagan teachings and Christianity mean the latter should not be more hateful (20-22)
- Justin outlines the three main points of his argument (23):

a) Christian teaching from Christ and the Jewish prophets is older than other writers and true, independently of similarities with other writers (24-29).

b) Jesus is the only proper incarnate Son of God whose teachings are for the restoration of the human race (30-53; these chapters are mostly about the fulfilment of Old Testament prophecies in the life of Jesus eg his birth, ministry, death, ascension).

c) Demons enabled pagan writers to anticipate and imitate Christianity (54-67; eg Plato got ideas from Moses; pagan religions imitate baptism and the Eucharist; demons inspire persecution and heresy).

The apology concludes as it began, with an appeal for the just treatment of Christians and also a warning of God's judgement if the appeal is not heeded. A copy of a letter by the previous emperor, Hadrian, is appended, containing his ruling that Christians should only be convicted of substantiated crimes, while unfounded accusations should be severely punished (*ANE* pp21, 22).

Second Apology

The *Second Apology* is a brief supplement to the *First Apology* and was written shortly after. Its fifteen chapters are addressed to the Roman Senate, and the emperor himself is specifically appealed to in the text (chapter 2). Justin begins by explaining that the recent unjust persecution of Christians in Rome by the prefect Urbicus (AD144-AD160) had moved him to write his apology. Urbicus had condemned to death Ptolemaeus – the catechist of a Christian woman who had divorced her pagan husband – and two other believers, merely for being Christians. Justin writes that he too expects such treatment at the instigation of people like Crescens, a Cynic philosopher opposed to Christianity. Justin's pupil, Tatian, also refers to Crescen's opposition to Justin (*Address*, 19) and Eusebius was of the opinion that this is what led to Justin's death (*Hist Eccl* 4. 16. 7-8).

The disjointed and jumbled nature of the *Second Apology* makes analysis of its contents difficult, but the following represents a broad summary of the work:

- Persecution by Urbicus and Crescens (1-3)

- Replies to Pagan Statements (4-6)
    - reasons why Christians do not kill themselves and why they are persecuted

- Eternal Punishment (7-9)
    - Christians preserve the world from God's judgement
    - demons and their servants will suffer eternal punishment

  – eternal punishment is more than a mere threat

- Christianity and Philosophy (10, 13)

    – philosophers knew the truth partially and contradicted each other; Christ brought the truth completely

    – Socrates was punished for the same 'crimes' as Christians

- Christian attitude to death (11, 12)

    – Christians' fearless contempt of death show that they are innocent of hypocritical pagan charges

- Appeal for publication

    – to dispel public ignorance of Christianity

    – to expose the error of Simon Magus' teaching

Dialogue with Trypho the Jew

While Justin's two apologies were addressed to the Roman authorities and public, his *Dialogue* appears to have a Jewish audience in view. In the apologies he sought to defend the morality and superiority of Christianity in the eyes of pagans; in the *Dialogue* he argues that both Christ and Christianity were predicted in the Jewish Scriptures (the Law/the Old Testament) and that the Church is the true Israel.

This is a very long work of 142 chapters and was written probably around AD160. It presents a dialogue or debate, possibly fictitious, between Justin and a Jew called Trypho and his companions at Ephesus, around the time of the Second Jewish Revolt against the Romans (AD132-AD135; Dial 16. 17; 1 Apol 47). The debate appears at times to be fairly courteous, though Trypho's companions seem to be less friendly. Tessa Rajak has stressed, however, the hostile anti-Judaism of the work in which Justin is talking at, rather than to, Trypho[1]. The *Dialogue* is certainly an important text for understanding relations between Christianity and Judaism and the former's perception of its relation to the latter in the mid second century.

The following outline of the *Dialogue* is a broad overview of its main contents.

Introduction (1-9)

- Justin's philosophical studies and conversion (see earlier under 'Life') – the limitations of the philosophers' knowledge about the soul

- God is known only through the Spirit and the truth is known from the Jewish prophets

---

[1] Rajak, Tessa 'Talking at Trypho: Christian Apologetic as Anti-Judaism in Justin's Dialogue with Trypho the Jew' in *Apologetics in the Roman Empire - Pagans, Jews and Christians. (op cit)*

The Law – a provisional prefigurement of Christianity (10-47)

- Trypho's main objection: Christians have rejected the Law (ie the Old Testament/Covenant)
- the Law/Old Covenant is now replaced by the New Covenant, which was promised in the Law itself
- some Old Covenant laws were due to the people's sins or hardness (eg circumcision, sabbaths, sacrifices)
- salvation and righteousness are not obtained through the Law, but through Christ
- the laws of Moses contain 'types' or 'figures' of Christianity: the offering of fine flour prefigured the Eucharist; the bells on the High Priest's robes prefigured the twelve apostles
- various Psalms speak of the divinity and adoration of Christ eg Psalms 45, 72, 110
- Jews have spread slanders against Christians throughout the world

Christ – the Law proves that he is God and predicted his coming (48-108)

- Christ appeared to the patriarchs and Moses as God, yet as distinct from the Father
- John the Baptist is the Elijah who was to come before the Messiah (eg Isaiah 40)
- the following events relating to Christ were predicted in the Old Testament: his two comings (Jacob-Genesis 49: 5, 8-11, 18, 24), virgin birth (Isaiah 7: 14), death on the cross (Psalm 22; also prefigured in various references to 'wood' such as Noah's ark, Moses' outstretched arms and the snake on the pole in the desert), resurrection (conclusion of Psalm 22; Jonah)
- Justin accuses the Jews of removing parts of the Old Testament (the LXX-Greek version) which refer to Christ eg Psalm 96: 10 – 'from the wood' (a supposed reference to the cross)
- the 'curse' of the Messiah hanging on the cross, offensive to Trypho, is explained as Christ bearing the curse due to us
- Justin affirms his belief, not shared by all Christians, in an expected millennial reign of Christ in Jerusalem
- Trypho objects to Justin's interpretations of various biblical passages and his application of them to Christ, and to his claim that the Jews altered the Bible.

The Gentiles – their conversion predicted by the prophets (eg Micah 4; 109-113). Christians – the true Israel predicted by the prophets (114-end).

- Christians, the true people of God, were foreseen by the patriarchs (Genesis 26: 4; 28: 14), Zechariah (2: 10-13; 3: 1, 2) and Malachi (1: 10-12)

- Christians have the true circumcision and are more faithful to God than the Jews.

Briefly outline the background and contents of Justin's main writings.

Apologetic method

In a context of political oppression by the Roman authorities, popular slander by the general public, philosophical criticism by pagan intellectuals and theological conflict with Judaism and Christian heresies, Justin both defended and commended Christianity politically, morally, philosophically and theologically.

Political arguments

We have seen in chapter 6 that early Christians were suspected, by the authorities in particular, of being politically disloyal and subversive. This was due largely to their refusal to worship Rome's gods, which earned them the name 'atheists', or to give divine honours to her emperors. Justin argues, however, that while Christians are atheists in relation to idols and false gods, they are not so in relation to the true God.

Thus we are called atheists. And we confess that we are atheists, as far as gods of this kind are concerned, but not as regards the most true God, the Father ... Him and the Son and the host of other good angels ... and the Spirit of prophecy, we worship and adore ...

(1 Apol 6; ANE p60)

Further, while worshipping God alone, Christians pray for and obey the emperor in every other respect, and pay their taxes. After quoting Jesus' words about giving to Caesar what belongs to Caesar, Justin writes,

Therefore to God alone we render worship, but in other things we gladly obey you, acknowledging you as kings and rulers of men, and praying that your royal power may be found wise and prudent.

(1 Apol 17)

Justin also protests that the only 'crime' that Christians are convicted of and condemned for is that of having the name Christian (compare Pliny's letter to Trajan). Rather, as with any other citizen, charges of criminal activity should be investigated and substantiated before conviction and punishment (1 Apol 2-4, 7).

Moral arguments

Justin had to deal also with popular suspicion and accusations of immorality against Christians. He refuted such charges and argued positively for the moral superiority of Christianity compared with paganism. Christians are not guilty of the practices that pagans accused them of, such as cannibalism and sexual immorality (Dial 10). Trypho accepts this. Christian conversion, rather, has made them good and virtuous people,

> *And we who were full of war, mutual slaughter and every kind of wickedness, have each throughout the whole earth changed our weapons of war, our swords into ploughshares and our spears into farming implements, and we cultivate piety, righteousness, the love of man, faith and hope which comes from the Father himself through him who was crucified, each sitting under his own vine, that is, each enjoying his own married wife.*

> *(Dial 110; ANE p59)*

Indeed, the patience and honesty of Christians have resulted in the conversion of their pagan neighbours (1 Apol 16; *ANE* pp58-59). Justin quotes from the Sermon on the Mount to show that Christ himself expected high moral standards from his followers, who reject lust, adultery, sexual immorality, magical arts, materialism, racism and lying (1 Apol 14-16). Also, the confident attitude to death which Christians display shows that they are good people, innocent of charges of which pagans themselves are guilty (2 Apol 11, 12). To dispel pagan claims that Christians engaged in immoral practices and ceremonies in their secretive meetings, Justin provided accounts of such meetings and ceremonies, including Sunday worship, baptism and the Eucharist, which give us important information on second century church life and sacramental practice and theology (1 Apol 61-67; *ANE* pp62-65; see pp10, 11, 24-26 of this book).

Philosophical arguments

Justin himself, as we have seen, had a philosophical background and pilgrimage through Stoicism, the teachings of Aristotle, Pythagoras and, most satisfactorily, Plato before his conversion to Christianity. But his was not a conversion from philosophy to Christianity, but rather from inferior philosophy to the best philosophy. Thus he writes of his Christian faith, "I found this philosophy alone to be safe and profitable. Thus, and for this reason, I am a philosopher." (Dial 8).

The challenge for Justin and the other second century Apologists was to defend the claim that Christianity was indeed the best philosophy. Educated pagans in the Roman world were familiar with the teachings of Greek philosophers such as Socrates, Plato, Aristotle and Zeno (the founder of Stoicism). By the time of the Apologists the philosophy of the average literary pagan was a mixture of Platonism and Stoicism, and Justin found teachings in both that were agreeable to Christianity, as well as teachings that needed to be corrected by the superior philosophy. In the preceding century, Paul had faced the same challenge of how to present the gospel of a crucified Jew to philosophically-minded Gentiles in terms they would understand, without compromising the essentials of the Christian message (eg Acts 17: 16-34; 1 Corinthians 1: 18-31; see also Colossians 2: 2-4, 8). And as Justin writes, it is in the face of philosophical critique from pagans, such as Crescens, a Cynic philosopher (2 Apol 3).

Justin's main apologetic weapon in his defence of Christianity as the best philosophy was his use of the 'logos' concept (*logos* is Greek for 'reason' or 'word'). The term 'logos' was used frequently by the Greek philosophers. In the sixth century BC Heraclitus regarded the logos as the principle of order and stability in the universe. The Stoics, founded by Zeno (335-263 BC), taught that the logos is God's reason in the world, the creative force of nature. We find the term applied to the Son of God, before his birth as a human, in John's Gospel (1: 1-18). While John's use of logos may be due to Jewish influence (eg Old Testament references to God's powerful word), its use in Greek philosophy would have been apparent to some readers.

Justin's creative use of the logos concept enabled him to argue that any wisdom found in the Greek philosophers came from the pre-incarnate Son of God, the logos, in whom all people shared.

I confess that I prayed and strove with all my might to be found a Christian, not because Plato's teachings are different from Christ's, but because they are not in all respects similar, as neither are the teachings of the others, Stoics, poets and prose-authors. For each spoke well according to the share he had in the divine generative logos [word, reason]. But those who contradict themselves on the more important matters seem not to have the invisible wisdom and irrefutable knowledge. Whatever has been rightly said by any man belongs to us Christians; for next to God, we worship and love the logos who is from the unbegotten and ineffable God, since on our account he became man, becoming a partaker of our sufferings that he might bring us healing. For all the authors were able to see reality darkly, through the seed of the logos implanted in them.

(2 Apol 13; ANE p61,62)

Indeed Justin claims that all those before Christ who lived 'with the logos' (ie according to Christ) were Christians – Greek philosophers as well as Jewish prophets (1 Apol 46; *ANE* p61). Philosophers like Socrates believed things similar to Christianity and suffered like Christians for such beliefs (2 Apol 10).

However, the philosophers contemplated the logos only partially and thus contradicted each other (2 Apol 10). In Christ, however, the logos came fully (2 Apol 8, 10). Thus, Christianity is complete wisdom, whereas before this philosophy was incomplete. Thus, the complete must judge and correct the incomplete. Christianity must reject what is wrong in philosophy (Dial 4-6).

Justin used another argument to defend the superiority of Christianity over Greek philosophy. Not only did the philosophers get any wisdom they had from the Son of God, as the pre-incarnate logos, but they also got wisdom from the Jewish prophets in the Old Testament – ancient writings that pre-dated Christianity, yet foretold its coming (1 Apol 31). For example, Justin claims that Plato borrowed ideas about creation from the first chapter of the Bible (1 Apol 59). This line of argument had been used before Justin by Jewish apologists such as Josephus in *Against Apion* and Philo in his commentaries on the first five books of the Bible. It was a common claim of the Christian Apologists too that the Jewish Scriptures were older than pagan writings and this has been called a 'battle of literatures'[1]. Thus, Justin was able to argue that although Christianity had only recently appeared, it actually pre-dated the great Greek philosophers and, through the logos and the Jewish prophets, was the source of any wisdom they had.

Theological arguments

As well as dealing with political, popular and philosophical hostility from the pagans, Justin responded to the theological challenges of Judaism on the one hand and heretical Christianity on the other (eg 1 Apol 26 – Simon, Marcion; Dial 35).

In his *Dialogue with Trypho the Jew*, Justin argues that the Jewish Bible (the Old Testament) finds its fulfilment in Christianity and that the Church is the true Israel. He repeatedly uses the argument from prophecy to defend his case. In his *First Apology*, addressed to pagans, reference is made to Jewish prophecies and their fulfilment in Christ to show the antiquity of Christianity and its divine origins (1 Apol 31-53). But especially in the *Dialogue*, Justin argues that the Old Covenant with the Jews was a provisional prefigurement of Christ and Christianity. After quoting Jeremiah's prophecy concerning the New Covenant (Jeremiah 31:31) and referring to Christ's miracles, Justin states:

> *... it is possible for everyone to understand that he* [Christ] *is the new law and the new covenant, and the hope of those who from every people wait for the good things of God. For the true spiritual Israel, and descendants of Judah, Jacob, Isaac and Abraham ... are we who have been brought to God through this crucified Christ ...*
>
> *(Dial 11)*

---

[1] Young, Frances, 'Greek Apologists of the Second Century' in *Apologetics in the Roman Empire – Pagans, Jews and Christians*, p93 *(op cit)*

Following in the tradition of Philo the Jew and the Christian author of the *Letter of Barnabas*, Justin interpreted the Old Testament allegorically by regarding its contents as being symbolic of greater things. Christ and Christianity are hidden in types and symbols which Justin decodes. Justin complains that Jewish interpretation of the Bible is too literalistic and trivial (Dial 112, 114, 115). On the one hand he says that the meaning of the Scriptures are self-evidently clear (Dial 55, 76), yet on the other he argues that they cannot be understood without God's grace (Dial 92, 99). Not only in Scripture but also in everyday life Justin could see the shape of Christ's cross symbolised eg in sails, ploughs, digging tools and banners (1 Apol 55).

Trypho, however, was not impressed by Justin's perceived misinterpretation and misapplication of the Jewish Scriptures (eg Dial 32, 74, 77, 87), nor by his claim that the Jews had altered the Scriptures to remove references to Christianity (Dial 73). That God should become human (Dial 68) and that the Messiah should be cursed by God on a cross (Dial 89) were incredible claims to Trypho. His view of Christians is that "having accepted a worthless rumour, you invent a Messiah for yourselves and perish for him unthinkingly." (Dial 8).

Against heretical forms of Christianity, particularly Marcionism and Gnosticism (1 Apol 26; Dial 35), Justin affirmed that the only God is the Creator (eg 1 Apol 16), that Christ was truly human (eg Dial 98, 99) and that humans have free will (eg Dial 141; see later chapter on Heresy).

Thus Justin marshalled various lines of evidence to defend the faith politically, morally, philosophically and theologically in the face of both pagan and Jewish opposition.

Summarise the main arguments used by Justin in response to pagan and Jewish challenges to Christianity.

2. TATIAN

Tatian was born in the AD120s in Assyria and was converted about AD160 in Rome through reading the Scriptures. He became a pupil of Justin and returned to his homeland after his teacher's martyrdom. According to Irenaeus, he turned to an ascetic form of Gnostic heresy (*ANE* p100). Two of his works have survived – his *Address to the Greeks* and his *Diatessaron* (the first harmony of the four Gospels; *ANE* pp125, 126).

In his *Address to the Greeks* he seeks to demonstrate the superiority of Christianity over Greek philosophy and polytheism by using arguments found in the writings of his teacher, Justin eg the dependence of Greek philosophers upon Moses, and the logos as God's agent of creation and revelation. However, unlike Justin, he had a negative attitude to Greek philosophy and did not regard any of the pagan writers as 'Christians before Christ.'

3. ATHENAGORAS

Athenagoras of Athens wrote his *Plea for the Christians* around AD177. It was addressed to the emperor, Marcus Aurelius, and his son and successor, Commodus. Like Justin, Athenagoras protests that Christians are unfairly punished merely for the name of Christian. They are not guilty of the charges made against them (atheism, cannibalism and incest, see pp74, 75 of this book). Rather, they are morally good people and loyal citizens of the emperor (*ANE* pp66, 67). Athenagoras focuses particularly on the charge of atheism and argues that Christians worship the one true God, who is Father, Son and Spirit. Unlike other Apologists who rejected the pagan gods as mere idols, he argued that such 'gods' were originally humans. Like Justin, he had a positive attitude to Greek philosophy and referred to God's logos as the agent of creation and order in the universe. Athenagoras also wrote a work on the *Resurrection of the Body* in which he defended this Christian belief.

4. THEOPHILUS OF ANTIOCH

Theophilus, bishop of Antioch in Syria, wrote a work entitled *To Autolycus*, about AD180, to convince a pagan friend of the truth of Christianity. In the three books of *To Autolycus*, Theophilus responds to Autolycus' praise of pagan gods. These gods are but the names of dead men. The true God, unlike the pagan gods, made all things out of nothing. The philosophers were deceived and those who follow them are as bad. The Christians' Scriptures are older than the writings of the Greeks and Theophilus provides a biblical chronology and history of the human race to prove the antiquity of Christian faith. Theophilus also contrasts pagan immorality and Christian righteousness.

5. ARISTIDES

Aristides (or Aristeides) of Athens wrote an apology in the AD140s, dedicated to the emperor, probably Antoninus Pius. The work is mentioned by Eusebius (*ANE* p58) and is the most Jewish of the early apologies. While paganism is denounced, Judaism is praised. However, Christians alone worship God acceptably. The Jews erred in worshipping angels. The truth and superiority of Christianity are seen in the morality and charity of its followers, as well as in their teachings (*ANE* pp52-55).

6. MELITO OF SARDIS

Melito, bishop of Sardis in Asia Minor, wrote an apology in the AD170s to the emperor Marcus Aurelius. Fragments of this work are preserved in Eusebius (*ANE* p65, 66). He protests about the harassment of Christians in his region due to recent decrees. It is claimed, for the first time it seems, that Christianity has brought prosperity to the Empire. The Christian 'philosophy' began under Augustus and was honoured by the current emperor's predecessors, apart from Nero and Domitian who were misled into acting against Christianity. Melito's Easter sermon on the Passover gives us an insight into the growing hostility between Jews and Christians. While Melito accepted the Jewish origins of Christianity, he attacked the Jews for rejecting and killing their Messiah. Like Justin, he interpreted the Old Testament as a prefigurement of its superior completion in Christianity. The Passover lamb of Exodus 12 was but a symbol of Christ's sacrifice.

7. QUADRATUS

Quadratus, who probably lived in Asia Minor, addressed an apology to the emperor Hadrian in about AD125. WHC Frend has called him 'the father of the post-apostolic Apologists'[1]. In the one fragment of his work preserved by Eusebius (*ANE* p58), Quadratus appeals to the miracles of Jesus in defence of Christianity. It has been suggested that the lost apology of Quadratus is actually the *Letter to Diognetus* which is traditionally, but inappropriately, classed along with the Apostolic Fathers (see p102).

Task

List the names and outline the work of second century Apologists other than Justin Martyr.

THE VALUE OF THE APOLOGISTS

In conclusion we shall assess the value of the second century Apologists in general and of Justin in particular, for the study of early Christianity.

Of crucial importance was their role in defending and defining the new faith in relation to the Judaism from which it was emerging and to the Gentile context in which it was developing. Their writings reveal that the Church was self-consciously further along the road from Jewish sect to Gentile religion

---

[1] Frend WHC, *The Rise of Christianity,* Fortress Press: Philadelphia, 1984, p235

than is apparent in the earlier writings of the Apostolic Fathers. While Aristides is the most pro-Jewish of the Apologists and Melito appears to be the most anti-Jewish, there is a clear sense overall that the future of Christianity is increasingly Gentile. Justin and Melito, like Barnabas before them, claim the Jewish Scriptures for the Christian Church by interpreting them allegorically and Christologically. Thus, the Apologists represent an important link between Jewish and Gentile Christianity and a witness to early Christian interpretation of the Old Testament.

The Apologists also provide an insight into the relationship between Christianity and the Roman authorities. The regular appeal for just treatment rather than punishment for the name of Christian, as well as the rejection of popular slanders and the evidence of martyrdoms (eg Justin), all testify to the difficulties faced by the growing Church in this area. However, ironically persecution led to the growth of the Church (Justin, Dial 110). Important too is the evidence of the Church's positive attitude to the authorities (prayer, taxes) and Melito's claim that the Empire's prosperity is due to the presence of the Church.

The Apologists were also the first Christian writers to relate Christianity to Greek philosophy and thus to demonstrate its intellectual validity. Justin's creative use of the logos concept provided a comprehensive Christian explanation of wisdom in all cultures and races. Without this, it could be argued that the Church would have been completely ignored by educated pagans. However, it is not clear if the apologies had much of a pagan readership at all. Indeed, Tertullian in the early third century could say concerning Christian writings; '... no-one reads them unless he is a Christian already.' (*On the Testimony of the Soul* 1.4). However, it is possible that the pagan intellectual Celsus wrote his attack on Christianity because of Justin's writings. Also, it has been argued that in their appeal to and use of Greek philosophy, the Apologists compromised the Christian message – what the early Church historian Adolf von Harnack (1851-1930) called the 'Hellenization of Christianity'. Justin seems to have been unaware of the extent to which the Platonic view of God's transcendence and distance from the world (eg 1 Apol 25) is incompatible with the Judaeo-Christian view of God's immanence and nearness to creation. Ideas such as God's impassibility (inability to suffer or feel) and incomprehensibility (beyond human intellect), owe much to Greek philosophy and little to biblical teaching (Athenagoras, *Plea for the Christians*, 10). Yet, we have seen that Justin was prepared to criticise Plato when he contradicted Christian teaching (eg Dial 4-6).

Justin in particular is important for providing us with the earliest detailed accounts we have of Christian Sunday worship and baptismal and eucharistic services. However, while he tells us that Christian writings were read along with the Old Testament at such services, he provides little insight into the state of the developing canon of the New Testament. He refers to the Gospels as 'the memoirs of the apostles' (1 Apol 66), probably reflecting terminology used by the students of pagan philosophers, and may have had a harmony of the Gospels. He probably knew all four of our Gospels and makes mention of the book of Revelation (Dial 81).

The impact of the Apologists and Justin in particular on later Christian writers was considerable. The Latin writer Tertullian entitled one of his works, *Apology*, in conscious continuity, it seems, with his Greek predecessors. The Apologists laid the foundation for later developments of the doctrine of the Trinity. We note the emphasis on the 'threeness' of God in Justin (eg 1 Apol 13) and Athenagoras (Plea 10), the latter providing one of the first explanations of the relation of Father, Son and Spirit. Justin's use of the word *prosopon* (face, person; eg 1 Apol 36; Dial 25) was influential for later trinitarian terminology.

The Apologists' use of the logos concept of Greek philosophy to refer to God's Son was not only apologetically useful but theologically important in the development of early Christian Christology. Justin also provided a Christian theology of history which was developed by later writers, particularly in Irenaeus' doctrine of 'recapitulation', in which all things are summed up in Christ (see Irenaeus' quotation of Justin in *Against Heresies* 4.6.2; and Justin in Dial 45; 79-81; 100).

While the Apostolic Fathers display little theological reflection, the apologetic literature of the second century may be rightly viewed as the mother of Christian theology. In this respect, its authors also prepared the ground for later developed rejection of Christian heresy. We have made reference already to Justin's rejection of Marcion in particular and Gnosticism in general (eg 1 Apol 26; Dial 35). The true God is the Creator of the physical world and the logos became truly human.

The failings and limitations of the second century Christian Apologists are apparent with the benefit of hindsight. But as early Christianity evolved from its Jewish past into its Gentile future, the Apologists defended it against contemporary attacks and marked out the main lines of its future development.

Tasks

a. What do the Apologists contribute to our understanding of the development of early Christianity?

b. Comment on the claim that the Apologists successfully defended apostolic Christianity.

Practice Essay Titles

1. *Outline your knowledge and understanding of the life and writings of Justin Martyr. (30)*

   Evaluate the impact of his writings on the development of early Christianity. (15)

2. *Outline and discuss the work of the second century Apologists. (30)*

   Assess the importance of these writers for early Church historians. (15)

Sin and Repentance

Sin and repentance – with particular reference to the writings of Hermas, Hippolytus and Tertullian.

(CCEA Specification)

Objective

In this chapter we shall gain a knowledge and understanding of the early Church's teaching and practice in relation to sin and repentance, referring particularly to the writings of Hermas, Hippolytus and Tertullian.

Task

Define the terms 'sin' and 'repentance'.

VERY EARLY IN THE history of the Church a problem arose concerning post-baptismal sin. As we have seen in chapter one, it was generally held that all sins were forgiven through the act of baptism, the rite of initiation into the Christian Church. But what about sins committed after baptism? Was there forgiveness for any, all or some post-baptismal sin? And if so, how could this forgiveness be obtained? We shall see that while some post-baptismal sins were regarded by the Church as unforgivable, other such sins would be pardoned and the offender restored to fellowship with God and the Church when (s)he submitted to a required discipline or penalty known as 'penance' (from the Latin *poena*: penalty, punishment). Those undergoing such discipline were known as 'penitents'.

THE NEW TESTAMENT

In the New Testament certain passages appear to teach that some sins are unforgivable, including sins committed after baptism – blasphemy against the Holy Spirit (Matthew 12: 31, 32), apostasy (falling away from the faith; Hebrews 6: 4-6; 12: 16, 17; 2 Peter 2: 20-22), deliberate sin (Hebrews 10: 26-31) and the 'sin that leads to death' (1 John 5: 16, 17). The last passage makes a distinction between forgivable and unforgivable sin, which became the basis for the later distinction between venial and mortal sins. Note also the Old Testament distinction between unintentional and intentional sins, eg Numbers 15: 22-31. However, it has been argued that genuine, rather than merely nominal, Christians cannot commit such sins (1 John 3: 6, 9; 5: 18). In other passages it is clear that Christians do commit sin and that forgiveness is available to those who repent (eg 1 John 1: 8-2: 2; 1 Corinthians 5: 1-5; 2 Corinthians 2: 5-11; Galatians 6: 1; James 5: 14-16; 2 Thessalonians 3: 14, 15; Luke 22: 31-34).

Peter in particular and the apostles in general had the authority to administer discipline (the 'binding' and 'loosing' in Matthew 16: 17-19; 18: 18; see also 1 Timothy 1: 20; 5: 20), and to forgive or to 'retain' sins (John 20: 21-23). Church discipline was administered also by the local church as a whole (Matthew 18: 15-17; 1 Corinthians 5: 4, 5, 11-13; 2 Thessalonians 3: 14, 15; Titus 3: 10, 11). These references show that such discipline involved exclusion from the fellowship, 'handing over to Satan' and 'destruction of the flesh,' to ensure the ultimate salvation of the offender. It is unclear, however, what such terminology implies in practical terms.

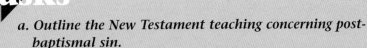

Tasks

> *a. Outline the New Testament teaching concerning post-baptismal sin.*
>
> *b. In the New Testament, who administered church discipline?*

HERMAS

The *Shepherd of Hermas*, as we have seen (chapter 7), is one of the collection of early Christian writings known as the Apostolic Fathers. According to the late second century Muratorian canon, Hermas was the brother of Pius, bishop of Rome (about AD140-AD154). The book consists of five Visions, twelve Mandates and ten Parables (or Similitudes). Divine revelation is mediated to Hermas first by a woman symbolising the Church

Eusebius, Historian and Bishop of Caesarea

André Thevet, 1584

(Vis 1-4) and then by a shepherd (Vis 5), who instructs Hermas to write down the Mandates and Parables that follow. Thus, Hermas' teachings are presented as divine revelations which he has received and, as a prophet, is communicating to the Church. His views on sin and repentance are thus given the status of divinely authoritative statements, to ensure their acceptance by the book's readership. Hermas' difficult writing style (eg long sentences, repetition) and poor logic mean that his views on sin and repentance are at times ambiguous and incoherent. However, the following points may be noted.

Sin

The book begins (Vis 1) with an account of Hermas' personal sin, that of his family and also of his church in Rome. Some time after admiring and assisting a beautiful woman bathing in the River Tiber, he confessed his sins to the Lord. In a vision, a woman, symbolising the Church, said that she had come to convict him of his sins before the Lord. He is told to pray to God "and he will heal your sins and those of your whole house and of all the saints." (Vis 1.1.9). Hermas is confronted with the wickedness of his family, whose moral well-being he has neglected (Vis 1.1.3; 2.2-3; *ANE* p50, 51; also Par 7.2). His children have rejected and blasphemed God, betrayed their parents and engaged in orgies, while his wife has a loose tongue. The church too has sinned (Vis 2.2.4), including its leaders (Vis 2.2.6) and deacons (Par 9.26.2). The moral failure of Hermas, his family and his church thus sets the scene for the rest of the book.

Sin is defined, in language similar to that used by the Rabbis, as 'evil desire' within the heart (eg Vis 1.1.8; 1.2.4;), the opposite of 'good desire' (eg Mand 12.1-2). This evil impulse originates with the devil (Mand 12.2.2 – 'a daughter of the devil'; 4.3.6) and is in essence self-indulgence (Par 6.5). Hermas frequently condemns 'double-mindedness' (eg Vis 2.2.4; Par 8.7.1), which Carolyn Osiek[1] understands to be doubt in one's relationship with God more than moral uncertainty (see Mand 9; compare James 1: 5-8; 4:8).

Sexual sin too is regularly censured and indeed the book begins with a reference to Hermas' guilt in this area (eg Vis 1.1.7-8; 1.2.4). Adulterous and similar sexually immoral thoughts are regarded as a 'great sin' (Mand 4.1.1-2). Actions that are 'the most wicked of all in the life of men' include adultery, sexual immorality, lawless drunkenness, evil luxury, many kinds of food, the extravagance of wealth, boasting, snobbery, arrogance, lying, slander, hypocrisy, malice and blasphemy (Mand 8.3-4; 12.1.3-2.1). Materialism and being over concerned with business affairs are also condemned (Vis 3.6.5; Mand 10.1.4; Par 8.8.1; 9.20.1).

---

[1] Osiek, Carolyn *The Shepherd of Hermas*, Hermeneia, Fortress: Minneapolis, 1999, p123, 124

The sins that are specifically mentioned throughout the book, particularly those that are frequently condemned (double-mindedness, sexual immorality, materialism), reflect the pagan Roman society with which Hermas and the church in Rome were morally compromising. It may be that in a period of relative peace between persecutions past (Vis 3.2.1; 3.5.2) and impending (Vis 4.3.6), the Roman church had become nominally Christian, morally lax, socially compromised and materialistically oriented.

Tasks

a. *Outline the moral situation in Hermas' life, family and church which gave rise to his book.*

b. *What particular sins does his book address?*

Repentance

The moral laxity and spiritual decline of the church provoked Hermas' prophetic call for repentance. Repentance (Greek: *metanoia*), and in particular the possibility of repentance and forgiveness for post-baptismal sin, is indeed the leading theme of the book. The following passages present Hermas' views on the matter.

In Vision 2, Hermas records what was written in a book given to him by an old woman. These things were to be reported to God's chosen people.

After you have made known to them these words, which the Master commanded me to reveal to you, then all the sins which they have previously committed will be forgiven, if they repent wholeheartedly and put away double-mindedness from their heart. For the Master has sworn by his glory concerning his elect, that if sin still occurs, now that this day has been fixed, they shall not have salvation, for repentance for the righteous has an end; the days of repentance have been fulfilled for all the saints, but for the heathen there is repentance until the last day.

(Vis 2.2.4-5; ANE p50, 51)

In Mandate 4, Hermas questions the shepherd about the possibility of post-baptismal repentance and forgiveness.

I have heard from certain teachers that there is no other repentance except that when we went down into the water and received forgiveness of our previous sins.

He said to me, 'You have heard correctly, for that is so. For the one who has received forgiveness of sins should never sin again, but should live in purity. But since you inquire so carefully about everything, I will show you this also, not to give an excuse to those who are about to believe or to those who have just now believed in the Lord. For those who have just now believed, or those who are about to believe do not have repentance of sins, but they do have forgiveness of their previous sins. Therefore, for those who were called before these days the Lord has established repentance. For since the Lord knows the heart and knows everything in advance, he knew human weakness and the craftiness of the devil, and that he would do something bad to God's servants and commit evil against them. But the Lord, who is very compassionate, had compassion on his creation and established this repentance, and to me was given authority over this repentance. But, I tell you,' he said, 'if, after this great and venerable call, any one is tempted by the devil and sins, he has one repentance. But, if he sins repeatedly and repents, it is of no benefit to such a person, for he will scarcely live.'

(Mand 4.3.1-6; ANE p51)

It is clear from these passages that in Hermas' view, while there was no opportunity for post-baptismal repentance and forgiveness for recent or prospective converts, there was one such opportunity for those who had been Christians for some time. However, only one post-baptismal repentance was allowed – to sin and repent repeatedly after baptism was unacceptable. The need to avail oneself of this one opportunity for repentance was urgent since after the disclosure of Hermas' prophecy the opportunity would be gone.

Further, the end of all things was near. The building of the tower (the Church) was almost complete, but its construction was temporarily halted by the mercy of God to allow a second repentance (Vis 3.5.5; Par 8.9; 9.14.1-2; 10.4). For the heathen (ie the unbelievers), there is the opportunity for repentance until the day of judgement. The repentance itself, if it is to be effective and gain God's forgiveness, is not an act but rather a process of self-humiliation and self-affliction (Par 7; Vis 3.7.5-6). Its sincerity is proven by obedience to God's commands (Mand 2.7; Par 9.33). And this single post-baptismal repentance is available even for the serious sins of adultery (Mand 4.1.7.4-8) and apostasy, unless it was from the heart (Par 9.26.3-6; 9.19; 8.6.4).

Hermas appears to be the first to deal seriously with the problem of post-baptismal sin. In his distinction between different sins and sinners, Norbert Brox sees the beginnings of the need to regulate penance[1]. A moral reformer, Hermas sought to avoid a strictly rigorist position which allowed no opportunity for post-baptismal repentance and forgiveness and a morally lax position which allowed repeated opportunities for post-baptismal repentance and forgiveness. As Michael Holmes has stated, Hermas sought to strike a balance between God's justice and mercy[2]. His apparent slight relaxation of

---

[1] Brox, Norbert *A History of the Early Church*, SCM: London, 1994, pp107, 108

[2] Holmes, Michael *The Apostolic Fathers*, Baker Books: Grand Rapids, 1999, p328

the traditional position on post-baptismal sin reflected a balance between pastoral realism and moral idealism. If he was indeed the brother of Pius I, bishop of Rome, and if his brother shared his views, then the Roman church may have begun a trend which would gather pace, as can be seen a generation later under Callistus (see below under Hippolytus).

Carolyn Osiek sees in Hermas' teaching on sin and repentance an awareness that the morality of the Church was developing to take account of the fact that, while post-baptismal sin is not permitted, it is also inevitable. Thus, repentance (or 'conversion') is a constant reality for the Church[1]. Important too for understanding the teachings of Hermas (and indeed any Christian teacher) on sin and repentance, is his ecclesiology ie doctrine of the Church. The Church was created before all things, and indeed the world was created for her sake (Vis 2.4.1-3; *ANE* p51, 52). While sinners may be found in the Church as a historical institution, only those who repent have a place in the eternal congregation of the purified[2].

Tasks

a. Outline the key points of Hermas' views on post-baptismal repentance.

b. Assess the claim that his teaching on sin and repentance struck a good balance between moral idealism and pastoral realism.

HIPPOLYTUS

Hippolytus (about AD160-AD235) was a presbyter in Rome who rejected the views of Callistus, his bishop (about AD217-AD222), concerning post-baptismal sin and repentance. Hippolytus became a rival bishop of a schismatic church in Rome, outraged at Callistus' practice of pardoning and restoring to fellowship penitent church members who had committed serious sins.

But it was not just Callistus' views on penance that Hippolytus objected to. In a very prejudiced, highly critical and, at times, even vicious account of Callistus, he presents his rival as having a morally corrupt past. As a slave he apparently embezzled his master's money. He also accused him of holding theologically erroneous views concerning God, charging him with stressing the unity of God to the point of denying that there were three distinct persons ie

---

[1] Osiek, Carolyn *The Shepherd of Hermas*, Hermeneia, Fortress: Minneapolis, 1999, p115

[2] So Pernveden, L *The Concept of the Church in the Shepherd of Hermas*, Lund: Gleerup, 1966

modalism. And, undoubtedly with some professional jealousy, Hippolytus also represents Callistus as one who manipulated his way into the prestigious office of bishop of Rome (on all the above see *Refutation of all Heresies* 9.11.1-3; 9.12.1-19; *ANE* p146-151).

Hippolytus' perspective on Callistus' doctrine and practice of penance is presented in the following passage:

The impostor Callistus, having ventured on such opinions, set up a school in opposition to the Church, adopting the previously mentioned teaching. And he first invented the strategy of conniving with men in regard to their pleasures, stating that everyone had his sins forgiven by himself. For if anyone attends someone else's congregation, and is called a Christian, should he commit any sin, they say that the sin is not reckoned to him, provided he rushes off to the school of Callistus. And many were gratified with his proposition, as being conscience-stricken, simultaneously having been rejected even by numerous sects; while some of them, in accordance with our sentence, had been by us forcibly put out of the Church. Such disciples as these went over to them and served to crowd his school. He propounded the view that if a bishop was guilty of any sin, even a mortal sin, he should not be removed from office. During his time, men who had been twice and three times married began to be ordained to office as bishops, priests and deacons. If also, however, anyone in holy orders were to get married, Callistus allowed such a person to remain in holy orders as if he had not sinned. And he argues that what has been spoken by the apostle has been declared in relation to this: 'Who are you that judges another man's servant?' But he asserted that similarly the parable of the weeds speaks in relation to this, 'Let the weeds grow along with the wheat', or, in other words, let sinners remain in the Church. But also he stated that Noah's ark was made for a symbol of the Church, in which were both dogs and wolves and ravens and all things clean and unclean; and so he argues that the case should apply likewise to the Church. And as many passages relating to this as he could collect, he interpreted in this way.

And his hearers, delighted with his teachings, continue to deceive both themselves and as many others, and crowds stream together into his school. So his pupils increase in number and they rejoice in the crowds who attend for the sake of pleasures which Christ did not allow. But in contempt of him, they put no restriction on the commission of sin, saying that he forgives those who are in his favour. For he permitted women, if they were unmarried but of marriageable age and burned with passion, if they did not want to overturn their own status through a legal marriage, to have whatever man they chose, slave or free, as a bedfellow and to regard this man as a husband without being legally married. [Hippolytus then goes on to say that such women had abortions to avoid having children to men of low status]. *See into how great sacrilege the lawless one has advanced, by teaching adultery and murder at the same time!*

And beyond these bold acts, they – and they are past shame – attempt to call themselves a Catholic Church. And some, supposing that they will benefit themselves, run to them. During his time they first presumptuously practised a second baptism.

(Refutation of all Heresies 9.12.20-26; ANE p151-153)

We can see that Hippolytus considered his own congregation to be worthy of the name 'church' while the congregation of Callistus is but a 'school', a term normally used for heretical sects. Also, Hippolytus is clearly annoyed that Callistus' perceived penitential laxity is undermining the standards of other congregations, since people disciplined by other churches, and even by heretical sects, simply went to Callistus' school where they found acceptance. Such a liberal attitude to post-baptismal sin made Callistus' congregation very popular so that its numbers were increasing, an observation which Hippolytus may have made with a tinge of jealousy.

Specifically, Callistus is presented as one who pardoned any post-baptismal sin, even the most serious, upon repentance. However, Hippolytus' prejudice gives the unfair impression that Callistus favoured the sins themselves. Even church leaders were treated liberally. If a bishop was guilty of a 'sin unto death' (compare 1 John 5: 16, 17), that is a serious sin such as adultery or murder, he was not removed from his position. Men who had been twice or three times married were ordained to all three orders of ministry, and men in office were allowed to be married, in conflict with clerical celibacy. Hippolytus also states that a 'second baptism' was practised at the time of Callistus. Hippolytus had condemned a sect called the Marcites for a similar practice – *Refutation* 36.6.

Further, Callistus is charged with relaxing the Church's teaching on marriage. A Christian could marry only another Christian. The problem was that there were not enough men of high social status in the Church for Christian women of similar status to marry. Unwilling legally to marry men of a lower class, these Christian women were permitted by Callistus to enter into relationships which were not recognised by Roman law. Such women also performed self-induced abortions to avoid having children to lower class fathers, whose status the children would take. Thus, says Hippolytus, Callistus condoned murder as well as adultery.

Of interest are the biblical passages that, according to Hippolytus, Callistus appealed to in order to justify the readmission of penitents to the Church – Paul's condemnation of those in the church of Rome who judged fellow-believers (Romans 14: 4 – the context is differences over dietary rules); Jesus' parable of the wheat and the weeds/tares (Matthew 13: 30), where the wheat and the weeds must grow together until the harvest (ie the sons of the Kingdom and the sons of the evil one must remain together in the Kingdom until the end of the age; Matthew 13: 40-43); and the mixture of clean and unclean animals in Noah's ark (eg Genesis 7: 2), interpreted as a symbol of the co-existence of good and bad within the Church. According to Hippolytus, these three passages are but a representative sample of a larger collection appealed to by Callistus.

Here we see, as we did with Hermas, different views on the nature of the Church. For Hippolytus the Church is a 'holy society' composed of those who lived righteous lives (*Commentary on Daniel* 1. 17). Both the garden of Eden and Susannah are seen as types or symbols of the purity of the Church, in which sinners and heretics should not be found and from which those who lapse must be removed (*Commentary on Daniel* 1. 15 onwards). However, Callistus' ecclesiology was clearly broader than this, informed by his interpretation of various Scriptures and expressed in his more lenient attitude to post-baptismal sin. As JND Kelly observes, Callistus was the first to introduce as a principle of ecclesiastical policy a more liberal attitude to serious sins, introducing penitential reforms which impacted his understanding of the nature of the Church[1]. Thus, his views on penance and on the Church affected each other. The tension between ecclesiastical idealism and pastoral realism is thus again brought into sharp focus. Though Hippolytus accepted that a bishop could pardon some post-baptismal sin (*Apostolic Tradition* 3. 5). J Stevenson defended Callistus' attitude to penance as a practical necessity to prevent penitents going back to paganism (*ANE* p152). MA Smith's view was that both Hippolytus and Callistus were right: the former in wanting to maintain moral standards and the latter in wanting to offer forgiveness to the truly penitent. The problem was the practical outworking of these principles[2].

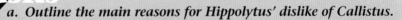

Tasks

a. *Outline the main reasons for Hippolytus' dislike of Callistus.*

b. *According to Hippolytus, which post-baptismal sins should not have been pardoned by Callistus?*

c. *What biblical passages did Callistus refer to in defence of his actions?*

d. *How far did different views of the nature of the Church account for this dispute?*

---

[1] Kelly, JND *Early Christian Doctrines*, A&C Black: London, 1977, p201, 218

[2] Smith, MA *From Christ to Constantine*, IVP: London, 1971, p120, 121

TERTULLIAN

Tertullian (about AD160-AD220) was a Roman theologian who lived in Carthage, North Africa. Possibly a converted lawyer, Tertullian had morally strict views which became even stricter when he became a supporter of the Montanists (see pp177-183) in about AD206.

In his book *On Repentance*, written before his Montanist period, Tertullian allowed one repentance for post-baptismal sin. The book begins by dealing with the repentance of the non-Christian (1-6), where Tertullian states that 'all sins' of whatever kind are forgiven through repentance. This repentance sinners must hurry to embrace as a shipwrecked man grasps at a plank for protection – 'This will lift you up when you are sunk in the waves of sin and will carry you into the harbour of the divine mercy' (*On Repentance* 4). Tertullian then (7 onwards) deals with the matter of post-baptismal sin and permits a single second repentance, the first being expressed in baptism.

> *These poisons of his* [the devil], *therefore, God saw beforehand, and although the gate of forgiveness has been shut and fastened with the bolt of baptism, he has permitted still some opening. In the hallway he has stationed the second repentance to open to those who knock, but only once, because it is the second time; but never again because the last time it opened in vain.*
>
> (7; ANE p174)

Tertullian then provides the first detailed account of the process of post-baptismal repentance which, he says, is known by the Greek name *exomologesis* (ie confession), the 'handmaid' of repentance (*On Repentance* 12). It is a public penance of self-humiliation. There is as yet no evidence of private penance imposed by a priest after a personal confession. The repentance is tested laboriously so that it is seen to be not just a guilty conscience but also expressed in actions.

> *This action, normally expressed and commonly referred to by its Greek name, is* exomologesis *by which we confess our sin to the Lord; not indeed as if he were unaware of it, but inasmuch as satisfaction is settled by confession, and repentance is produced by confession, and by repentance God is placated. And so* exomologesis *is a discipline for prostration and humiliation, creating a demeanour designed to attract mercy. With regard also to the very dress and food, it requires the penitent to lie in sackcloth and ashes, to cover his body in mourning, to cast down his spirit in sorrows, to exchange his sins for severe treatment; to have no food or drink, except what is plain – not for the stomach, but for the soul; generally, to feed prayers with fastings, to groan, to weep and moan to the Lord his God, to prostrate himself at the feet of the presbyters and to kneel before God's dear ones; to call upon all the brothers to be ambassadors to carry his prayer for mercy. The purpose of this* exomologesis *is to enhance repentance, to honour God through fear of danger; by itself passing judgement on*

the sinner to stand as a substitute for God's indignation; and by temporal affliction, I will not say to frustrate, but to discharge eternal punishment. So, while prostrating the sinner, it raises him; while it covers him with squalor, it makes him more clean; while it accuses, it excuses; while it condemns, it acquits. Believe me, the less you spare yourself, the more God will spare you.

(9; ANE p174, 175)

Thus we can see both the procedure and the purpose of the one post-baptismal repentance. In his Montanist work, *On Modesty*, he describes how in the Catholic Church (as distinct from schismatic groups such as the Montanists), similar public repentance was performed by adulterers begging for re-admission to the Church – the wearing of a hair shirt, covered in ashes, trembling, public prostration before the widows, and presbyters, seizing the hems of their garments, licking their footprints, grasping their knees (13). And in his pre-Montanist *Apology* Tertullian writes of the Church's godly discipline, and censure and excommunication of those who have sinned, who are no longer regarded by the Church as Christians (39, 46).

In his Montanist period, Tertullian made a clear distinction between pardonable and unpardonable sins. Daily sins which all Christians are liable to, such as unjustified anger, physical violence, careless slander, rash swearing, breaking promises and lying, are forgiven by God through Christ's intercession with God. Serious sins, however, such as murder, idolatry, fraud, apostasy, blasphemy, adultery, fornication and any other violation of God's temple are not forgiven. Indeed a Christian will never commit these sins and would cease to be a Christian if he did (*On Modesty*, 19; in *Against Marcion* false witness is also listed as a capital sin). In the closing decades of the second century the Church generally regarded adultery, murder and idolatry (apostasy) as unforgivable. These sins were reserved and the offender was excluded from the Church, being left to the judgement of God. Tertullian was outraged when a certain bishop published an edict stating that he would pardon, upon the performance of appropriate penance, adultery and fornication. Tertullian's moral disgust and biting sarcasm are evident in the following passage.

The Supreme Pontiff, the Bishop of Bishops, issues an edict: 'I remit to all who have discharged the requirements of repentance the sins both of adultery and of fornication'. O edict on which cannot be inscribed 'Good deed'! And where will this liberality be posted up? On the very spot I imagine, on the very doors of lust, under the very trade signs of lust. There is the place to publish such a penance, where the sin itself occurs! There is the place to announce the pardon, where men will enter in the hope of it! But this edict is read in the Church, and is pronounced in the Church – and the Church is a virgin! Let such a proclamation be far removed from Christ's betrothed!

(On Modesty 1; ANE p176, 177)

Tertullian may well be referring here to Callistus, the bishop of Rome, or his predecessor Zephyrinus; though, it is possible that Agrippinus, the local bishop in Carthage, is in view. Tertullian also protested that Hermas permitted a second repentance for serious sins and scathingly termed his book the 'Shepherd of adulterers', rejecting it as uncanonical (*On Modesty* 16; 20), though in his pre-Montanist *On Prayer* (12) he quoted it as an authoritative work. As far as Tertullian was concerned the Roman bishop, as Peter's successor, had no power to forgive capital sins. He may 'loose' (forgive) sins against men (Peter was told to forgive such sins seventy times seventy), but he must 'bind' (retain) sins against God (*On Modesty* 21). A bishop may pardon lighter sins but God alone can pardon greater and unforgivable sins (*On Modesty* 18).

The Church thus has power to forgive some sins, as indeed the Montanist prophets declare in the Spirit, but the same prophets withhold such forgiveness lest sin is encouraged (*On Modesty* 21). Further, while in his pre-Montanist book, *To the Martyrs* (1), he implies that Christian prisoners awaiting martyrdom could bestow the peace of forgiveness on fellow Christians, in his Montanist work, *On Modesty* (22), he opposes such a practice, arguing that while a 'martyr' can cleanse his own sins, he cannot pardon sins reserved to God. No wonder, then, with such strict views concerning post-baptismal sin that even the pre-Montanist Tertullian urged the delay of baptism (*On Baptism* 18; see p14 of this book). Indeed, 'clinical' baptism, ie baptism near the time of one's death, became an increasingly popular practice from about the mid third century.

Tertullian's morally strict views may have been due in some degree to the legal background that many assume he had. Certainly influential was the perceived moral laxity of the Church, not least in the willingness of bishops (eg Callistus) to pardon and restore to the full communion of the Church those who had committed grave sins. This was undoubtedly one reason for Tertullian's support for the Montanists, whose moral views were compatible with his own.

As with other early writers, Tertullian's attitude to post-baptismal sin was closely related to his ecclesiology. Kelly states that Tertullian's understanding of the nature of the Church was radically transformed when he became sympathetic to the Montanists[1]. Instead of viewing the Church as a single, visible, hierarchical institution, the Montanist Tertullian conceived of the Church as a charismatic community; pure, undefiled Spirit, consisting only of spiritual people – while in the Catholic Church there were 'natural' men (Greek: *psychikoi*) , the Montanists were the 'spiritual' men (Greek: *pneumatikoi*). Such ideas are apparent in, for example, *On Modesty* (21) and *On the Exhortation to Chastity* (7). If the Church is pure, so must its members be.

---

1 Kelly, JND *Early Christian Doctrines* A&C Black: London, 1977, p200

Tasks

a. Identify the key differences between Tertullian's pre-Montanist and Montanist views on sin and repentance.

b. Outline the procedure and purpose of the 'exomologesis'.

CONCLUSION

We see then that the early Church's theology and practice in relation to sin and repentance, specifically regarding those who were already baptised, emerged and developed gradually in the first two centuries. In the earliest period, the scarcity of information in our sources means that we cannot say much about the Church's penitential theology and procedures, if there were any. Certainly, post-baptismal sin was treated seriously and we have seen that Hermas allowed only a limited post-baptismal repentance because of the critical urgency of the imminent end of the age. Other Apostolic Fathers too allowed forgiveness for sins committed after baptism – the *Didache* required public confession (4.14; 14.1); Ignatius accepted that schismatics could be readmitted to the Church after repentance (Phld 3.2; 8.1); and Polycarp anticipated the restoration of the presbyter Valens and his wife to the Philippian church upon their repentance (Pol Phil 11.4).

While, as we have noted, Norbert Brox detected the beginnings of a desire to regulate and formalise penance in Hermas' distinction between different types of sins (see p127), it was not until the early third century that penitential practice began to be standardised. While there was not as yet, nor for some time to come, any private penance in which a priest prescribed penance to an individual after confession of sin, there was a process of public penance for serious sins. This *exomologesis* involved public confession, a period of penance and eucharistic exclusion and, finally, absolution of sins and restoration to fellowship, normally by a bishop. And it was to be permitted once only (so Hermas and Tertullian above; Clement of Alexandria in *Stromateis* 2.13, 56-59). Lesser sins were dealt with personally through prayer, good works and the intercession of Christ (see Tertullian above; Origen, *Sermon on Leviticus* 2.4).

An important shift in penitential theology at this time was the development of a more liberal attitude concerning which post-baptismal sins could be forgiven by the Church. Hippolytus and Tertullian opposed such leniency while their contemporary, Callistus, appears to have been the innovator. By the time we come to the middle of the third century, Cyprian, bishop of Carthage (where Tertullian had lived), provides us with evidence that sexual immorality was pardonable (*Epistle* 55. 20 onwards). Cyprian reveals too that while idolatry was unpardonable before the Decian persecution (AD250-AD251), it was not absolutely so afterwards, in recognition of the reality that many had lapsed during the persecution (*Epistles* 3.28; 55.6, 17). The mid third century Syrian *Didascalia Apostolorum*, while recognising that post-baptismal evil-doing merits condemnation to hell, urges bishops to restore all who repent, even of the sins of idolatry, murder and adultery.

Thus as the Church grew, idealism was gradually tempered by realism. Henry Chadwick notes that the success of the Church's mission highlighted the difficulty not only of moral rigorism, but also of the public nature of penitence. Eventually, he says, two tendencies converged – penance became more therapeutic than judgmental, and private (to a priest or bishop) rather than public[1]. The tension between preserving the moral integrity of the Church, while at the same time extending pastoral compassion and restorative pardon to the truly repentant, is a tension which the Church, ancient and modern, has to live with. Some will stress one more than the other, which will thereby shape their views of Church discipline. Not least, one's views of the nature of the Church – a society of saints or a school for sinners – will determine such views. Serious sin in the lives of church members still raises a number of important and challenging issues – theological (what we believe), moral (what is right and wrong) and pastoral (what can be done), to mention a few. As in the early Church, the challenge is to strike a balance between the need for holiness on the one hand and the grace of forgiveness on the other.

Practice Essay Titles

1. **Outline your knowledge and understanding of sin and repentance in the early Church. (30)**

   Assess the view that the early Church did not have a definite penitential system. (15)

2. **Describe the developments that occurred in Tertullian's understanding of penance during his Christian life. (30)**

   Evaluate the claim that the modern Church can learn much from the development of penitential doctrine and practice in the early Church. (15)

---

[1] Chadwick, Henry *The Church in Ancient Society*, OUP: Oxford, 2001, p691

Church Government

The development of Church government

(CCEA Specification)

Definition

Church government is concerned with how the Church is organised in terms of leadership and ministry. This is sometimes referred to as Church order or polity.

Objective

In this chapter we shall gain a knowledge and understanding of how the government/leadership of the early Church and churches developed over time from the New Testament until the Council of Nicaea (AD325).

Particular attention will be paid to the offices and roles of bishops, presbyters and deacons; the beginnings of the papacy (ie the growing influence of the Pope/Bishop of Rome); Church councils; and the claim that during our period the Church increasingly became less charismatic and democratic and more institutional and hierarchical.

THE NEW TESTAMENT

THE GENERAL VIEW OF New Testament scholars is that Jesus himself did not provide a set pattern of Church government. Rather, this developed gradually as the early Church adopted and adapted existing Jewish models. In the Gospels Jesus appoints twelve 'apostles' (from the Greek for 'send'), as his authoritative representatives (eg Mark 3: 13-19; Matthew 18: 18; John 20: 19-

23). Among the twelve, Peter is presented as the leading apostle (Matthew 16: 18, 19; John 21: 15-17).

In the early chapters of the book of Acts, the apostles in general and Peter in particular oversee the Jerusalem church. In this church, seven men were chosen by the congregation and appointed by the apostles to distribute food to widows. While they are not called 'deacons' (Greek *diakonos*: servant), it is often suggested that their ministry formed the basis for the later office of deacon (Philippians 1: 1; 1 Timothy 3: 8-13). Later in Acts we read that the Jerusalem church also had 'elders' and that James, the brother of Jesus, took a leading role (11: 27-30; 15: 4, 6, 13, 22, 23; 21: 17, 18). After their first missionary journey, Paul and Barnabas appointed elders (or had elders appointed) in each of the churches (14: 23). The elders (Greek: *presbuteroi*) of the church in Ephesus are also called 'bishops' (Greek: *episkopoi*: overseers) who are to pastor (ie shepherd) their flock (Acts 20: 17, 28). The word 'elder' had a Jewish background in particular (eg elders in the synagogues). However, the word translated 'bishop' or 'overseer' was used in classical Greek of supervisors of various kinds and not in an exclusively religious sense. The book of Acts also refers to prophets and teachers in the churches (13: 1; 15: 22,32), though the former appear not to have been strictly local ministers (eg 11: 27, 28). The so-called Council of Jerusalem (Acts 15) provides us with the earliest example of churches in conference in an effort to resolve a theological dispute.

In the latter half of Acts the emphasis is on Paul as the apostle to the Gentiles. Since he was not one of the twelve, he had to defend his apostolic status continually (eg 1 Corinthians 9: 1, 2; 15: 7-10; Galatians 1: 1). In the Pauline literature there is both a charismatic ministry of many church members exercising various gifts of the Spirit, and an official ministry of leadership in the churches. It has been argued that while the earlier Pauline letters are charismatic, with no church officials (Romans 1: 1; 12: 6-8; 1 Corinthians 12-14; 1Thessalonians 5: 19-21; Galatians 3: 5), the later Pauline letters reveal an institutionalised church with leaders in office (Ephesians 4: 11-13; 1 Timothy 3: 1-13; Titus 1: 5-9). However, it is clear that from the beginning both charismatic and official ministries existed and that they were not regarded as incompatible (compare 1 Corinthians 12-14 with 16: 16; 1 Thessalonians 5: 12, 13 with 19-21; Galatians 3: 5 with 6: 6; also 1 Peter 4: 11, 12 with 5: 1-5). Indeed, leadership itself is a charismatic gift (Romans 12: 8; 1 Corinthians 12: 28; Ephesians 4: 7-13; 1 Timothy 4: 14; 2 Timothy 1:6).

As regards official leadership in the Pauline literature, there appear to have been two orders of ministry in local churches – bishops/overseers (Philippians 1: 1; as in Acts 20: 17, 28 and 1 Peter 5: 1-5, they are also called presbyters/elders – see 1 Timothy 3: 1-13; 5: 17; Titus 1: 5-9), and deacons (Philippians 1: 1; 1 Timothy 3: 8-13). Both types of minister were to be of the highest moral character and bishops were specifically required to be able to teach. While there is no New Testament evidence that the office of bishop was held by females (1 Timothy 2: 11-15; compare 1 Corinthians 14: 33-35), it appears that there were female deacons (Romans 16: 1 and 1 Timothy 3: 11 may be interpreted in this way), as well as female prophets (Acts 2: 16-18; 21: 8, 9; 1 Corinthians 11: 5).

The general picture of New Testament ministry then is of a foundational ministry of largely itinerant apostles and prophets as well as evangelists (Ephesians 2: 20; 4: 11) and later a settled, localised ministry in which typically each church had a team of bishops assisted by deacons. There were clearly charismatic ministries performed by various believers in the churches and no sharp clergy-laity distinction. Indeed, while the word 'priest' is never used of a church leader in particular, the church in general is a priesthood (eg 1 Peter 2: 5, 9; Revelation 1: 6). There is no evidence that the Lord's Supper or baptism were to be administered only by church leaders. Church members participated in decision making and discipline matters (eg Acts 1: 15-26; 6: 3, 5; 15: 22; 1 Corinthians 5; Matthew 18: 15-17), while submitting to their leaders (eg 1 Thessalonians 5: 12, 13; Hebrews 13: 17; 1 Timothy 5: 17).

Tasks

a. *Explain the distinction between itinerant and local ministries.*

b. *Outline the New Testament evidence relating to bishops.*

c. *Assess the view that within the New Testament there is a development from an initial charismatic ministry to an official ministry.*

THE APOSTOLIC FATHERS

The earliest Christian writings outside the New Testament provide important evidence on the development of Church government from the late first to mid second century. *1 Clement*, a late first century letter from the Roman church to the Corinthian church, addressed a situation where the presbyters had been removed from office. The church at Corinth appears to have the twofold ministry of bishops and deacons apparent in New Testament writings. However, for the first time we read of the laity (people) as distinct from the leaders, and of apostolic succession – the idea that bishops and deacons are successors of the apostles (see earlier, p98).

Clement states that the apostles knew that there would be strife over the bishop's office and therefore appointed bishops and deacons and made provision that on their death (ie the death of the bishops and deacons, though it could refer to the apostles) other approved men should succeed to their ministry. The appointment of such leaders required the approval of the whole church. Also in *1 Clement,* the Church is compared to the Roman army and its different ranks and to three orders of the Old Testament priesthood – the high priest, the priests and the Levites, though no equation is made between these and bishop, presbyter and deacon. The analogy with the Jewish sacrificial priesthood may be the beginnings of a sacerdotal (ie priestly) view of the Christian ministry. Clearly these analogies imply a hierarchy of leadership within the Church (*1 Clement* 27; 40 *ANE* p7-9).

The *Didache* reveals a tension between itinerant ministers (apostles/prophets: 'your chief priests', 13.3) who travelled around the churches and the local, resident ministers (the twofold ministry of bishops and deacons). The latter were to be appointed by the churches and, as in the New Testament and *1 Clement,* were to be morally upright. They were not to be looked down on since they too carried out the ministry of prophets and teachers and were to be honoured along with them (see p99). In the *Shepherd of Hermas* we find that the mid second century Roman church was governed by a number of presbyters (Vis 2.4.3; *ANE* p51, 52).

Among the Apostolic Fathers the letters of Ignatius are of the greatest significance in relation to the development of Church government. In Ignatius we first find what has been called 'monarchical episcopacy' or 'monepiscopacy' – each church has a single bishop (*episkopos* is Greek for bishop/overseer) who is assisted by presbyters (elders) and deacons. This threefold ministry appears to be a development of the twofold ministry (where 'bishops' and 'presbyters' refer to the same leaders) apparent in other early Christian writings such as the New Testament, *1 Clement,* the *Didache* and the *Shepherd of Hermas.* Unlike *1 Clement,* the idea of apostolic succession is not used despite Ignatius' high view of the bishop – in fact, the presbyters rather than the bishops correspond to the apostles (see pp93,94 for details and references).

Clearly in Ignatius, bishop (overseer) and presbyter (elder) are no longer interchangeable terms for the same leaders, as they were in the New Testament and appear to be in other early Christian writings. Thus the bishop (singular) is distinct from the presbyters (plural) and deacons (plural) in each church. We find this threefold structure in six of his seven letters. Romans is the exception. Ignatius himself is the monarchical bishop of Antioch and his friend Polycarp had the same position in Smyrna. Indeed, Ignatius appears to have authority over churches of which he is not the monarchical bishop; he is almost, in later terms, a metropolitan bishop. It may be that his impending martyr status earned him an episcopal primacy in the region. However, while in Asia Minor monarchical episcopacy is common, further west it is not so. Neither Ignatius' letter to the Roman church nor Polycarp's letter to the Philippian church indicate the existence of such an episcopacy in these churches. Further, the Roman writings, *1 Clement* and the *Shepherd of Hermas*, as we have seen, reveal a twofold ministry of bishops and deacons. Indeed, Ignatius' repeated insistence on the threefold ministry may indicate that it was a new or recent pattern of ministry even in Asia Minor, though the evidence could be interpreted in the opposite way. That is, Ignatius may have been reinforcing the traditional pattern of ministry, particularly the centrality of the bishop, in the face of the threats of heresy and schism.

But the question remains, how did monarchical episcopacy and the threefold ministry develop historically from what appears in the sources to be an earlier twofold ministry where bishop and presbyter were synonymous and equivalent? Did the monarchical episcopate in fact arise from the apostolate (the apostles) or later from the presbyterate (from among the presbyters/ elders)?

Arguments for the apostolic origins of the monarchical episcopate include:

- the position of James as leader of the Jerusalem church (Acts 15: 13; 21: 18);

- the apostolic delegates who appointed presbyters in churches, such as Timothy and Titus (1 Timothy 3; Titus 1: 5);

- the seven angels of the seven churches in Asia Minor (Revelation 1-3) who may have been leaders of individual churches in the same region where monarchical episcopacy clearly appears within two decades in Ignatius;

- Clement of Alexandria (about AD150-215) states that the apostle John appointed bishops on return from his exile (*Quis Dives Salvetur*, 42) and various early writers state that John appointed Polycarp bishop of Smyrna (eg Irenaeus, an acquaintance of Polycarp, *Against Heresies* 3.3);

- the succession lists of bishops in churches going back to the apostles (eg Irenaeus, Tertullian).

Arguments for the later development of monarchical episcopacy as a development from the order of presbyters in each church include:

- the equivalence of bishops and presbyters in the New Testament (Acts 20: 17, 28; Philippians 1: 1; 1 Timothy 3; 5: 17; Titus 1: 5-7; 1 Peter 5: 1, 2);

- the existence of corporate episcopal oversight in other early Christian writings into the second century (*1 Clement*, the *Didache*, the *Shepherd of Hermas*; for references see above);

- Jerome (about AD345-419) states that the churches were originally governed corporately by elders and then later by one of the elders to combat schism. This development, he says, is a matter of ecclesiastical custom rather than divine institution (*Ad Titum* 1.7; Epist 83 and 85).

It seems that one of the body of presbyters/elders governing each church gradually rose to prominence. The chairman of the eldership would naturally come to the fore. Certain tasks would also elevate such an individual – president at the Eucharist, secretary and representative of the church and manager of the church's property and funds. The need for decisive and focused leadership in the face of persecution, heresy and schism also undoubtedly contributed to the emergence of the monarchical bishop. Biblical precedents, though not strictly analogous in name or function, were found in individuals such as James of Jerusalem. The monarchical bishop also provided a Christian counterpart to the ruler of the local synagogue and may have been modelled on the superintendents of the Essene community at the Dead Sea.

We should note here that around the same time as Ignatius, Pliny mentions the existence of deaconesses among the Christians in Bithynia (see p82).

Tasks

a. *Define 'monarchical episcopacy' and outline the evidence for its emergence in the letters of Ignatius.*

b. *Outline factors that may have contributed to the emergence of the threefold ministry.*

c. *What developments in Christian ministry appear for the first time in 1 Clement?*

d. *What tensions in Christian ministry appear in the Didache?*

JUSTIN MARTYR

In his *First Apology*, written in mid second century Rome, Justin refers in his account of Christian worship to 'the president of the brothers' or, as it could be translated, 'that one of the brothers who was presiding'. This person who presided at the Eucharist gave thanks at length for the bread and wine, preached a sermon, received an offering collected by others and distributed it to the needy. Reference is also made to 'deacons' who distributed the bread and wine to those present and to absentees (see pp24-26 and *ANE* p62-65).

IRENAEUS

Irenaeus (about AD130-200) was bishop of Lyons, Gaul (AD177-200). While Ignatian episcopacy was congregational (a bishop in charge of each church), in Irenaeus, episcopacy appears to be more diocesan, ie a bishop was in charge of the churches and their leaders in his 'diocese' (from the Greek for an administrative area – the Church adopted existing imperial administrative regions). His interchangeable use of the terms 'bishop' and 'presbyter' indicates that as yet there was not a universally sharp distinction between the two offices (*Against Heresies* 3.2; 4.26; 5.20; 26.2).

As earlier in Clement, we find the idea of "the episcopal succession: for to the bishops the apostles entrusted the care of the church in each place, which has come down to our time." (*Against Heresies* 4.33.8). He used this as an effective weapon against Gnostic heretics (see next chapter) who claimed to have secret apostolic teachings – "We can enumerate those who were appointed bishops in the churches, and their successions down to our own time, who never taught nor knew absurdities such as these heretics produce" (*Against Heresies* 3.1; *ANE* p114). Irenaeus appealed to succession lists of bishops in churches founded by apostles to demonstrate that apostolic teaching had been faithfully preserved and transmitted in these places down to his own day. The church at Rome, in particular, had been founded by Peter and Paul and all churches must agree with the apostolic tradition preserved in this church through its succession of bishops (*Against Heresies* 3. 2, 3; *ANE* pp114, 115; see pp148, 149). With Irenaeus then, the diocesan bishop is the custodian of apostolic tradition, while in Ignatius the congregational bishop had been the focus of ecclesiastical unity. In both cases the role of the bishop was essential as a defence against the threat posed to the churches by heresy.

Tasks

a. **Explain how Irenaeus used the concept of apostolic/episcopal succession as an effective weapon against heretics.**

b. **In what ways is Irenaeus' episcopacy different from Ignatian episcopacy?**

HIPPOLYTUS

In his *Apostolic Tradition*, the early third century Roman presbyter Hippolytus provides evidence of the status and roles of bishops, presbyters and deacons (see the first two chapters of the present book for details in relation to baptism and the Eucharist). The bishop, assisted by the presbyters, ordained church leaders. He also remitted sins, imposed penances and offered the Eucharist and the eucharistic prayers. FF Bruce states that in Hippolytus the bishop is assisted in liturgical acts by the deacons rather than the presbyters, the latter acting as his administrators, and that with the emergence of the monarchical bishop, presbyters had a minor liturgical role for several centuries[1]. Norbert Brox observes that in Hippolytus there is a clear division of the church into clergy and laity on the basis of ordination (*Apostolic Tradition* 8-10, 19) and a notable change in vocabulary. The ministry is thought of less in terms of service and more in terms of authority[2].

Outline the functions of bishops, presbyters and deacons in Hippolytus (see also the first two chapters of this book).

TERTULLIAN

Around the beginning of the third century in Carthage, Tertullian, like Irenaeus, used the argument of episcopal succession from the apostles to refute Gnostic claims to secret apostolic traditions. He challenged the heretics to provide similar succession lists (*On the Prescription of Heretics*, 32). However, unlike Irenaeus, he consistently distinguishes between bishops and presbyters. By the early third century the threefold ministry and its corresponding terminology was clearly established. In *On Baptism* (17) he states that the bishop ('the supreme priest') has the right to baptise but may delegate this to presbyters and deacons and, if need be, to the laity (apart from women). In *On the Veiling of Virgins* (9) he does not permit women to speak in church, nor to baptise, nor to offer the Eucharist, though in *Against Marcion* (5.8) he notes that Paul allowed women to prophesy. Both these works were written in Tertullian's Montanist period.

Tertullian is the first to understand the Christian ministry specifically as a priesthood, though we have noted that Clement drew a parallel between Old Testament priests and Church leaders. In the third century the term priest became increasingly and exclusively used of ministers, especially bishops. However, while before his Montanist period Tertullian protested that heretics applied priestly functions to laymen (*On the Prescription of Heretics*, 41), in his Montanist *On the Exhortation to Chastity* (7) he says that laymen are priests also (quoting Revelation 1: 6). In cases of necessity, then, laymen could act as priests. The distinction between the order of clergy and the laity was due, he says, to the authority of the Church and the honour of a special bench where

---

[1] Bruce, FF *The Spreading Flame*, Eerdmans/Paternoster: London, 1958, p207

[2] Brox, Norbert *A History of the Early Church*, SCM: London, 1994, p79

the clergy sit in the church. The order of widows had a special bench as well – *On the Veiling of Virgins*, 9. Finally, in Montanist writings Tertullian refers to Church synods/councils which settled matters of controversy such as the canonical status of early Christian writings (*On Fasting* 13; *On Modesty*, 16).

Task

Outline Tertullian's views on Church government with particular reference to the priesthood of the ministry.

CYPRIAN

Cyprian, bishop of Carthage (AD249-258), was a very influential theologian in relation to the development of episcopacy. He has been called 'the Ignatius of the West' because of his emphasis on bishops and contributed greatly to formalising and institutionalising episcopacy. His views were developed against the background of his own legal training and the Decian persecution and its aftermath (see later chapter on Persecution, p185).

The Decian persecution (AD250-251) had resulted in schismatic churches and bishops due to disagreement over the discipline of those who had compromised or lapsed at the time. In his *On the Unity of the Catholic Church* Cyprian argued that the unity of the Church is founded and centred in its bishops, individually and collectively, who are the successors of the apostles and the glue which binds the Church together. In the manuscript tradition of this book there are two different versions – one is episcopalian and stresses the equality of all bishops (the 'Textus Receptus') while the other is papal and stresses the importance of the bishops of Rome as Peter's successors (the 'Primacy Text'; see *On the Unity of the Catholic Church* 4-6; *ANE* pp228-230). While all the apostles were equal in power and honour, Christ built his Church on one man to show from the beginning that the Church is one. Cyprian had a collegiate or federal view of the episcopacy. Each bishop possessed and shared in the totality of the universal episcopate, much like a share-holder in a large institution. Thus: "The episcopate is one; the individual bishops have each a part" (*On the Unity of the Catholic Church*, 5). And yet, the bishops are independent as well as inter-dependent. At the Seventh Council of Carthage (1 September AD256) Cyprian stated: "For none of us sets himself up as a bishop of bishops ... since every bishop in the free use of his liberty and power has the right of reaching his own judgement and can no more be judged by another than he can himself judge another" (*ANE* pp243, 244). Thus, Cyprian rejected

Stephen's attempt, as bishop of Rome, to impose his views on schismatic baptism on the African bishops (*ANE* excerpts 214, 217).

Further, the Church may be found only where the bishop, as the successor of the apostles, is found and only his ministries (such as baptism, the Eucharist and penance) are valid and effective. After referring to the Church being originally built on Peter, Cyprian says:

Thereafter, age has followed age and bishop has succeeded bishop, and the office of bishop and the system of church government has been handed down, so that the Church is founded on the bishops and every act of the Church is directed by those same presiding officers.

(Letter 33.1)

Also:

... the church is made up of the people united to their priest and the flock that cleaves to its shepherd. Thus, you should know that the bishop is in the Church, and the Church in the bishop, and that if anyone is not with the bishop he is not in the Church ...

(Letter 66.7)

The bishop is in the place of God and of Christ. He is the overseer of the brotherhood, the head of the people, the shepherd of the flock, the governor of the Church, the representative of Christ, the priest of God (*Letter* 59.4-6; *Letter* 66.5). Thus, the bishop and not the 'confessors' (those who remained faithful in persecution) are in charge of discipline. In Ignatius the stress is on the bishop as the focus of Church unity; in Irenaeus, as the guardian of apostolic tradition; in Cyprian, as the representative of Christ's authority.

While Tertullian, fifty years earlier in the same place, was the first specifically to use priestly terms for Church leaders, Cyprian was the father of the sacredotal view of the ministry (*sacerdos* is Latin for priest). In Cyprian, bishops are normally described as priests and Old Testament passages about the priesthood are applied to Church leaders (eg Deut 17: 12, 13 in *Letter* 59.4-6 and Numbers 20: 25 following in *Letter* 67.4). The Christian minister, as a priest, offers the sacrifice of the Eucharist to God (*Letter* 63.14).

Further, despite Cyprian's high view of the authority of the bishop, we may note that the bishop worked in consultation with fellow bishops, lesser clergy and even the laity. Thus, for instance, bishops are chosen and appointed by neighbouring bishops in the presence and with the approval of the people who can vouch for their moral integrity. For Cyprian, the approval of the people in episcopal appointments was an apostolic and virtually universal requirement (*Letters* 60. 3,4; 59. 5; 55. 8; 67. 2, 3-5). Finally, Church leaders were not to be involved in secular affairs (*Letter* 55).

A contemporary of Cyprian, Cornelius bishop of Rome, provides us with information about the number and variety of church officials in the church of Rome in the mid third century – forty-six presbyters (possibly heads of house churches in the city), seven deacons (based on the number of 'deacons' in the Jerusalem church in Acts 6), seven sub-deacons (deacons' assistants), forty-two acolytes, fifty-two exorcists, readers and door-keepers (in Eusebius, *Hist Eccl* 6.43.11-12; *ANE* pp232).

Tasks

a. *Why is Cyprian important in the development of episcopacy?*

b. *Explain his views on the interdependence and independence of bishops, and how they were developed against the aftermath of the Decian persecution.*

c. *Why is Cyprian sometimes regarded as the father of the sacerdotal view of the Christian ministry?*

d. *What evidence is there to support the view that in Cyprian bishops are not dictators?*

A HIERARCHY OF BISHOPS

While Cyprian argued for the solidarity and equality of all bishops, gradually different ranks of bishops appeared, their relative status being determined by the apostolic origins of their churches and/or the political importance of their cities or 'sees' (areas of episcopal oversight). The political or territorial organisation of the Church reflected the political division of the Empire. Just as the provinces were governed by their respective capitals in imperial administration, so the bishops of the capital cities, the so-called 'metropolitans' (Greek for 'mother city'), were accorded an authority over the bishops and churches in their provinces. It was from these cities that rural areas were evangelised. Synods (regional gatherings of bishops) were held in these cities from the third century and the metropolitans presided over such councils. They also ordained bishops in the provinces and supervised discipline. By the end of the fourth century each province had a metropolitan bishop. Below the metropolitans, and the city bishops generally, were the so-called *chorepiscopi* or country bishops, who ranked between the city bishops and the presbyters. We hear of them first in the councils of Ancyra and Neo-Caesarea (AD314).

Another and higher rank developed among the metropolitans. Certain city churches were known to hold a special status due to apostolic associations and/or political importance. Thus in AD325 the Council of Nicaea ratified the traditional importance of the bishops of Rome, Alexandria and Antioch as having power over more than one province (canon 6; *ANE* p340). The bishops of Jerusalem and Constantinople (the New Rome) were also regarded as having special status. The term 'patriarch', which previously had been used of all bishops in the East, was applied in the fourth century to the bishops of these five important centres of Christianity.

Explain how an episcopal hierarchy developed in the early Church.

THE BISHOP OF ROME

In the early period of Church history we see the beginnings of the development of the papacy – the overall authority of the bishop of Rome in the Western Church. Paul's letter to the Romans (about AD57) is addressed to the whole church and provides no information about the Church's leadership. The late first century fraternal letter from the Roman church to the Corinthian church known as *1 Clement* makes no claim for Roman authority over the Corinthians and, as we have seen, appears to indicate that the Roman church was governed by a plurality of bishops. Notably, while Ignatius in the early second century is aware of monarchical bishops in the churches of Asia Minor, he makes no reference to such a bishop in his letter to the Romans. Though he does say in the preface that the Roman church 'presides in the place of the region of the Romans' and has a 'primacy of love'.

In mid second century Rome the church appears still to have a collective episcopal leadership, as is apparent in the *Shepherd of Hermas*. Around this time Justin in Rome makes no special claim for his church's leadership and refers to 'that one who presides over the brothers' in worship. However, in the late second century struggle with Gnosticism, there appear succession lists of bishops of apostolically founded churches, to demonstrate that the Church is the true heir of the apostles eg Irenaeus (*Against Heresies*, 3.1-3; *ANE* pp114, 115) and Tertullian (*On the Prescription of Heretics*, 32). Indeed, Irenaeus refers to the Roman church as the greatest and oldest church, known to all, founded and set up by the two most glorious apostles, Peter and Paul. He then writes: "Because of its position of leadership and authority each church must agree with [or, resort to] this church." (*Against Heresies* 3. 1)

While we have here late second century evidence of the esteem in which the Roman church was held, there are some historical problems to note. Far from founding the Roman church, Paul appears not to be acquainted with their members (Romans 1: 10-15). Also, we have no early evidence of Peter's role in relation to the Roman church. The late second century succession lists are theologically motivated responses to Gnosticism, rather than historically researched chronicles. We have already seen that there is no evidence of monarchical bishops in Rome in the earlier period, and we may note too that Irenaeus and Tertullian disagree over who was appointed bishop by Peter. Irenaeus says Linus and Tertullian says Clement, who is third in Irenaeus' list. It is clear also that the lists are all about apostolic heritage, with no claim to Roman primacy over the whole Church at this stage. However, in his Montanist work *On Modesty* (1. 13) Tertullian scathingly rejects the perceived penitential laxity of 'the Supreme Pontiff, the Bishop of Bishops' – and 'blessed Papa'. This may be a reference to a Roman bishop (Callistus or Zephyrinus) but could also refer to the local bishop of Carthage, Agrippinus.

About AD190, in the so-called Quartodeciman controversy over the date of Easter, the Eastern bishops rejected the attempt of Victor, bishop of Rome (AD189-199), to impose his views on them. The Western bishop Irenaeus opposed Victor's authoritarianism. However, it is not known on what basis Victor sought to impose his authority on other churches, even if it is clear that other bishops and churches saw no necessity to submit. Rather, it is with the mid third century schismatic/heretical baptism controversy (see pp15, 16) that the claim to Roman supremacy or primacy was born. Stephen was the first Roman bishop (AD254-257) to appeal to Matthew 16: 18, 19 (Peter is the foundation of the Church and has the keys of the Kingdom) and claim that as Peter's successor he had authority over the whole Church. We have already noted Cyprian's response to and rejection of such claims. In time more such claims would be made by Roman bishops and eventually the bishop of Rome would attain overall authority in the Western Church.

Due to the Roman church's prestigious location in the capital and power-base of the Empire, the tradition that it was founded by the two greatest apostles and the fact that it was the only apostolically founded church in the West, its bishop was accorded honour and eventually supreme authority in the West. Since the East had several patriarchates it has always resisted any attempt at centralisation of episcopal authority (see previous page for the Council of Nicaea's rulings).

Task

In the form of a flow diagram, outline the sources relevant to the development of the papacy in our period.

CHURCH COUNCILS

In the development of the government of the Church we should also note the role of Church councils/synods – gatherings of bishops to rule on matters of faith, order and discipline. In the New Testament we have, of course, the Council of Jerusalem. This is the earliest example of churches in conference and was convened to deal with a theological dispute, namely, the grounds on which Gentiles would be admitted to the Church (Acts 15). As well as apostles and elders, non-official church members participated (Acts 15: 6, 7, 12, 13, 23). After this, we do not hear of Church councils again until the mid-late second century when such gatherings were held in Asia Minor to reject Montanism and to excommunicate its followers (Eusebius, *Hist Eccl* 5.16. 6-10; *ANE* pp102, 103). Around the same time several gatherings of bishops met in various places to deal with the controversy over the date of Easter (Eusebius, *Hist Eccl* 5.23-25; *ANE* pp138-141). In the third century councils were convened to deal with various matters of controversy, particularly in the middle of the century in Carthage to rule on the discipline of the lapsed and heretical baptism. A synod of bishops met in Antioch in AD268 and, for the first time, excommunicated a bishop – Paul of Samosata (a suburb of Antioch) – for erroneous views about the person of Jesus.

Diocesan synods included the diocesan bishop, his presbyters, deacons and lay people too. These existed from at least the third century. Provincial or metropolitan synods met once or twice a year in the metropolis under the chairmanship of the metropolitan bishop. There is evidence of lay membership and participation in such councils (eg Cyprian, *Letters* 11, 13, 66, 71), but increasingly bishops alone had a voice and a vote, not as representatives of their churches but in their own right as successors of the apostles. Presbyters and other clergy acted as secretaries to or representatives of the bishops. This was particularly so after the Council of Nicaea in 325, the first ecumenical (universal) council of the Church – ecumenical at least in intention if not in fact (see chapter 13). In the early fourth century a number of important councils, dealing largely with matters of church government and morality, paved the way for the first ecumenical council. These included the councils of Elvira in Spain (*ANE* pp290-3), Arles in Gaul (*ANE* pp293-296), Ancyra in Asia Minor (*ANE* pp313, 314) and Neocaesarea in Cappadocia (*ANE* p293). Church councils had important unifying and standardising roles in the development of Church government. As the Church grew numerically and spread geographically, Church councils of various levels attempted to provide organisational uniformity, particularly in matters of controversy.

Task

Describe the development and importance of Church councils in relation to the regulation of the Church during our period.

CONCLUSION

In this chapter we have surveyed "the development of Church government" in the first two centuries or so. The evidence suggests that the Church gradually became less charismatic (ie less dependent on the gifts and ministries of its members) and more institutional (ie more dependent on officials and structures). The Church appears to have become less democratic and more hierarchical and bureaucratic as power gradually shifted from its corporate membership to a select number of ranked officials.

Some have had an idealised picture of an initial charismatic phase which soon gave way to institutionalism, eg late nineteenth and early twentieth century Continental scholars such as Rudolph Sohm, Adolf von Harnack and Hans von Campenhausen. For instance, the latter held that Paul's charismatic view of the Church clashed with the official view of the church in Jerusalem which eventually resulted in second century episcopacy[1]. However, as we have seen, in the New Testament itself both charismatic ministry and church leadership co-existed from the beginning, though a tendency away from the former to the latter is discernible. Even in the post-apostolic period charismatic ministries are still apparent, though their relation to official ministries was a source of some tension, as can be seen in the *Didache* and in Montanism (see next chapter). Charisma, however, became routinised with the passage of time.

There is no doubt that the sources reveal a growing hierarchicalism and clericalism – witness 1 Clement's distinction between clergy and laity and its comparison of the Christian ministry with the Old Testament priesthood and the military, as well as its episcopal succession; Ignatius' monarchical episcopacy, in particular; Tertullian's and, more so, Cyprian's sacerdotal conception of the ministry; the growth of various subordinate church offices (as reported by Cornelius); the development of diocesan, metropolitan, patriarchal and papal episcopacy; and the power of synods culminating in ecumenical councils. The role and authority of the bishop in particular was enhanced and guaranteed by all these factors so that gradually sacramental and ecclesiastical functions and ministries were only valid if performed by the

---

[1] von Campenhausen, H *Ecclesiastical Authority and Spiritual Power*, SCM Press: London, 1969

bishop or his delegate. We have seen that episcopacy in Ignatius was especially the focus of Church unity, then in Irenaeus the guarantee of apostolic orthodoxy and finally in Cyprian the focus of ecclesiastical authority. The growing importance of the bishops was but part of a wider trend towards formalism and institutionalism generally, apparent also in credal development, liturgical standardisation and the formation of the New Testament canon.

Such developments may be seen as inevitable and even essential to ensure that the rapidly growing Church would be efficiently organised and in order to secure theological, liturgical and ethical uniformity. In the face of persecution, heresy and schism, bishops, individually and collectively, preserved the unity, orthodoxy and integrity of the Church.

However, the increasing institutionalism and hierarchicalism of the Church may be perceived as having harmful effects. Colin Bulley has recently shown that in the early centuries of the Church, clergy and laity were increasingly separated, resulting in a denial of the priesthood of all Church members.[1] To view Church leaders as mediating priests without whom the Church's sacraments or ordinances are invalid is regarded by many as a departure from the New Testament and apostolic conception of Christian ministry, where the Church as a whole is a royal and holy priesthood, some of whom, nevertheless, are appointed as its spiritual pastors.

Practice Essay Titles

1. **Outline the developments that occurred in Church government in the early Church. (30)**

   Assess the claim that over time the Church's ministry became less charismatic and more institutional. (15)

2. **What do early sources tell us about the roles and ministries of bishops, presbyters and deacons? (30)**

   Evaluate the claim that the development of episcopacy in the early Church was essential for the Church's progress. (15)

---

[1] Bulley, Colin *The Priesthood of Some Believers* subtitled 'developments from the general to the special priesthood in the Christian literature of the first three centuries', Paternoster: Carlisle, 2000

Heresy

The emergence and teaching of Gnosticism, Marcionism and Montanism and the Church's response with particular reference to Irenaeus' polemic against heresy.

(CCEA Specification)

Definition

In traditional Christian understanding 'heresy' refers to any belief or opinion which is not in agreement with the teachings of the Church. Such beliefs are described as 'heretical' and those who hold them as 'heretics'. Heresy or 'heterodoxy' is usually contrasted with the 'orthodoxy' or correct teaching of the Church.

Objective

In this chapter we shall gain a knowledge and understanding of the emergence (origins/beginnings) and teaching of three early movements, traditionally regarded by the Church as heresies, namely, Gnosticism, Marcionism and Montanism. We shall also study the Church's response to these movements, focusing especially on Irenaeus' polemic against heresy.

THE WORD 'HERESY' COMES from the Greek word *hairesis* (literally 'choice') which initially meant a 'sect' or 'party' such as the Pharisees and the early Christians (eg Acts 15: 5; 24: 5, 14). In the New Testament the word is also used of divisions and factions disrupting the unity of the Church (eg 1 Cor 11: 19; Gal 5: 20). At least one New Testament passage may use the word in its later sense of erroneous teaching (2 Peter 2: 1 – 'destructive heresies/opinions'), which seems to be one of its meanings in Ignatius in the early second century (eg Eph 6:2; Trall 6.1).Originally it appears to have meant much the same as the Greek word 'schisma' (a 'tear' or 'crack'; see 1 Corinth 11: 18 – 'schismata'; v19 – 'haireseis'). However, 'schism' is now often used to refer to division due to difference in church practice or discipline, apart from the theological disagreement implied by the word heresy.

The word `heresy` has gone out of favour in recent study of early Christianity since, it is argued, it represents a value-judgement unsupported by the historical evidence. Walter Bauer challenged the traditional view by arguing that the distinction between orthodoxy and heresy was a late development and that in 'earliest' Christianity (by which he meant the second century!) so-called 'heretical' and 'orthodox' churches existed together, the latter eventually dominating more because of Church politics than loyalty to some original set of correct beliefs.[1]

Despite scholarly criticism of weaknesses in Bauer's work[2] his thesis is still largely accepted. The traditional view, in fact, has been turned on its head so that many regard the early 'heretics' as the authentic representatives of early Christianity while the early Fathers who opposed them are presented as the villains[3].

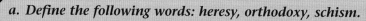

Tasks

a. Define the following words: heresy, orthodoxy, schism.

b. Explain why the word 'heresy' has been considered inappropriate by many recent studies of early Christianity.

---

[1] Bauer, Walter *Orthodoxy and Heresy in Earliest Christianity* German Original, 1934; English translation, Fortress: Philadelphia, 1971

[2] eg Turner, HEW *The Pattern of Christian Truth: A Study in Relations Between Orthodoxy and Heresy in the Early Church*, Mowbray: London, 1954. Also Robinson, TA *The Bauer Thesis Examined*, Edwin Mellen Press: Lewiston, New York, 1988

[3] A trend criticised by Henry, P, 'Why is Contemporary Scholarship so Enamored of Ancient Heretics?', in *Studia Patristica*, 17,1: 123-126; cited by McGinn, Sheila E, in *The Early Christian World* Vol 2 ed P Esler, Routledge: London/New York, 2000, p894

1. GNOSTICISM

Our study of Gnosticism is structured as follows:

a) Definition
b) Sources
c) Emergence
d) Teachers
e) Teachings
f) The Church's Response

Definition

'Gnosticism' is a modern term referring to a variety of ancient religious and philosophical movements which flourished particularly in the second and third centuries AD and focused on *gnosis* (Greek: 'knowledge') as the means of salvation. Ancient opponents of these movements, including pagan philosophers as well as early Church Fathers, referred to them as 'Gnostics' (Greek: *gnostikoi*: 'knowers'). However, these movements or groups used a variety of names for themselves. Of the many different groups that Irenaeus described in the late second century, only one, he says, specifically called themselves Gnostics (*Against Heresies* 1. 25.6). None of the uncovered texts composed by Gnostics include the term as a self-designation. In fact, many of these groups called themselves 'Christians', according to Justin in mid second century Rome (*Dialogue with Trypho* 35.6). The Church Fathers often referred to the groups by the names of their founders or teachers or by a leading concept in their teaching. Thus, we see that while ancient opponents of these diverse groups referred to them as Gnostics, the groups themselves used a variety of self-designations and that many of them regarded themselves as Christians – a claim, of course, rejected by the early Church Fathers.

The word 'Gnosticism' appears to have been used first by the seventeenth century English philosopher and theologian Henry More[1] (the term was used by More in relation to the teachings of Jezebel in Revelation 2: 20). Many scholars have argued that the use of this modern term to cover such a variety of diverse ancient groups is unsatisfactory since there is no clear view on what it means or how it relates to 'gnosis'. In 1966 at a Gnosis Conference in Messina an attempt was made to clear up the confusion about terminology. Scholars attending approved the definition of the general term 'gnosis' as knowledge of divine mysteries for an elite, and the definition of the specific term 'Gnosticism' as referring to a group of religious systems from the second century AD onwards. However, these definitions have not satisfied all scholars.

---

[1] More, Henry, *An Exposition of the Seven Epistles to the Seven Churches*, published in 1669

Michael Williams has argued that, since there is no agreement among scholars as to a definition of 'Gnosticism', the term should be abandoned[1]. Due to the problems of definition it is safer to operate with a broad definition, of the type with which this section began.

Tasks

a. Define the words 'gnosis' and 'Gnosticism'.

b. Explain the difficulties involved in providing a definition of 'Gnosticism'.

Sources

Ancient sources that provide information on Gnosticism are classified in various ways by modern scholars. Here we will present them under three broad categories: Church Fathers, pagan philosophers and Gnostic authors.

(i) Church Fathers

A number of early church fathers provide us with information about Gnostics and even quotations from Gnostic works:

Justin in Rome, in his mid second century *First Apology*;

Irenaeus of Lyons, in his five volume *Refutation and Overthrow of Knowledge (Gnosis) Falsely So-Called*, known by the shorter name *Against Heresies*, particularly Book 1 which provides details on the history and teachings of Gnosticism. This was probably written in the AD180s (see *ANE* pp76-85, 91);

Clement of Alexandria (writing in the late second and early third century; in his *Stromateis* see *ANE* p78, 85); Tertullian of Carthage (writing around the same time as Clement of Alexandria; eg *On the Prescription of Heretics, Against the Valentinians, Against Marcion*; see *ANE* p79, 169); Hippolytus of Rome (early third century; *Refutation of all Heresies* – Books 5-9 cover thirty-three groups considered Gnostic in modern scholarship; see *ANE* pp72-76); Origen of Alexandria and Caesarea (first half of the third century; in his *Commentary on John* he opposes a second century Valentinian commentator on the same book, known as Heracleon – see also *ANE* p89, 90); and Epiphanius of Salamis, Cyprus (late fourth century; his 'Panarion' or 'Medicine Chest' against heresies, especially 21-40, discusses eighty heresies, about twenty of which would be considered

---

[1] Williams, Michael *Rethinking Gnosticism: An Argument for Dismantling a Dubious Category*, Princeton University Press: Princeton, NJ, 1996

Gnostic by modern scholars. Irenaeus in particular is especially important as a source for Gnosticism. However, the early Fathers cannot be uncritically relied on for accurate accounts of Gnosticism due to the biased, polemical nature of their writings and to the fact that sometimes they were recording unverified hearsay. For instance, nothing in the Gnostic texts discovered near Nag Hammadi, Egypt in 1945/6 corroborates the claim by early Fathers that some Gnostics were immoral.

(ii) Pagan philosophers

Neo-Platonic philosophers were also opposed to Gnosticism due to its perceived corruption of their philosophy. Thus some information on Gnostics is provided by the second century writer Celsus (preserved in Origen's *Against Celsus*) and the third century writers Plotinus (especially *Enneads* 2.9) and Porphyry (especially *Life of Plotinus* 16).

(iii) Gnostic authors

In 1945/6 a library of original Gnostic texts was found near Nag Hammadi, Upper Egypt, including eleven complete books and fragments of two others, containing a total of fifty-two texts. There is, however, no certainty about the dates of these texts. While they were all produced in the fourth century as Coptic translations, the Greek originals may go back to the second century and possibly earlier. The library includes Gospels (eg of Thomas,of Philip, of Truth), Acts (of Peter and the Twelve Apostles), Letters (eg of James, of Peter to Philip), Apocalypses (ie revelations, eg of Paul, of Peter, of James, Of Adam), Prayers (eg of Paul, of Thanksgiving), Hymns (eg 'The Thunder') and also non-Christians writings (eg 'The Discourse on the Eighth and the Ninth', a dialogue between the god Hermes and one of his disciples). See *ANE* excerpts 43-51 (pp68-72).

In addition, some other primary Gnostic texts (mostly from the second and third centuries) were available before the discovery of the Nag Hammadi Library – Ptolemy's Letter to Flora (see *ANE* pp85-89), Excerpts from Theodotus (see *ANE* p68), the Book of Baruch, The Naassene Hymn, The Great Exposition, The Hymn of the Pearl, The Two Books of Jeu, Pistis Sophia and four Gnostic works in the Berlin Codex.

Also, collections of Manichaean texts survive – discoveries from Turfan, Medinet Madi and Dakhleh, as well as a biography of the Persian teacher Mani (Cologne Mani Codex), the third century founder of Manichaeism which represents the conclusion of ancient Gnosticism. Finally, Hermetic sources (the Corpus Hermeticum) may provide insight into Gnostic ideas in the third century, and the Jewish texts known as the 'Hekhalot Literature' may represent a kind of ancient Jewish gnosis.

a. Outline briefly the main sources that exist for the study of Gnosticism.

b. Discuss the value of the early Church Fathers as sources for Gnosticism.

Emergence

Due to the nature of the sources, (eg biased polemic and uncertain dating), and due to the lack of any scholarly agreement on what ancient gnosis or Gnosticism is, there is much uncertainty and controversy over the beginnings of Gnosticism. Two main options exist. The traditional view, represented in the early Church Fathers, is that Gnosticism began in the second century AD as a heresy within the Christian Church. The modern view holds that Gnosticism was an independent, non-Christian, even pre-Christian, religion which began in the first century AD, if not before.[1]

Evidence for the traditional view may be found in the observations that no Gnostic texts clearly pre-date the second century and that the early Fathers present Gnosticism as a Christian heresy. However, arguments for the modern view include: some of the Nag Hammadi Gnostic texts seem to have been originally non-Christian works which Christians have only slightly edited (eg Eugnostos), and some first century texts do appear to reflect the existence of Gnostic ideas to some degree eg Philo of Alexandria's *The Legacy of the Divine* and various passages in the New Testament (eg the dualism of John's Gospel; 1 Corinthians 2: 14, 15; Colossians 1:19; 2: 8-10; Ephesians 1: 20-23; 1 Timothy 6: 20; 2 Timothy 2: 18; 1 John 4: 1-3; 2 John 7).

It seems then that while Gnosticism became a predominantly Christian heresy in the second century, its roots lie in the previous century at least. In its undeveloped first century form it is sometimes termed pre- or proto- or incipient Gnosticism. Early Church Fathers locate its origins in the first

---

[1] Representatives of the traditional view include, for example, Petrement, S *A Separate God: The Christian Origins of Gnosticism*, Harper San Francisco, 1990; Yamauchi, EM *Pre-Christian Gnosticism: A Survey of the Proposed Evidences*, 2nd edition, Baker: Grand Rapids, 1983; Logan, AHB *Gnostic Truth and Christian Heresy: A Study in the History of Gnosticism*, T&T Clark: Edinburgh,1996. Defenders of the modern view include, for example, Rudolph, K *Gnosis: The Nature and History of Gnosticism*, Harper and Row: San Francisco, 1983; Filoramo, G *A History of Gnosticism*, Blackwell: Oxford, 1990; Robinson, JM (ed) *The Nag Hammadi Library in English*, 3rd ed, Harper Collins: San Francisco, 1990

century, with Simon Magus (eg Justin: 1 Apol 1.26. Irenaeus: *Against Heresies* 1.23-2.3). DM Scholer[1] argues plausibly for the beginnings of Gnosticism in the first century in deviant Hellenistic Judaism (Judaism influenced by Greek ideas) and forms of the Platonic tradition in Greek philosophy, before it made its way into the Christian Church. Certainly, the biography of the third century Gnostic thinker Mani and traditions within the Nag Hammadi Gnostic texts seem to confirm the view that Gnosticism derived from heterodox Jewish speculation. Gnostic sects, however, were syncretistic in that they drew upon various sources. While the majority view is that Gnosticism emerged from Judaism originally[2], there was influence also from other sources along the way – Greek philosophy, eastern mysticism and astrology (Persia) and, of course, Christianity – traditions which were already in a process of mutual influence to various degrees.

Tasks

a. Summarise the two main views concerning the emergence of Gnosticism and the arguments for each.

b. Comment on the syncretism of Gnosticism.

Teachers

The following prominent Gnostic teachers may be noted:

(i) Simon Magus

The Church Fathers generally regarded Simon Magus (Acts 8) as the originator of Gnostic heresy and refer to his followers, the 'Simonians'. The picture we get from the Fathers is that Simon and his companion Helen were worshipped as divine beings. However, most scholars reject the reports of the Fathers, not least because they do not agree with the picture of Simon in the book of Acts.

(ii) Menander

The Fathers present Menander as a fellow-Samaritan and disciple of Simon, active in Antioch, Syria, in the late first century. He seems to have taught that the first power is unknown and that death could be avoided through Menander's baptism.

---

[1] *Dictionary of the Later New Testament and Its Developments*, IVP: Leicester, 1997, pp403, 404

[2] so Logan, AHB in *The Early Christian World* VolII p915, ed P Esler, Routledge: London, 2000

(iii) Saturninus

Next in Irenaeus' account of early Gnostics is Saturninus who also taught in Antioch in the early second century. He taught, among other things, that the first God is unknown, that the world was created by angels – one of whom was the God of the Jews, and that Christ, who was not really human, came to save humans from angelic powers. His followers apparently rejected marriage, reproduction and the consumption of meat.

(iv) Cerinthus

Cerinthus, in early second century Asia Minor, also taught that the world was not made by the first God, but by a lower power ignorant of the supreme God. He rejected the virgin birth of Jesus. Christ descended on the man Jesus at his baptism and then left him before his suffering and death, since the Christ could not suffer (see *ANE* pp49, 50). Irenaeus reports a tradition from Polycarp that the apostle John left a bath-house in Ephesus in a hurry when he heard that Cerinthus was there, fearing that the building would collapse (*ANE* p116)!

(v) Basilides

Basilides was active in second century Alexandria, Egypt. In addition to accounts of the Fathers, there are some authentic fragments of his teaching. These latter texts present a different picture of Basilides than that, for instance, in Irenaeus. This raises questions about the reliability of the Fathers' accounts, particularly in relation to reports that cannot be checked independently. In the fragments we see that he made a distinction between the supreme God and the god of creation, believed in the migration of souls and the importance of loving all things. In Irenaeus, Basilides is presented as teaching that the supreme God provided five partial aspects of himself, two of which (wisdom and power) united and produced many more inferior powers contained in 365 heavens. The powers of the last heaven, including its ruler (the 'God of the Jews') created the world. The supreme God sent his Mind, called Christ, to liberate those who believe in him from the powers that made the world. Simon of Cyrene was crucified in place of Jesus – who stood by laughing. Hippolytus also provides an account of Basilides which is somewhat different to that found in Irenaeus (see *ANE* excerpts 52-59).

(vi) Marcion

There is disagreement over whether this Christian leader in mid second century Rome should be considered a Gnostic. Details and discussion can be found later in the chapter.

(vii) Valentinus

Probably the most famous Gnostic, Valentinus taught (like Justin) in mid second century Rome, though he originated in Egypt. He was an impressive teacher and was even proposed as a candidate for high church office. A few fragments of his own writings have been preserved and some of the Nag Hammadi writings are considered Valentinian eg *The Gospel of Truth,* possibly written by Valentinus himself (see *ANE* excerpts 45-47, 49-51). In the surviving fragments, Valentinus regards humans to be the imperfect creation of angels who were nevertheless perfected by the creative act of the supreme God. Unlike many other Gnostics, he believed that the world was an orderly creation permeated by God's Spirit. God's revelation of himself through his Son Jesus leads to the moral purification of humans. Jesus Christ was human in that he ate and drank but demonstrated his divinity by not excreting – since God needs no nourishment, he does not need to digest.

Justin in mid second century Rome was aware of the existence of Valentinians. Indeed, in the Fathers it is not easy at times to differentiate between the teachings of Valentinus and his followers. In the late second century Irenaeus attributes a cosmological myth to Valentinus which basically provides a prequel and a sequel to biblical history: from the supreme God (*Bythos*: depth) proceed other divine aspects (*aeons*: eternities; whose names are often taken from John's Gospel). These thirty aeons make up the divine Pleroma (*pleroma*: fullness). The last aeon (*Sophia*: wisdom) falls due to her desire to know God. The result is that the Demiurge (*demiourgos*: craftsman) was produced – the creator God of Genesis, who does not know of his connection to the supreme God. After the fall of Sophia, an aeon called Christ, who comes from the 'firstborn' of the Father, completes the Pleroma. Humans have a spirit, placed in them without the knowledge of the Demiurge, and a body. The body, as matter, perishes and the spirit alone may be saved through knowledge. These three parts of human beings also represent the human race – the body standing for the materially dominated who will perish; the soul representing ordinary Christians who have faith and may be saved and the spirit signifying those who will certainly be saved (see *ANE* excerpts 61-67). Followers of Valentinus include Marcus, Heracleon, Ptolemy and Flora (see *ANE* excerpt 68) and Theodotus (see *ANE* excerpt 42).

Many other Gnostic groups are included in the writings of early Church Fathers such as a group called the Barbelo-gnostics by modern scholars, the Sethians, the Cainites, the Ophites etc. The ancient Gnostic movements reached their conclusion in a separate religion, the Manichaeism of the fourth century onwards, which originated with the Persian teacher, Mani (see *ANE* pp265-68).

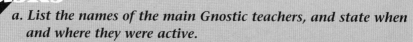

a. List the names of the main Gnostic teachers, and state when and where they were active.

b. Give details of the teaching of Valentinus, especially his cosmological myth (see also the relevant excerpts in ANE).

Teachings

There is difficulty in trying to provide a list of Gnostic beliefs and teachings due to the diversity of ancient Gnostic teachers and movements, which often held contradictory beliefs. The following teachings, however, were common to many Gnostic groups, as we have noted in the previous section.

(i) God

The supreme, transcendent and ultimately unknowable God is distanced from the inferior creator god (the Demiurge) by the multiplication of lesser divine beings (aeons) within the Pleroma (the divine fullness). A fall within the Pleroma resulted in the production of the Demiurge who is often identified with the God of the Old Testament. The distinction and distance between the supreme, spiritual God and the material creation is preserved by a hierarchy of hostile intermediary beings (archons, powers etc) between the Pleroma and the world.

(ii) Creation

The material world is inferior and even evil, produced as it was not by the supreme God who is Spirit, but by an inferior power.

(iii) Humanity

Trapped and slumbering within the material human body is a spiritual element, a divine spark which needs to be liberated. Some Gnostics, like Valentinus, classified humans into various groups according to their spiritual state.

(iv) Salvation

The supreme God sends a saviour from the Pleroma with liberating knowledge (*gnosis*) to release humans from ignorance about their origin, nature and destiny and from imprisonment in the body and the material world. Thus the serpent in Genesis 3 who points Adam and Eve to the tree of knowledge (*gnosis*) is on the same side as the supreme God. The creator god, on the other hand, wanted to keep *gnosis* from them. Some Gnostics claimed that they secretly received this saving *gnosis* from Jesus or the apostles. By means of this *gnosis*, including rites and passwords, the human spirit ascends the hierarchy of intermediary powers and demons to the supreme God. In Christian Gnosticism the redeemer is usually identified as Jesus. Since the human body is usually regarded as evil in Gnostic thought, the divine Jesus only 'appears' to be human. This denial of Jesus' humanity and suffering is termed 'docetism' (from the Greek for 'seem') since Jesus only seemed to be human. Thus it was not Jesus on the cross but a human substitute, put to death by the Demiurge and his intermediary forces.

(v) Ethics

In their own writings, Gnostics stressed the need for a morally ascetic (strictly disciplined) lifestyle. This asceticism, particularly related to marriage and reproduction, logically followed from their belief that the body was evil – to indulge its desires would be to serve its creator (the Demiurge). This conflicts with the view of Gnostic ethics presented by many of the Church Fathers who often characterise Gnostics as immoral and self-indulgent. It may be, however, that some Gnostics actually did draw an opposite logical deduction from their belief that the body is evil – to indulge it would not affect the spirit.

(vi) The Future

The eschatology (teaching about last things) of Gnostics included personal and cosmic dimensions. Personal eschatology (the destiny of the individual) involved a spiritualised idea of resurrection or belief in the immortality of the soul rather than the resurrection of the inferior, evil body. Cosmic eschatology (the destiny of the world) involved belief in the destruction of the cosmos and the return of the alienated divine sparks to the Pleroma.

Overall, we can see that a radical dualism, especially between the supreme God and the creator god and between spirit and matter, underlay much Gnostic thinking, resulting in a negative view of the material world in general and the human body in particular. Common too is the use of a cosmological myth or mythological drama to explain the origin, nature and destiny of the world and of God's elect people. These complex myths (such as that attributed to Valentinus – see p161) were philosophically informed attempts to make Christianity intellectually acceptable to educated pagans.

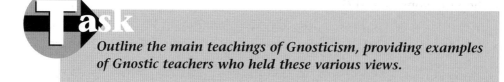

Task

Outline the main teachings of Gnosticism, providing examples of Gnostic teachers who held these various views.

The Church's response

The early Church's response to heresy in general is evident in a number of developments. The growing importance of bishops as the focus of Church unity, the custodians of inherited apostolic orthodoxy and the exclusive mediators of sacramental grace (see previous chapter), was in large part shaped by the challenge posed by heretics and schismatics. Also, the emergence and development of early Christian creeds, especially the second century 'rule of faith', represented to a large degree the Church's desire to distinguish itself theologically from rival claims to apostolic Christianity (see chapter 3). Further, the development of the New Testament canon, a fixed list of authoritative Christian writings, was spurred on, if not created, by Marcion's canon and by heretical use of spurious and apocryphal writings (see pp167, 172, 173). We may note too the role that Church synods and councils played in response to the challenge of heresy (see p41, 150).

Specific responses to Gnosticism were made by various early Fathers (see p156, 157), including the early third century writer Hippolytus who argued that Gnostics drew their ideas from pagan philosophy rather than the Church's Scriptures, as did his contemporary Tertullian (see final chapter for details). The early Fathers rejected Gnostic teachings which conflicted with the Church's apostolic traditions, such as the doctrine of two gods (and consequent rejection of the Old Testament), the inferiority or wickedness of matter (specifically creation and the body), a hierarchy of intermediaries between God and humanity, salvation as release of the spirit from the body, secret apostolic knowledge, fatalistic denial of human choice, the denial of Christ's real humanity (docetism), extreme asceticism or immorality and denial of the resurrection of the body.

In this section we shall focus on the main opponent of Gnosticism among the early Fathers – Irenaeus (about AD130-200), bishop of Lyons, Gaul. Irenaeus was born in Smyrna, Asia Minor and had been taught by Polycarp, bishop of Smyrna (see pp96, 97) and acquaintance of the apostle John. Irenaeus was sent in about AD150 to Lyons to be a presbyter among emigrants from Asia Minor. He avoided persecution there in AD177 because he had been sent to Rome to protest about heresies, particularly Valentinian Gnosticism, that had found their way from there to Gaul. He succeeded his martyred bishop in Lyons in AD177.

In the 180s he composed a five-volumed work against Gnosticism, usually known as *Against Heresies*, though its full title in Greek, variously translated into English, is *A Refutation and Overthrow of Knowledge* (ie Gnosis) *Falsely So-Called* (an obvious echo of 1 Timothy 6: 20). This was the first attempt at a critical investigation and refutation of Gnosticism, based on research into some twenty distinct Gnostic sects. The work was motivated by the adverse influence of Valentinian Gnostics, led by Marcus and his followers (Marcosians), upon his own church members, some of whom had defected to the Valentinians. Irenaeus' work was accepted as authoritative because of his connection with the apostle John and contributed to the eventual demise of Gnosticism. However, the discovery of primary Gnostic texts has thrown doubt on the reliability of Irenaeus (and other early Fathers) in his polemical portrayal of early Gnostics (see pp157, 160).

Before we consider the main arguments that Irenaeus used against the Gnostics, we will briefly outline the contents of his *Against Heresies*. However, it should be noted that the work is poorly structured, possibly due to additional insertions by Irenaeus which were not properly edited. Book 1 provides a history and description of Gnosticism and its diverse teachers and sects. The remaining four books are a refutation of Gnosticism by means of a variety of arguments.

Book 1 – an account of the beliefs of the Valentinians (chs 1-9)
　　　　 – a summary of the universal Church's beliefs (ch 10), contrasted with:
　　　　 – the diverse teachings of the Valentinians (ch 11-21) and
　　　　 – the diverse Gnostic teachers from Simon Magus to the Ophites.

Book 2 – the thirty-five chapters of this book refute Gnosticism mostly on rational and philosophical grounds and criticise Gnostic misuse of the Scriptures.

Book 3 – Gnostic teachings are contrasted with the apostolic tradition of the Church preserved by episcopal succession (chs 1-4) and with
　　　　 – the teaching of the Scriptures in both Testaments (chs 5-12);
　　　　 – the unity of apostolic teaching, particularly between Peter and Paul whom some Gnostics contrasted (chs 12-15);
　　　　 – Christ is not an aeon separate from the man Jesus, rather Jesus is divine and human (chs 16-18);
　　　　 – rejection of docetism: Jesus was begotten of the Father and born of the virgin (chs 19-22);
　　　　 – criticism of Tatian and Marcion and review of arguments (chs 23-25)

Book 4 – the forty-one chapters of this book argue (against Marcion) that there is one God, the Father and Creator, revealed and proclaimed in both covenants. The Old Testament prophets predicted the coming of Christ, who affirmed the unity of the two covenants. The Church, in which alone the Scriptures are properly interpreted, affirms the common divine author of the two covenants.

Book 5 – in the thirty-six chapters of the final book the resurrection of the body is affirmed against Gnostic denials of it. Arguments are used from both the Old (eg the translation of Enoch and Elijah) and New Testaments (eg Christ's resurrection of others and his own; the body as the temple of the Spirit). Reference is made also to end time events other than the resurrection eg the coming of antichrist and an earthly millennium.

We may note the following main ways by which Irenaeus sought to refute Gnosticism.

(i) ***description of Gnostic systems*** – Irenaeus exposed what appeared to him to be the complexity and absurdity of Gnostic teachings, as well as the mutually contradictory beliefs of various Gnostics. He wrote: "merely to describe such doctrines is to refute them."[1] . Indeed, Eric Osborn states that this was Irenaeus' main objection against the Gnostics – their teachings were incredible and incoherent, in contrast to the credible and coherent teachings of the Church[2]. We may note here Irenaeus' sarcastic dismissal of the names invented by Gnostics in their myths and his suggested replacements of Cucumber and Melon (*Against Heresies* 1.11)!

(ii) ***apostolic succession*** – Gnostics often claimed that their teachings were secret apostolic traditions (*Against Heresies* 3.3.1) eg Valentinians said that their leader had been taught by a disciple of Paul named Theudas. However, Irenaeus contrasted the consistent and public traditions of the churches founded by apostles and preserved by their successive bishops with the inconsistent, secret and alleged apostolic traditions of the Gnostics (see previous chapter for details and references, p143). While many Gnostics claimed to have secret traditions from the apostle John, Irenaeus himself had a link to this apostle through Polycarp (see p165).

(iii) ***biblical interpretation*** - Irenaeus criticised Gnostic misinterpretation and misapplication of the Scriptures as unreasonable and perverse. He accused Gnostics of misusing the Bible to produce weird theories, like someone

---

[1] cited by Tony Lane in *The Lion Concise Book of Christian Thought*, Lion: Tring, 1984, p16.

[2] 'Irenaeus: Rocks in the Road', in *The Expository Times* Vol 114, No 8, May 2003 p255, T&T Clark: London. (Osborn cites *Against Heresies* 2.10.4)

dismantling a mosaic of the emperor and with the pieces making a picture of a dog or fox (*Against Heresies* 1.1.15). For example, Irenaeus rejected Gnostic claims that the twelve apostles were a type or symbol of aeons and similarly that Jesus' baptism in his thirtieth year symbolised thirty aeons (*Against Heresies* 2. 21-22); and that Paul's statement that 'flesh and blood cannot inherit the Kingdom of God' (1 Cor 15: 50) was a denial of the resurrection of the body (*Against Heresies* 5.9; see also 1. 3, 8, 18-20; 2.10). He laid down principles for proper interpretation of biblical passages (eg 2.27) and argued that only in the Church could the Scriptures be properly interpreted (eg 4.26.5; 4.32.1; 5.20.2).

(iv) *apostolic teachings* – from the second century on there arose summaries of the teachings of the apostolically founded churches, usually known as the 'rule of faith' (see p38-39 and *ANE* pp111, 112). It was the criterion by which heretical interpretations of the Scriptures could be tested, since it contained the apostolic and universal faith of the Church.

(v) *apostolic writings* – in his controversy with Gnostics, Irenaeus recognised the need for agreement on what constituted authoritative Christian writings (*Against Heresies* 3. Preface) and knew that there was a distinction between 'the writings of truth' and 'the mass of apocryphal and spurious writings' (1.20.1) which Gnostics appealed too. He certainly argued for the authority of our four Gospels and criticised those who would increase or reduce their number (3.11.8; *ANE* pp117, 118) – possibly a reference to second century Gnostic Gospels and Marcion's acceptance of Luke alone (see p171). He appeals to or reflects most of the books which eventually were recognised as New Testament Scripture. The formation of the New Testament canon undoubtedly owed something to the Church's controversy with heretics.

(vi) *theological critique* – Irenaeus' polemic against Gnosticism on a theological level required a positive statement of those beliefs of Church tradition which Gnosticism compromised or rejected. The most important point for Irenaeus was that there was one God, who is also the Creator (2.1.1.). By means of his Word and his Wisdom, or Spirit, he created the world (2.30.9). Also, Irenaeus stressed the unity of the man Jesus and the heavenly Christ (eg 3.16.8), repeatedly using the formula 'one and the same' (eg 1.9.2; 3.16.8). He insisted too on the real humanity of Jesus (eg 4.6.7) as essential to human salvation (5.14.2f; see also *ANE* p119). Further, far from being evil, the human body is included in the divine image in which humans were made (5.6.1; 5.16.2), is redeemed in Christ (5.14.2f) and will be raised to eternal life (most of Book 5). Finally, Irenaeus' doctrine of 'recapitulation' provides a biblical scheme of creation, fall and redemption which counteracted the speculative cosmological myths of Gnosticism. As Paul had compared and contrasted Adam and Christ (Romans 5: 12-21; 1 Corinthians 15: 22, 45) so Irenaeus, following Justin, stated that as the first Adam was the head of a disobedient human race condemned to death, so Christ, the second Adam, had established a new, redeemed humanity. This 'recapitulation' or summing up of all things in Christ (compare Ephesians 1: 10) means that what was lost through union with Adam is restored through union with Christ (eg 3.16.6; 3.21.10; 3.22.3, 4; see also *ANE* p120, an excerpt from Irenaeus' second main surviving work: *Demonstration of the Apostolic Preaching*).

Tasks

a. What developments occurred in the early Church in its response to heresy in general?

b. Apart from Irenaeus, how did the early Church respond to Gnosticism?

c. Discuss the importance of Irenaeus' Against Heresies *in his opposition to Gnosticism.*

d. Summarise the main arguments used by Irenaeus in his polemic against Gnosticism.

2. MARCIONISM

Sources

Our knowledge of Marcion and Marcionism comes mostly from early Church Fathers who opposed their teaching in the second century and beyond.

Justin: *First Apology, Dialogue; ANE* p93 Irenaeus: *Against Heresies; ANE* pp92, 94, 96, 114-117 Tertullian: five books *Against Marcion; ANE* pp94-96 and *On the Prescription of Heretics; ANE* pp93, 169, 170	Hippolytus: *Refutation of all Heresies* Clement of Alexandria: *Stromateis,* Origen: *Against Celsus; Commentary on Genesis; ANE* p98 Eusebius: *Ecclesiastical History; ANE* pp96-98 Epiphanius: *Panarion.*

Emergence

Marcionism was founded by Marcion (about AD80-155) from Sinope in Pontus, Asia Minor, on the shore of the Black Sea. He was a wealthy shipowner or export trader whose father, a bishop, excommunicated him, probably because of his views rather than the immorality claimed by Epiphanius. About AD140, after travelling around Asia Minor, he went to Rome and joined the church there, donating to it a considerable sum of money. In Rome he came under the influence of Cerdo (or Cerdon), from Antioch, Syria, who was a pupil of the Gnostic teacher Saturninus and whom the Roman church excommunicated. Marcion himself was excommunicated from the church in Rome more than once and on the last occasion, in AD144, his money was returned to him. He apparently applied for readmission to the church and was told that first he would have to restore to the church all those he had led astray. He agreed, but died before he could fulfil this requirement, sometime after AD150 (Tertullian, *On the Prescription of Heretics*, 30; *ANE* p93)

As early as the mid second century Justin claimed that Marcionism had spread to every nation (*1 Apology* 1.26) and around the end of that century Tertullian claimed that it had filled the entire world (*On the Prescription of Heretics* 5.19). An uncovered inscription identifies a Marcionite place of worship about twenty kilometres south of Damascus, constructed in AD318/19. At the end of the fourth century, according to Epiphanius (*Panarion* 42.1), Marcionite churches were to be found in Rome and Italy, Egypt, Palestine, Arabia, Syria, Cyprus and even as far as Persia. In the mid fourth century Cyril of Jerusalem advised Christians to check when going to a strange church lest it be Marcionite (*Catechisms* 18.26). And in the early fifth century a North Syrian bishop claimed that he had eradicated Marcionism from eight villages (Theodoret of Cyrrhus, *Letter* 81). One of Marcion's immediate and well know disciples was Apelles (see *ANE* p98).

a. Outline the main events in Marcion's life.

b. What evidence is there for the growth of Marcionism?

Teaching

Basic to Marcion's theology is his distinction between the supreme God and the inferior god who created the world. This distinction was made by early Gnostic teachers and indeed by Marcion's teacher Cerdo, who taught that the God of the Old Testament was not the Father of Jesus Christ and that while the former was known and righteous, the latter was unknown and good. For Marcion these were the two first principles – the good God whom Jesus first revealed and the Demiurge who created this world. The God of the Law and the Prophets, according to Marcion, was 'a worker of evils, a lover of wars, inconsistent in judgement and self-contradictory', to be distinguished from the God who sent Jesus, 'the Father, who is above the god that made the world' (Irenaeus, *Against Heresies*, 1.24; 25.1; *ANE* p92 – see also excerpts 72, 75, 76).

In his now lost *Antitheses*, Marcion contrasted the two gods, the two testaments and law and grace (*ANE* p94). The God of the Old Testament, the God of the Jews, the God who created this material world was incompetent and vindictive – allowing sin to enter the world and harshly judging those who commit it, creating evil (Isaiah 45:7), demanding 'an eye for an eye and a tooth for a tooth' (Exodus 21:24), contradicting himself by both forbidding the making of images and commanding the creation of the bronze snake. Also, he gave the Sabbath command yet ordered his people to march for seven days around Jericho. Further, he told the Hebrews to plunder the Egyptians. Ignorant, he had to ask where Adam was. Losing his temper at the people's idolatry, he was calmed by Moses' prayer. He was a God who changed his mind (unacceptable to Greek philosophy's immutable God) as when he decided not to punish the Ninevites in Jonah's day. He was a God who demanded sacrifices and ordered the extinction of whole races. Marcion's literal interpretation of the Old Testament, in contrast to the symbolic or allegorical interpretation of many early Fathers and Gnostics, produced for him an inferior god of wrath unlike the God of love and grace revealed by Jesus and proclaimed by Paul. The imperfections of the creator god are also apparent in his imperfect creation, which contains poisonous insects and plants, fierce animals and, repulsively, the indignity of sexual intercourse and pain of pregnancy and childbirth.

This fundamental dualism, no doubt aided by the anti-Jewishness caused by the recent Jewish Revolt (AD132-135) and the synagogue-church conflict, caused Marcion to reject the Old Testament and its god. He was the first to draw up a New Testament canon, a list of authoritative Christian writings, which he termed Gospel and Apostle. However, it included only one Gospel, that of the Gentile Luke, edited in accordance with Marcion's anti-Judaism and his rejection of Jesus' human birth. Thus the very Jewish first two chapters, if original, were removed and, beginning with 3:1, his version of Luke jumps ahead to 4:31. Can you guess why?

In addition to Luke, Marcion included ten letters of Paul, excluding 1 and 2 Timothy and Titus. Paul, Luke's companion, was Marcion's hero because of his contrast between law and grace. The sections in Paul's letters which clearly affirm the Old Testament and its god were regarded by Marcion as later insertions by Judaizing Christians. Galatians was placed first, possibly because of its antithesis, in Marcion's view, between Paul and the Jerusalem apostles, between Gentile and Jewish Christianity. Yet, even it had to be edited because of apparent Judaizing corruption, eg 3:6-9, 15-25.

Due to his belief that creation and matter were the inferior work of a lower god, Marcion had a docetic view of Christ – Christ was not really human but only appeared to be so. For him the idea of God becoming incarnate was incredible (see *ANE* excerpt 77). Yet, inconsistently, while rejecting Christ's birth he affirmed the reality of his sufferings and death. The Demiurge mistook Jesus for his own Messiah and caused his crucifixion. Realising his mistake, he repaid Jesus by giving him the souls cursed by the law in exchange for his death on the cross. Now, through the death of the Saviour sent by the supreme God, there was forgiveness for breaches of the Demiurge's harsh law. Jesus descended into Hades and released those imprisoned there – but not those who followed the Demiurge under the Old Testament, such as the patriarchs and prophets, since they suspected that the Demiurge was tempting them again and therefore rejected Jesus (see *ANE* excerpt 78). Marcion expected no future return of Jesus or resurrection of the dead. Fellowship with God would be wholly spiritual.

Marcion's rejection of the Demiurge's inferior, material creation resulted in a strict asceticism. Marriage and sex were the Demiurge's inventions and were forbidden. The married could be baptised only if they vowed to abstain from sexual intercourse. Wine, even in the Eucharist, and meat were disallowed, though fish was permissible. Pagan religion and entertainment were to be avoided.

It is clear that Marcion held some beliefs commonly regarded as Gnostic, particularly his teaching concerning two gods and his inconsistent docetic Christology. Underlying this was a philosophical dualism which contrasted matter and spirit. However, if the definition of Gnosticism is problematic generally, then it is particularly so in relation to Marcion. In contrast to beliefs normally regarded as Gnostic, Marcion believed in salvation by faith rather than gnosis; he had no cosmological myth such as that found in Valentinus; he interpreted the Bible literally rather than allegorically (unlike many in the Church as well as Gnostics); he did not divide the human race into various pre-determined categories; he had no magical rituals and, also, he founded a schismatic church rather than a Gnostic school. While Marcion was a pupil of Cerdo, who himself was a pupil of the Gnostic teacher Saturninus, he may have been influenced also, and possibly more so, by the dualistic asceticism of various Hellenistic philosophies and religions, such as the Cynics and Mithraism. That he had a lot in common with mainstream Christianity in the second century is due no doubt to his background as a son of a bishop in the Catholic Church.

Tasks

a. Summarise the principal teachings of Marcion.

b. Assess the view that Marcion was a Gnostic.

The Church's response

In our outline of Marcion's life we saw that Marcion was excommunicated by his father and several times by the church in Rome. Thus at an early stage the Church showed its disapproval of his teachings. We noted earlier too, a number of ways in which the early Church responded to heresy in general and Gnosticism in particular, several of which were of particular relevance to Marcionism. The Church's insistence that its bishops, as the legitimate heirs of the apostles, transmitted a common apostolic tradition contradicted Marcion's claims that Paul alone had preserved the teaching of Jesus and that the twelve apostles had defected. Christian creeds, especially the rule of faith, were shaped, amongst other things, by the Church's rejection of Marcionism (see pp38, 39).

Particularly important too was the role that Marcion played in the development of the New Testament canon. While some scholars[1] have argued that Marcion's canon was the first and that the Church was forced to create its own in response, others[2] have stated that the process of canonisation was already under way in the Church and that Marcion lent urgency to the development. It may well be that the list of New Testament books known as the Muratorian canon and reflecting the canon recognised by the church at Rome in the late second century, was drawn up partly in response to Marcion's canon. It explicitly rejects, among other writings, Marcionite works (*ANE* excerpt 103). Also, in some Latin manuscripts, early prologues to the Gospels of Luke and John appear to reflect a reaction against Marcionism. For example, the prologue to Luke affirms the necessity of its opening chapters.

Irenaeus reports that when Polycarp of Smyrna was asked by Marcion if he recognised him, he replied that he did – as the firstborn of Satan (*ANE* p116). In his critique of Gnosticism, *Against Heresies*, Irenaeus rejected Marcion's two gods (*ANE* excerpts 71 and 75; as did Justin before him, *ANE* excerpt 72), his reduced and mutilated canon (*ANE* excerpt 71) and his teaching on the salvation of the soul but not the body (*ANE* excerpt 78). We have seen that he also stressed the unity of the Old and New Testaments, which came from the one God, and the reality of Christ's incarnation. Important too is Irenaeus' insistence that the Scriptures must be interpreted within the Church and in line with the rule of faith.

Tasks

a. Explain how the Church's response to heresy in general was also a rejection of Marcionism in particular.

b. Comment on the claim that the New Testament was Marcion's idea.

c. Read again the section on Irenaeus in this chapter and identify anti-Marcionite material in his Against Heresies.

Tertullian (about AD160-220) in Carthage also wrote against Marcion. Like Irenaeus he argued that the true Christian faith was found in the apostolically founded churches and their rule of faith – any departure from or distortion of this, including Marcionism, was heretical (*On the Prescription of Heretics*; *ANE* excerpts 142-144). However, he went further than Irenaeus in claiming that since heretics are not Christians they have no right to the Christian Scriptures

---

1 eg Adolf von Harnack, Hans von Campenhausen
2 eg Theodore von Zahn, Bruce Metzger

– 'Indeed Marcion, what right have you to chop my wood?' – and protested that Marcion 'used the knife and not the pen' in relation to the Scriptures (*ANE* excerpt 147 and note). He traced heresy's origins to pagan philosophy – including the superior and tranquil god of Marcion – and claimed that Marcion was a Stoic (*ANE* excerpt 145).

Tertullian's largest work was his five-volume *Against Marcion*, written in his Montanist period in the early third century. It is not possible to provide a neat outline of its contents but we may note Tertullian's main points as he seeks to refute Marcion's teaching.

In **Book 1** Tertullian identifies Marcion's leading doctrine as his separation between the law and the gospel, each with its own god (*ANE* excerpt 74). He stresses the unity and uniqueness of God against Marcion's plurality of gods and deals with arguments used to support the latter. While Marcion's God is unknown and recent, the true God has revealed himself in creation from the beginning. While Marcionites devalue creation, it is a worthy witness of God. Jesus Christ revealed the true God, the Creator, and his teaching did not contrast law and gospel. Nor can the latter be contrasted by setting Paul and Peter against each other. Indeed, Paul, whom Marcion favoured, contradicts Marcionism. Tertullian argues against the 'goodness' of Marcion's superior God. For example, why did he wait so long to save humans and why only their souls? He affirms that the true God is more than merely good. Marcion's God is also criticised for not justly punishing sin, a view of God that could result in immorality (*ANE* excerpt 76). Tertullian concludes Book 1 by defending marriage against Marcion's rejection of it.

In **Book 2** Tertullian argues that man's fall into sin does not reflect badly on the Creator, but rather was due to the free will of both man and the Devil, granted to both by the Creator. God's goodness and justice belong together, the latter regulating the former, and are not the attributes of two different gods. God is responsible for penal evil (judgement) but not criminal evil. Tertullian defends Old Testament laws of the Creator against Marcionite criticisms eg God's command that a bronze snake be put up on a pole is not inconsistent with his forbidding of images. God's repentance, as in the case of the Ninevites, is defended, as is the incarnation of God.

Book 3 is mostly concerned with Old Testament prophecies concerning the coming of Christ and subsequent events, demonstrating the unity of the two Testaments and their one God. Thus, for example, reference is made to Isaiah's prophecy of a virgin giving birth to Immanuel and to various prophecies and types of Christ's death. The reality of Christ's body is stressed against Marcion's docetism (*ANE* excerpt 77). The call of the Gentiles and the dispersion of the Jews were also prophesied. The book ends with Tertullian's belief in a future earthly kingdom of Christ lasting a thousand years, followed by the heavenly kingdom.

Nero Claudius Caesar Drusus Germanicus, Roman Emperor.

Vecelli ('Titian') engraved by J Pass

In **Book 4** Tertullian shows from many passages in Marcion's own edition of Luke's gospel that the Christ of the Gospel is the same as the Christ of the Creator and are not to be separated. The Christ of Luke's Gospel is the one prophesied in the Old Testament. While Tertullian demonstrates these points using Marcion's own preferred Gospel, he rejects Marcion's mutilation of Luke and also argues for the antiquity and authority of the other Gospels. Marcion's docetism is also refuted.

In the **fifth and final book** of Tertullian's *Against Marcion*, he used Marcion's own edited and selective edition of Paul's letters to refute his teachings (as he had done with Marcion's Luke in the previous book). After stating that Paul was sent by the Creator and that he did not introduce a new god, he then demonstrated from Paul's letters, among other things, that Paul's teaching was in agreement with the Old Testament and that its God was his God. He also argued that Paul was in basic agreement with the other apostles. Marcion's docetism is rejected and the resurrection of the body affirmed, against Marcion's misinterpretation of Paul. Tertullian also criticised Marcion's mutilation of Paul's letters, particularly his Roman letter.

 Tasks

> *a. In what way did Tertullian go beyond Irenaeus in his refutation of heresy?*
>
> *b. Comment on Tertullian's view of the relationship between pagan philosophy and Christian heresy.*
>
> *c. Outline the key points of Tertullian's* **Against Marcion**.

3. MONTANISM

Sources

As with Marcionism, our knowledge of Montanism comes mostly from early Church Fathers and writers who opposed the movement in the second century and beyond. Some of these sources were preserved by Eusebius in the fourth century (eg Apollonius and the 'Anonymous', both from the late second century; *ANE* chapter 8). Other sources include Epiphanius (*Panarion*; *ANE* excerpt 89), Clement of Alexandria (*Stromateis*), Hippolytus (*Refutation of all Heresies*), Firmillian of Caesarea's letter to Cyprian (Cyprian, *Letter* 75), Origen (*On First Principles*) and Jerome (*Letter* 41). Writings from Tertullian's Montanist period provide an important sympathetic source. Montanist oracles or sayings have been preserved in Tertullian, Epiphanius and Eusebius (*ANE* excerpt 89). Due to the sparsity, hostility and lateness of most of the sources, it is difficult to reconstruct Montanism accurately, particularly in its early stages and in the different regions to which it spread.

Emergence and teaching

Opponents of the movement referred to it as 'Montanism', a term first used in Christian literature by Cyril of Jerusalem in the fourth century. Its adherents were referred to as 'Kataphrygians', due to its origins in Phyrgia, Asia Minor. However, its earliest followers probably termed it the 'New Prophecy' and this was the name used by Tertullian.

Our sources provide conflicting evidence concerning when the movement began. While Epiphanius places its origins in about AD157, Eusebius dates its beginnings to AD172 (*ANE* excerpt 84 note). Certainly by the later date the new movement was making its presence felt.

The usual name for the movement comes from Montanus who, according to Jerome in the fourth century, was a second century pagan priest of Cybele in Phrygia, Asia Minor. Soon after his conversion to Christianity, according to Eusebius' anonymous source (*ANE* excerpt 84), Montanus, who had a longing for a position of leadership, began to prophesy in a state of ecstasy and frenzy, making strange sounds (possibly speaking in tongues?). The source characterises his style of prophesying as unlike that traditionally performed in the Church. It may be that Montanus' manner of prophesying was what he was used to in his pre-Christian days as a pagan priest. The prophetic utterances of Montanus which have been preserved are worded as direct utterances of God in the first person, not because he identified himself with God nor the Holy Spirit but rather to underline the divine source and authority of the prophecies. Thus, "Behold, man is like a lyre and I fly over it like a plectrum; man sleeps and I am awake; behold, it is the Lord who changes men's hearts and gives a heart to men", and "I am the Lord God, the Almighty, dwelling in man. Neither angel nor ambassador, but I the Lord God, the Father, have come." (*ANE* excerpt 89). It appears that such ecstatic prophecies were conceived of as being given through a passive, unconscious prophet.

Montanus was joined by two women who deserted their husbands, Priscilla (Prisca) and Maximilla, who prophesied in a similar way to Montanus (*ANE* excerpt 84). Epiphanius attributes a prophetic vision to Priscilla (though he states that it may have come from Quintilla, a later prophetess) in which Christ came to her in the form of a woman, gave her wisdom and revealed that Pepuza in Phyrgia was holy and that Jerusalem would descend there from heaven (*ANE* excerpt 89). Tertullian referred to her as the mouthpiece of the Paraclete, a term in John's Gospel for the Holy Spirit (*On the Resurrection of the Flesh* 11.2). It has been suggested that she may have been the source of anonymous oracles preserved by Tertullian such as: "Do not hope to die in your beds or in miscarriages and mild fevers, but rather as martyrs", a saying particularly relevant for women[1].

Maximilla's sayings, "Do not listen to me, but listen to Christ" and "I am word and spirit and power" (*ANE* excerpt 89) reflect her belief that she was delivering divine revelation. Her prophecies had a note of eschatological urgency, predicting the coming of wars and declaring, "After me there will be no prophetess any more, but the end." (*ANE* excerpt 89). Her death in about AD180 marked the end of the earliest phase of the movement.

It seems that Montanism's three earliest leaders may have regarded themselves as introducing the age of the Paraclete which replaced the age of Christ, who himself had predicted the coming of the Paraclete. This fuller revelation of God marked the three out as the prophets of the last days, and very soon the End would come when the New Jerusalem would descend on Pepuza.

Task

Outline the beginnings of Montanism in the activities of its first three prophets in Asia Minor.

The movement spread from its origins in Asia Minor to other areas such as North Africa. There Tertullian in Carthage, probably attracted by its strict discipline, became at least sympathetic to the movement and may even have

---

[1] Trevett, Christine, in *The Early Christian World*, Ed P Esler, Routledge: London, 2000, p939

joined it in about AD206. A comparison of his writings before and after he aligned with Montanism reveals that he developed stricter views on marriage, post-baptismal sin, flight in persecution and fasting (see pp132-134; Tertullian's Montanist works include, for example, *On Monogamy*, *On Repentance*, *On Flight in Persecution* and *On Fasting*). In North Africa there appears to have been more tolerance towards Montanists, who could actively continue in the churches. Thus, in his Montanist *On the Soul* (9) Tertullian describes what appears to be the charismatic actions of a Montanist woman in church meetings. This woman, he says, experienced ecstatic visions and revelations relating to healing, amongst other things (*ANE* excerpt 153). Also in North Africa, *The Passion of Perpetua and Felicitas* seems to be a Montanist account of a number of Christians who were martyred in about AD203 near Carthage. Reference to visions and prophecy on the part of the martyrs may indicate that they were Montanist Christians, though this is debated. A group in the region known as 'Tertullianists' may have been Montanists during or after Tertullian's lifetime. While Augustine of Hippo knew of their existence in North Africa in the early fifth century, it appears that by the middle of that century the movement had died out.

In early third century Rome, Gaius, an anti-Montanist presbyter, debated in correspondence with Proclus, a Montanist leader in Asia Minor, and apparently rejected John's Gospel with its Paraclete teaching, much liked by the Montanists. Another opponent of Montanism in Rome was Praxeas, whom Tertullian blamed for influencing the Roman bishop (possibly Eleutherus, 175-89) against the movement after he had shown initial sympathy for Montanists in Asia Minor. Praxeas had driven out prophecy and put to flight the Paraclete (*ANE* excerpt 146).

Hippolytus of Rome, a contemporary of Tertullian, referred to the many writings of Montanists, the Montanist elevation of Priscilla and Maximilla above the apostles and even Christ and their introduction of novelties such as new feasts, fasts and diets. Honorius, the Western emperor (395-423), issued laws against the Montanists and banned their books, and in the early fifth century, Innocent I, bishop of Rome, exiled some of the movement. Montanism also spread to Gaul which had close links with the churches in Asia Minor (*ANE* excerpt 90).

Task

Give details of the development of Montanism beyond Asia Minor.

While Montanism was not uniform in each stage of its history nor in each place where it developed, we may note the following general characteristics and teachings of the movement. Clearly it was a prophetic movement, as our consideration of its three early leaders has shown. Its prophets understood themselves to be passive agents of the Paraclete through whom divine revelation was communicated. It was also an eschatological movement in that its apocalyptic prophecies, such as those given by Maximilla, declared that the End was near and that the New Jerusalem would soon appear. With the introduction of the age of the Paraclete and his prophets, the last days had arrived. Related to this was the idea that persecution and martyrdom should be welcomed as a sign of the end times and as a proof of genuine prophecy (*ANE* excerpt 85; in this source, Eusebius' 'Anonymous' rejects claims of Montanist martyrdoms).While Tertullian's encouragement of such things (eg *On Flight in Persecution*) may not have been typical of Montanism in general, it appears that it did play an important role in its development (see p178 for a possible prophecy by Priscilla relating to martyrdom, preserved in Tertullian).

It was also a charismatic movement in the sense that it encouraged the involvement of all believers and the use of their spiritual gifts in church life, including females (Priscilla, Maximilla and the woman referred to by Tertullian above are examples). Quintillian Montanists quoted Paul's words that there were no gender distinctions in Christ (Galatians 3:28). Not that Montanism was anti-clerical as such or opposed to order in the Church. It had its bishops, presbyters and deacons. However, the validity of ministry was not determined by an ordination rite but rather by the gifts of the Spirit. And, in what some regard as a first in Church history, the movement had salaried leaders, something which Apollonius criticised (*ANE* excerpt 86). Montanism was also an ascetic movement which stressed the need for discipline, self-denial and holiness of life. Remarriage was frowned upon while fasting and a simple diet were favoured. We have noted above Tertullian's stricter morality in his Montanist writings as compared with those before. He regarded Montanist ethics as avoiding Catholic laxity on the one hand and rejection of bodily appetites on the other, as practised by some Gnostics and others.

Overall, Montanism may be seen as a renewal movement within the Church[1]. It can be understood as a protest movement against the increasing formalism, institutionalism, clericalism, intellectualism, urbanisation and moral laxity of the Church. Many were alienated from these tendencies and attracted rather to the divine revelations, charismatic ministries and moral standards of Montanism.

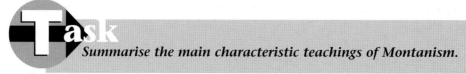

Task

Summarise the main characteristic teachings of Montanism.

[1] so Aune, DE *Prophecy in Early Christianity*, Eerdmans: Grand Rapids, 1983

The Church's response

The emergence of Montanism presented a difficulty for the Church because theologically it was largely orthodox in terms of the Church's developing beliefs. Thus if heresy be defined as doctrinal deviation from orthodoxy then the term would seem to be inappropriate for a movement in which the majority of adherents held to the Church's theology. Rather the term schism, understood as deviation in practice or discipline, appears more fitting. Indeed, Montanism may have been the first schism in the history of the Church. However, even in its practices it could be argued that Montanism was emphasising and recovering aspects of apostolic teaching and Church tradition which were declining. In fact, it has been asserted that all the main characteristics of early Montanism can be found in the apostolic writings[1].

Thus, Montanism's prophetic activity could be seen as a continuation of the charismatic gift of prophecy found in the New Testament (eg 1 Corinthians 12-14). Right through the second century prophets and prophecy continued in the Church. Among the Apostolic Fathers evidence of this may be found in the *Didache*, Ignatius and the *Shepherd of Hermas*. In the middle of the century Justin affirmed that prophetic gifts remained to his time among both men and women (*Dialogue* 82.1; 88.1). Later in the century, Irenaeus rebukes heretics for rejecting prophecy and Paul's affirmation of male and female prophesying (*Against Heresies* 3.11.9) and states that many in the churches had prophetic gifts (5.6.1). Eusebius records that an anti-Montanist had made a list of genuine Christian prophets, noting that the apostle's view was that the gift of prophecy would remain in all the Church until the coming of the Lord (*Hist Eccl* 5.17.4).

However, it was the manner of Montanist prophesying that seemed to be a departure from the traditional practice. Thus, Eusebius' anonymous source, as we have seen, characterised the prophesying of the three early Montanist leaders as an abnormal, frenzied, incomprehensible ecstasy, 'prophesying in a way contrary to that received by the Church through the generations from the beginning.' Some regarded Montanus' actions as Satanic and rebuked him while others regarded him as a true prophet (*ANE* excerpt 84). The same source argued that the Montanist style of prophecy had no precedent in either the Old or the New Covenants (*ANE* excerpt 88). Critics claimed that Montanists had introduced pagan style prophecy into the Church (Eusebius, *Hist Eccl* 5.16.6-9). Some bishops even attempted to exorcise Priscilla and Maximilla.

---

[1] Giles, KN, in *Dictionary of the Later New Testament and Its Developments*, Ed RP Martin and PH Davids, IVP: London, 1997, p975

Not only the style but also the status of Montanist prophecies presented a problem. New revelations posed a threat to the authority of the apostles and their heirs, the bishops, especially if the age of the Paraclete was regarded as having superseded the age of Christ and the apostles. We may note Hippolytus' complaint that Priscilla and Maximilla were elevated above the apostles and even Christ, and the reluctance of Eusebius' 'Anonymous' to write a treatise against the followers of the Montanist leader Miltiades, lest he too add or remove anything from the word of the New Covenant (*ANE* excerpt 87). Further, some Montanist prophecies had clearly failed, such as Maximilla's predictions of wars and her claim that after her there would be no more prophetesses but the End, which discredited the movement in the eyes of its critics.

The Montanists were regarded as divisive, insisting that their prophecy be accepted in the churches (Eusebius' 'Anonymous', *Hist Eccl* 5.16.9; *ANE* excerpts 84 and 87). When excommunicated, they set up their own schismatic churches and leaders, who were seen as rivals to the Catholic Church and leadership, and drew many from its membership.

Ironically, in the light of their high moral standards, Montanist leaders, particularly in later stages of the movement, were criticised for immorality. Apollonius condemned Montanus for dissolving marriages (he may have approved of Priscilla and Maximilla leaving their husbands) and his financial dealings. He found fault too with the prophetesses for deserting their husbands and for their pride and love of money. Apollonius also criticised later Montanist leaders – a certain Themiso who apparently bribed his way out of martyrdom and dared to write a 'catholic epistle', and a certain Alexander, a self-styled martyr whose robberies were on public record. He criticised other 'prophets' too for their worldly appearances and lifestyles (*ANE* excerpt 86). Yet, on the other hand, Stuart Hall states that the 'chief unorthodoxy' of the Montanists was their belief that the Paraclete had brought in a stricter discipline than Jesus himself[1] (see p241).

In what are the earliest known councils of the Church, after the Jerusalem Council of Acts 15, the Christians in Asia Minor examined and condemned Montanism and excommunicated its followers from the Church (*ANE* excerpt 84). Also in Asia Minor, in the early third century, a large synod in Iconium rejected Montanist baptism and required the re-baptism of those who would join the Catholic Church, while acknowledging their orthodoxy (Firmillian's letter to Cyprian: Letter 75.19; see *ANE* excerpt 217 note). Serapion, bishop of Antioch in the early third century, declared that the New Prophecy was regarded as abominable by the Church throughout the world (Eusebius, *Hist Eccl* 5.19). And the Council of Constantinople (AD381) refused to recognise

---

[1] Hall, Stuart G *Doctrine and Practice in the Early Church*, SPCK: London, 1991, p46

Montanists as Christians. Certainly, its members suffered persecution. Maximilla complained of being driven like a wolf from the sheep (*ANE* excerpt 89).

However, Irenaeus did not condemn the Montanists and, as noted already, criticised rather those who rejected prophetic gifts in the Church. Tertullian, of course, became at least a Montanist sympathiser and composed seven books (*On Ecstasy* – now lost) defending Montanism (mentioned by Jerome).

As with Marcion, some have regarded Montanism as influencing the Church to create, or at least to close, its canon of authoritative writings as a response to Montanist claims of new revelation. Henry Chadwick states that it is difficult to decide if Montanism added strength to an already existing idea of a closed canon or if it was influential in creating it, and feels that the former is more likely[1]. In the absence of clear evidence it is possible to overstate the influence of Montanism, and Marcionism, on the development of the New Testament canon.

In conclusion, it appears that while Montanism was generally orthodox in Catholic terms, both the style and status of its prophecies unsettled the Church. By the late second century the Church was becoming less charismatic and more hierarchical. Apostolic authority was located not in charismatic prophets but in the bishops who were regarded as the heirs of the apostles and the prophets of the Church. In this climate Montanism was seen as a threat to the developing institutional Church from which it was increasingly alienated.

 Tasks

> *a. Explain why the Church found Montanism to be a more difficult challenge to meet than Gnosticism or Marcionism.*
>
> *b. Why was the Church opposed to Montanist prophecies?*
>
> *c. On what other grounds did the early Church object to Montanism?*
>
> *d. Outline the role of Church councils in the rejection of Montanism.*

---

[1] Chadwick, Henry *The Church in Ancient Society*, OUP: Oxford, 2001, p115

Practice Essay Titles

1. Describe the origins and main teachings of Gnosticism. *(30)*

   Evaluate the effectiveness of Irenaeus' polemic against Gnosticism. *(15)*

2. Outline the life and teachings of Marcion. *(30)*

   Assess the claim that Marcion should be classified as a Gnostic. *(15)*

3. Describe the emergence and main characteristics of Montanism. *(30)*

   Comment on the view that the Church was wrong to reject Montanism as heretical. *(15)*

Persecution

Persecution in the early Church: origin, extent and impact. The problem of the lapsed.

(CCEA Specification)

Objective

In chapter 6, we considered the persecution of the Church during the reigns of Nero, Domitian, Trajan and Marcus Aurelius. In this chapter we shall gain a knowledge and understanding of the origin, extent and impact of the persecution of the Church from the close of the reign of Marcus Aurelius (AD180) until the emperor Constantine ended persecution by extending religious toleration to the Eastern provinces of the Empire (AD324). Pupils should review the definition and general causes of persecution in chapter 6 before working through the present chapter.

Task

In bullet point form outline the general causes of the persecution of the early Church.

COMMODUS

IN THE EARLY YEARS of the reign of the emperor Commodus (AD180-192), all the Christians of a certain city presented themselves before Arrius Antoninus, proconsul of Asia, who ordered the execution of a few and told the rest to find their own means of death if they wished to die (*ANE* excerpt 136). According to Hippolytus (*ANE* excerpt 125), Fuscian, Prefect of Rome in the latter half of the AD180s, had Callistus (later bishop of Rome) sent to a mine in Sardinia on the charge of being a Christian. Other martyrs in the Sardinian mine were released due to the influence of Commodus' mistress, Marcia, who was at least sympathetic to Christianity, if not a Christian herself.

SEPTIMIUS SEVERUS

In AD197, Tertullian could complain that Christians were blamed for any natural disasters that occurred and the pagan cry was, 'the Christians to the lion.' He added mockingly, 'What! So many of them to one lion?' In the same book he argued that persecution, far from destroying the Church, led ironically to its growth, since pagans were impressed by the courage of its victims – 'the blood of the Christians is seed' (Tertullian, *Apology* 40.2, 50.13-15; *ANE* excerpt 135).

At the start of the third century, the imperial authorities appear to become more aware of the Church's growing numbers and influence and persecution became more and more a matter of imperial action than merely local or popular hostility. In the opening years of the century Septimius Severus (AD193-211) became concerned about the increasing influence of the Church, though in the earlier part of his reign he appears to have been tolerant towards Christians, even within his court. It is possible that he issued an edict forbidding conversion to Judaism or Christianity. If so, this was the first official edict against the Church. From AD202-206 Christians were arrested in Carthage, Rome, Corinth and Alexandria. Converts rather than clergy felt the force of the persecution and paid for their faith with their lives. In AD202/3 a number of Christians in Carthage, mostly catechumens, were arrested, imprisoned and then thrown to starving beasts, such as leopards and bears, in the amphitheatre on the emperor's birthday. But it was not the wounds inflicted by the animals that resulted in their deaths, but rather the sword of a gladiator. Among them were the well-to-do Perpetua, a twenty-two year old married woman with a baby boy, and Felicitas, a pregnant slave-girl who gave birth to a baby girl in prison, and Saturus, a presbyter who had instructed those preparing for baptism. The account of these events, *The Passion of Perpetua and Felicitas* (which includes Perpetua's own account of her imprisonment and visions), is generally regarded to be a reasonably trustworthy record of what took place. Other victims of persecution at this time include a number of Christians, mostly catechumens, in Alexandria, notably Leonides, the father of Origen who was about seventeen at the time (*ANE* excerpt 168; Eusebius *Hist Eccl* 6).

MAXIMIN

The Church enjoyed a period of relative peace in the four decades from the death of Septimius Severus (AD211) until the infamous persecution by Decius (AD250/1). Some persecution, though, did occur in the first years of Caracalla's reign (AD211/212). Tertullian protested to Scapula, proconsul of Africa, for his persecution of Christians (*ANE* excerpt 136), who were being burnt alive for their faith, a fate which criminals did not suffer (*To Scapula* 4). Callistus, bishop of Rome, was killed in AD222 by a mob who threw him into a well.

The main persecution in this period of comparative relief for the Church was inflicted by the emperor Maximin (AD235-38). He disliked the tolerance shown to Christians by his predecessor Alexander Severus (AD222-35), during which time the Church and its clergy had made notable progress. Maximin, as a soldier, was unimpressed by Alexander's military failure and removed him, acting against those he favoured, including Christians in his court. About AD236 he initiated a persecution against the Church's leadership to reduce an influence which often went beyond their churches. This attack specifically on the clergy became characteristic of the later persecutions of our period, compared with the previous century. The Roman bishops Hippolytus and Pontian were exiled to Sardinia. Pontian and his successor Anteros were martyred. Earthquakes in Cappadocia and Pontus resulted in popular hostility towards the Christians under the legate Serenianus, a cruel persecutor. Origen's patron Ambrose and Protoctetus, a presbyter in Caesarea (Palestine), also suffered, which moved Origen to write his *Exhortation to Martyrdom*.

Task

Summarise the course of persecution during the reigns of Commodus, Septimius Severus and Maximin.

DECIUS

In the middle of the third century, the reign of Decius (AD249-251) brought a drastic turn of events for the Church. Under the previous emperor, Philip the Arabian (AD244-49), the Church had enjoyed toleration and even protection. However, animosity to Christians was still evident. According to Origen (*Against Celsus*, 3.15), at the millennial celebrations of the foundation of Rome in April AD247 there was resentment at the toleration extended to Christianity and at its growing influence in the Empire. Origen felt that soon persecution would no longer be local but universal (*Commentary on Matthew*, 39). In AD248, before Philip's rule ended, there was a massacre of Christians by mobs in Alexandria, including lynchings and forced sacrifices in the pagan temples (Eusebius *Hist Eccl* 6.41). Around the same time, the Goths were making inroads across the frontier. Philip, unable to halt their progress, was replaced by one of his commanders, Decius, who became emperor in the autumn of AD249. Decius was a conservative who, in the face of threatened invasions and disunity within the empire (due not least to the Church), sought to restore the traditional values and religion of Rome. That he assumed the name of an illustrious predecessor (Trajan), restored the old Republican office of Censor (Valerian became his deputy), minted coins recalling former imperial worthies and, of course, required universal sacrifice to Rome's gods, demonstrated his instinctive traditionalism.

The Persecution

An edict was issued by Decius on 3 January AD250 requiring that all citizens of the Empire sacrifice to the Roman gods. For the first time – apart possibly from Septimius Severus (see p186) – an imperial decree was directed, albeit indirectly, against the Church. Further, as Origen had foreseen, persecution was now universal and not local. Persecution was now systematic rather than spontaneous. Decius allowed no local variation.

A date was set by which sacrifice to the gods had to be made and those who failed to comply were to be regarded as Christians (Cyprian, *On the Lapsed* 3). The edict was to be enforced throughout the Empire – in small towns, villages and private estates as well as in large cities. In the presence of specially appointed commissioners and officials in the temples, citizens had to offer a sacrificial victim (goat, sheep, ox), or at least incense and a drink offering. Christ had to be renounced (*On the Lapsed* 8) and a sacrificial meal partaken of.

Upon completion of this process the commissioner issued a certificate (*libellus*) to confirm compliance with the decree. Over forty of these *libelli*, some fragmentary, have been preserved in Egypt. They typically contained details of the citizen (name, home town/village, age, distinguishing marks), his signature confirming that he had complied with the decree by offering a sacrifice, making a drink offering and partaking of the sacrificial victim, a request that the commissioner certify this to be so, the signatures of a witness and the commissioner and the date and name of the emperor concluding the document (see *ANE* excerpt 193 for examples and comment).

The enforcement of the decree had a devastating impact upon the Church throughout the Empire. In Carthage, North Africa, Cyprian's writings provide us with detailed insight into its effects in that region. Compliance with the edict, and thus apostasy from the faith, was widespread. So many took the initiative in offering to sacrifice that the officials had to ask them to return the next day (*ANE* excerpt 195). As far as Cyprian, their bishop, was concerned, the persecution was a divine test and judgement upon the moral laxity, spiritual decline and worldly behaviour of many in the Church, including materialistic bishops, which had developed during the previous long period of peace (*ANE* excerpt 194). Cyprian himself went into hiding, not out of cowardice (he would later die as a martyr), but to shepherd his persecuted flock from a safe distance by means of many letters – 'a prudent retirement to save oneself for the Lord' (*On the Lapsed*, 3). In areas neighbouring Carthage, whole churches sacrificed to the gods, including one led by its bishop.

The bishop of Alexandria, Dionysius, wrote to his colleague Fabius in

Antioch, describing the fear that the edict brought to his church. As in Carthage, there were those who came forward and willingly sacrificed. Others, however, were dragged by the mob. Many eminent persons and people in public positions complied. Others fled, while some were captured and imprisoned. Under torture some eventually yielded to the edict (*ANE* excerpt 192). A fifteen year old boy, named Dioscorus, remained faithful even under torture and was released by the magistrate who was impressed by his courage. Dionysius hid in his home for four days and then was persuaded to go to a more remote place for his safety.

The Martyrdom of Pionius records that in Smyrna, Asia Minor, the presbyter, Pionius, and his companions refused to sacrifice. Pagans mocked Pionius as he confessed his faith in the 'crucified one' and was ordered to be burnt alive, while in contrast, his bishop Euctemon, committed apostasy. However, other bishops were executed. Fabian in Rome was one of the first to be martyred, on 10 January AD250. He was, it seems, tried before Decius himself who said that he would rather have a rival for his throne than another bishop in Rome. No successor was appointed for fourteen months, so dangerous was the situation. Presbyters were also martyred in Rome but many, as elsewhere, eagerly yielded to the edict. The bishops of Jerusalem (Alexander) and Antioch (Babylas) also lost their lives. It seems to have been a matter of policy to eliminate the leadership in the hope that their flocks would conform and also to remove those loyal to the previous administration. The aim was not to make martyrs, apart from bishops, but to weaken the organisation and cohesion of the Church by removing its leaders and to win its rank and file back to Rome. In Caesarea, Origen, nearly seventy years old, suffered terribly on the rack, yet remained faithful. However, he died later of his injuries in AD254.

The persecution eased in the spring of AD251, just over a year after it had begun. The situation allowed a successor to Fabian to be appointed in Rome (Cornelius, March AD251) and shortly after, Cyprian returned to Carthage, where the persecution had relaxed somewhat in the previous November. The initial persecution had no planned follow-up and Decius was increasingly preoccupied with external threats to the Empire. The emperor was killed while at war with the Goths in June AD251. The persecution was over, but new problems were only beginning.

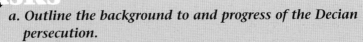

Tasks

a. *Outline the background to and progress of the Decian persecution.*

b. *Explain why this persecution marks a new stage in action against the early Church.*

The problem of the lapsed

This was the most difficult legacy of the Decian persecution for the Church. As we have seen, many Christians, whether nominal or otherwise, complied with the edict and committed idolatry and apostasy by sacrificing to the gods. Could these lapsed Christians (the *sacrificati*) be readmitted to the Church? And, if so, when and on what conditions? And what about those who purchased certificates without sacrificing (the *libellatici*) – was their guilt less than that of the lapsed and therefore their readmission to the Church easier? The books and letters of Cyprian provide us with details of the difficulties that these issues presented and of their eventual resolution.

At the beginning of the persecution (January AD250), Cyprian withdrew from Carthage and did not return until at least March AD251. In Rome, where the bishop had been martyred, presbyters tried to deal with the problem of the lapsed in consultation with the presbyters in Carthage (Cyprian, *Letter* 8). Cyprian, however, was shocked at the Roman presbyters' criticism of his withdrawal from Carthage and wrote to them in defence of it (*ANE* excerpt 200 and comment). There was opposition to Cyprian in Carthage as well, not least from five presbyters who had opposed his appointment as bishop in AD249. Near the end of AD250 the clergy apparently got the 'confessors' (those who had remained faithful and suffered during the persecution) to issue 'letters of peace' (*libelli pacis*) indiscriminately to the lapsed who had repented (see p85 for this practice in AD177). A letter written by Lucian on behalf of all his fellow-confessors, stated that they had granted peace to all whose behaviour subsequent to their lapse was acceptable to Cyprian. They wished Cyprian to make this known to other bishops and for him to be at peace with the martyrs (*ANE* excerpts 196, 197).

Cyprian was opposed to this solution to the problem of the lapsed. In *On the Lapsed* he argued that apostasy was serious yet pardonable where there is genuine repentance. And while he acknowledged that the confessors had gained 'privilege with God' which could benefit the lapsed (*ANE* excerpt 199), it was for the bishops in conjunction with the Church, taking into account the request of the martyrs, to examine each case. Indeed, the cases should be put on hold until after the persecution when Church councils would decide the process of readmission (*Letters* 55.4; 20.3). Thus, the presbyters in Carthage had acted hastily in restoring the lapsed to eucharistic fellowship. However, if any of the penitent lapsed who received letters from the martyrs became seriously ill, then a presbyter or deacon should hear their confession and lay hands on them, that they may go to the Lord in peace. Even the remaining penitent lapsed should receive pastoral encouragement (*ANE* excerpts 198 and 199). Such an interim policy was aimed also at restraining some among the lapsed who were violently demanding readmission on the basis of the *libelli pacis* (*ANE* excerpt 201). For Cyprian, ultimately, a general policy on the matter was required to ensure a consistent approach in the Church, and to readmit the lapsed immediately would be unfair to the faithful who had suffered during the persecution (*Letter* 19.2).

While Cyprian was in hiding, opposition was growing towards him in both Carthage and Rome. In his own city of Carthage there was a group, including the five anti-Cyprian presbyters led by Novatus, who took a more lenient attitude to the lapsed. However, Novatus and the other presbyters appear to have been motivated more by opposition to Cyprian's episcopacy. Conversely, in Rome a group headed by the presbyter Novatian, took a stricter line towards the lapsed than Cyprian and argued that they should not be readmitted to the Church at all. He was supported, ironically, by Novatus who had come to Rome from Carthage . When Cornelius was appointed bishop of Rome as successor to Fabian (March AD251), Novatian became a rival schismatic bishop in protest at what he perceived to be the new bishop's lax attitude to the lapsed.

Cyprian returned to Carthage after Easter (23 March) in AD251 and the Council of Carthage met soon after, from April to June. This council addressed, among other things, the question of the lapsed. The 'large number of bishops' present, according to Cyprian (*ANE* excerpt 202), after Scriptures were quoted on both sides, reached balanced decisions, not wanting on the one hand to deny all hope of restoration to the lapsed nor on the other to be morally lax and invite a hasty restoration. The letters of the confessors were not to be taken into account, rather each case should be judged on its own merits. The *libellatici* were to be restored to the Church after penances appropriate to each case. The *sacrificati*, however, could be restored only on their deathbed if they were penitent to the end. Those who refused to repent until near the end of their lives, however, should not be restored since fear rather than genuine repentance was the underlying motive. At the council, Cyprian read his *On the Unity of the Catholic Church* in which he emphasised the authority of each bishop in his own diocese and argued that each diocese should have only one bishop. Thus, clearly, Catholic bishops, rather than confessors, should rule on the discipline of the lapsed; schismatic bishops, such as Novatian, and their ministries, were invalid (*ANE* excerpt 205).

In AD252, as a plague sweeping through the Empire reached Carthage (*ANE* excerpt 219), Decius' successor, Gallus, renewed persecution against the Church, particularly its leaders, in an attempt to appease the anger of the gods. There were pagan demands in Carthage for Cyprian to be thrown to the beasts. Cornelius in Rome was exiled (as was his successor Lucius) and died soon after (June AD253). The Second Council of Carthage (May AD252), with its forty-two bishops chaired by Cyprian, responded to the renewed threat by deciding to re-admit the penitent lapsed to the Church so that the Church could present a united front. A letter from the Fourth Council of Carthage (autumn AD254) reveals Cyprian's opposition to the reinstatement to office of lapsed clergy, who could, however, be readmitted to penance. This position, he says, had long since been decreed by Cornelius in conjunction with all the bishops throughout the Empire (*ANE* excerpt 211; see also excerpt 188 for a summary of the Church's attitude to lapsed Christians, including clergy, just before the Decian persecution).

A related legacy of the Decian persecution was the issue of schismatic or heretical baptism. Novatian's schism was due to his opposition to Cornelius' perceived lenient policy towards the lapsed. What was the status of baptism performed by schismatics like Novatian? Should those who received such schismatic baptism be admitted to the Catholic Church without rebaptism? Cyprian said no, while Stephen, bishop of Rome (AD254-257) said yes (see p16). Three councils in Carthage (in AD255 and AD256) addressed the issue (see *ANE* excerpts 212-218). Rome and Carthage remained split on the matter until Carthage accepted Rome's position during the Donatist controversy of the early fourth century.

Tasks

a. What questions faced the Church as a consequence of the Decian persecution?

b. Give an account of the Church's responses to these questions.

VALERIAN

Valerian (AD253-260) appears initially to have favoured the Christians. Lucius, bishop of Rome, was permitted to return from exile and Dionysius, bishop of Alexandria, described Valerian's court as 'a church of God' (Eusebius, *Hist Eccl*, 7.10.4) – he would act, as we shall see, against his Christian civil servants. However, various factors appear to have combined to cause Valerian to take action against the Church in July AD257. The Empire was under pressure from barbarian invaders on many fronts, who in some cases received sympathy from Christians. Economically, the standard of living had been declining since the beginning of Philip's reign (AD244). Existing public buildings were being neglected and in North Africa, for example, fewer new ones were being erected. The value of currency was declining. The Church, however, was progressing numerically and financially despite the recent Decian persecution. The Roman church was able to support 1500 widows and needy persons (*Hist Eccl* 6.43.11) and in Carthage the clergy were salaried (Cyprian, *Letter* 34.4). Dionysius of Alexandria explained that Valerian's attitude to the Church was changed by his finance minister, Macrianus, who was also a leader of Egyptian magi (*ANE* excerpt 223). He may have had an eye on the Church's wealth and would have had no sympathy with the Church's opposition to magic.

Valerian issued two edicts against the Church. Though the texts of these edicts have not survived, their substance can be reconstructed from Cyprian's letters and Dionysius' letter to Bishop Herammon (*ANE* excerpts 221 and 223). The first edict, in the summer of AD257, required Christian leaders to profess their return to Roman religion and its gods or be exiled. Cyprian of Carthage and Dionysius of Alexandria, before different officials, refused to do so, affirming their faith in the one true God, to whom they prayed for the well-being of the Empire. Cyprian was exiled to the city of Curubis, some forty miles from Carthage, and Dionysius to Cephro in Lybia. This edict also forbade Christians to meet or to enter cemeteries (see note to *ANE* excerpt 221 and excerpts 222, 223). Nine Numidian bishops and others were condemned to the mines at Sigus, near Cirta, for holding meetings. Cyprian wrote a letter of encouragement to them and they replied in gratitude (Cyprian, *Letters* 76-79).

For reasons that are unknown, Valerian issued a second and more severe edict a year later in July AD258, addressed to the Senate. This is preserved by Cyprian (*Letter* 80.1; *ANE* excerpt 221). Bishops, presbyters and deacons were to be executed which, it seems, could not be prevented by recantation. Further, senators, lesser ranking officials and Roman knights would lose their positions and property, but not their lives – unless they continued as Christians. Upper class Roman women (matrons) would lose their property and be banished. Civil servants who were, or had been, Christians would similarly lose their property and be reduced to slavery on the imperial estates. Thus, while removing the leadership of the Church, as well as its upper class members, the Empire's own resources were increased with the confiscations that the edict required. This was, for the first time possibly, an attack specifically on the Church itself as an institution in an attempt to eliminate it altogether.

In Rome, the bishop Xystus II and four of his deacons were executed in the catacombs on 6 August AD258. In Carthage, Cyprian appeared before the proconsul Galerius Maximus and refused to conform to Roman religion. He was told that he had lived an irreligious life, was the ringleader of an illegal association of men and a professed enemy to Rome's religion and gods. An example would be made of him in his execution by the sword. He was martyred on 14 September AD258 (*ANE* excerpt 222). In the next year, Theogenes, bishop of Hippo in North Africa, was executed along with two other bishops. These were not the only clerical martyrs as anti-Christian mobs brought others before the judges.

Valerian's persecution drew to a close when he was captured by the Persians in June AD260. His son Gallienus, possibly recognising the potential political support of the numerous Christians in the East, in the face of invasions into the Empire and because of his own philosophical syncretism, issued a rescript of toleration in AD261 (*ANE* excerpt 224), addressed apparently to Dionysius and his fellow bishops in Egypt. Places of worship were to be returned to the Church, which was to be now free from harassment. Eusebius also refers to an order by the emperor allowing repossession of cemeteries. However, Christians were still required to sacrifice on public occasions under threat of execution (Eusebius, *Hist Eccl*, 7.15). Three years of political oppression of the Church were thus brought to an end.

asks

a. What factors combined to cause Valerian to act against the Church?

b. Describe Valerian's two edicts and their impact on the Church.

c. What were the reasons behind, and the terms of, Gallienus' rescript of toleration?

DIOCLETIAN

The 'Great Persecution' (AD303-312), which was initiated with the approval of the emperor Diocletian (AD284-305), was the Roman Empire's last major assault on the Christian Church.

The background

For some forty years, since Gallienus' rescript of toleration in AD261, the Church was largely free from imperial oppression, even if the emperor Aurelian (AD270-275) had intended to renew persecution in AD275 (*ANE* excerpt 231 and note). In this period of peace, the Church grew and prospered. Christians increasingly held positions in government (eg Eusebius, *Hist Eccl* 8.9.7; 8.11.2), their refusal to sacrifice often being overlooked. Large Church buildings were erected, not least the 'very lofty edifice', as Lactantius describes it, in Nicomedia, Diocletian's capital (Eusebius, *Hist Eccl* 8.1.5; Lactantius, *On the Deaths of the Persecutors* 12.5; *ANE* excerpt 238). The Church even had the confidence to bring an internal matter to the notice of the emperor Aurelian for resolution in the early AD270s (*ANE* excerpt 231). While the Church prospered, pagan religion was in decline in parts of the Empire, such as Numidia and Cyrenaica. The imperial authorities had enough on their plate in resisting barbarian invasions, without starting a fresh campaign against the Church.

For the first eighteen years of Diocletian's reign he left the Church untroubled. His own wife, Prisca, and daughter, Valeria, were catechumens and Christians held positions in his court. He focused his energies on a reorganisation and reformation of the Empire's administration, military and finances. Roman religion was also revived as pagan temples were rebuilt. Diocletian's action against the Manichees in the late third or early fourth century was motivated at least by a reverence for traditional and established religion (*ANE* excerpt 236). Traditional polytheism was defended by anti-Christian pagan intellectuals such as Porphyry of Tyre (about AD232-304; *ANE* excerpt 237)

In addition to this effort to restore Roman values and religion and to reform the Empire, there was a nervousness about the possible disloyalty of Christians in the army, especially in the face of external threats to the Empire. Diocletian's deputy, the anti-Christian Galerius, instigated the requirement that all soldiers must sacrifice to the gods. Initially, those who would not comply could leave, but some were executed (Eusebius, *Hist Eccl* 8.4). In AD298 Venturius, Diocletian's commander-in-chief, began removing Christians from the army and, according to Eusebius, from then persecution against the Church began little by little (*ANE* excerpt 238 note). Further, about AD298, when Diocletian and Galerius were at a public sacrifice in Antioch, its effectiveness was undermined by imperial servants who crossed themselves. Diocletian required that all in his court should sacrifice to the gods on threat of corporal punishment.

According to Lactantius, who was in Nicomedia between AD295 and AD305, Galerius' mother urged him to act against the Christians since they would not eat meat that she had offered to idols. However, Diocletian, realising the devastation that a universal persecution would cause and how eagerly Christians faced death, advised his deputy that more limited action was preferable – the prohibition of Christianity in his court and in the army. Galerius was not satisfied with this and so Diocletian took advice from a few civil magistrates and military commanders. Some felt that action should be taken against the Christians as enemies of Rome's religion and gods. Others privately disagreed but, wanting to keep Galerius on side, voiced a similar view. Diocletian, still not persuaded, decided to consult the oracle of Apollo near Miletus. Diocletian then yielded to Galerius' demand for action against the Church but ordered that it be conducted without the bloodshed that Galerius favoured (Lactanitius, *On the Deaths of the Persecutors*, 11; *ANE* excerpt 238).

Task

Outline the origins of the Great Persecution.

The Persecution

Appropriately, says Lactantius, 23 February 23 AD303, the feast of the Roman god Terminus, was the chosen date for the commencement of the imperial attempt to 'terminate' Christianity. At dawn, the church building in Nicomedia, in sight of the imperial palace, was forced open and its Scriptures burnt. Diocletian ordered that the building should be demolished rather than set ablaze, as Galerius had wanted, to prevent other buildings being damaged. In a few hours soldiers brought the tall building to the ground (*On the Deaths of the Persecutors* 12; *ANE* excerpt 238).

On the next day, the **first edict** of persecution was issued. According to Eusebius, it ordered the destruction of Church buildings, the burning of the Scriptures, the loss of all civil rights by Christians holding office and the loss of freedom by Christians in households (*ANE* excerpt 239 and note). The first edict apparently also forbade meetings for worship (Eusebius, *Hist Eccl*, 9.10.8) and required the surrender of Church property (*ANE* excerpt 240). Lactantius characterises this decree as depriving Christians of all honours and dignities, subjecting them to torture regardless of position or status, preventing them from taking legal action in cases of injury, adultery or theft and from gaining freedom if they were slaves (*On the Deaths of the Persecutors*, 13; *ANE* excerpt 238).

Compare and contrast Diocletian's first edict with those issued by Valerian.

A Christian in Nicomedia, who tore down the published edict in disgust, was burnt for treason. A fire in the imperial palace, which Lactantius blames on Galerius, resulted in the torture of some Christians in Diocletian's household. When a second fire occurred in the palace within a fortnight, Diocletian ordered his wife and daughter to sacrifice to the gods and officials in his court, accused of starting the fire, were executed. Many Nicomedian Christians were arrested and martyred and resistance to the edict was reported in some parts such as Antioch and Melitene. In Cirta, Numidia (May AD303) the clergy only reluctantly yielded to the mayor's demands for the Scriptures and other Church property to be handed over (*ANE* excerpt 240).

In the summer of AD303, Diocletian issued a **second edict** ordering the imprisonment of the clergy. However, the prisons became so overcrowded that there was no room left for criminals (Eusebius, *Hist Eccl* 8.6.9).

The **third edict**, associated with the twentieth anniversary of Diocletian's accession (20 November AD303), required the release of the imprisoned clergy upon sacrifice. The amnesty usually granted to criminals on such occasions was to be extended to the Church leaders. Torture was used as a means to ensure compliance with the edict, yet in some cases a token gesture, forced if necessary, was sufficient without actual sacrifice (Eusebius, *Martyrs of Palestine* 1.4). Many clergy, however, did sacrifice (Eusebius, *Hist Eccl* 8.3.1), while others refused, such as Hosius, bishop of Cordoba in Spain (later to be Constantine's theological adviser) and Donatus who remained six years in prison and endured torture on nine occasions (Lactantius, *On the Deaths of the Persecutors*, 35.1; 16.5).

Diocletian's ill health allowed Galerius to assume power and he issued the **fourth edict** of the persecution in the spring of AD304, requiring a general sacrifice throughout the Empire (*ANE* excerpt 241), as Decius had done over fifty years before. Until now in the Great Persecution the main target was the Church's leadership, but now that cautious Diocletian was out of the way, the reckless Galerius imposed the universal persecution that he had always argued for. While Diocletian had tried to suppress the Church by bloodless measures (the first three edicts), Galerius would make many martyrs. For example, in August AD304 Euplius, a deacon, was beheaded at Catania, Sicily, albeit at his own initiative and request. Such voluntary martyrdoms were discouraged by the Church. The Council of Elvira in Spain, held probably not long after the fourth edict, ruled that such people should not be included on the list of martyrs (canon 60; *ANE* excerpt 255). In December AD304 a certain Crispina was interrogated at Theveste by the proconsul Anulinus, who tried to persuade her to comply with the edict. She refused to sacrifice to the gods and was executed, along with five others. In Tunisia an inscription recorded the names of thirty-four martyrs who suffered under Diocletian and Maximian (emperor in the West). There were martyrdoms in Palestine too,where many were sent to work in the mines (Eusebius, *Martyrs of Palestine*, 8.1). Yet, Lactantius reports that many pagans were moved by the martyrdoms to leave the old gods and become Christians (*Divine Institutes* 5.22, 23; 13.1).

On 1 May AD305, Diocletian abdicated as emperor of the East, as did Maximian as emperor of the West. Galerius and Constantius (father of Constantine) became the new emperors in the East and West respectively. In the West, persecution was certainly not as prevalent as in the East. While some church buildings were destroyed by Constantius, some ten years later Donatists in North Africa reflected that he, unlike other emperors, had not oppressed the Church (Augustine, *Letter* 88.2). Thus, with the abdication of Maximian, the Great Persecution was largely brought to an end in the West after only two years. Even in the East there was some relief for nearly a year.

However, a **fifth edict** in Easter AD306 required another general sacrifice, enforced by the military who checked citizens' names on their lists (Eusebius, *Martyrs of Palestine* 4.8). In AD308 the persecution was relaxed somewhat when the usual capital punishment was reduced to lesser sanctions. However, later in that year, Maximin, Galerius' deputy, introduced a number of measures aimed at reviving paganism and further repressing Christianity. Pagan priests were installed in cities throughout his realm, including Palestine, Syria and Egypt. The priesthood was hierarchically structured, modelled it appears on clerical hierarchy. All, even babes in arms, were required to sacrifice. In Palestine, food in the markets was sprinkled with pagan drink offerings and the blood of animals that had been sacrificed to the gods. A propaganda war was waged against the Church in the form of a forged account of the Roman governor Pilate's trial of Jesus, which became part of the educational curriculum. In this apocryphal work Pilate's verdict against the founder of Christianity was, of course, viewed as a just decision. Slanders relating to immorality in Church meetings were invented and published throughout the Empire with Maximin's approval (*ANE* excerpt 245 and note). Martyrs in those times include Eusebius' friend Pamphilus (a presbyter in Caesarea) and eleven of his companions (1 February AD309).

Hope of relief came when, struck down by illness, Galerius published an edict on 30 April AD311 granting religious tolerance to the Church (*ANE* excerpt 246). Galerius admitted that attempts by imperial leaders to return the Christians to ancient Roman traditions had failed. Due to their folly and willfulness, the Christians had persisted in their own ways. Thus, the emperor decreed that Christians could exist again and re-establish their places of worship, as long as they did nothing against public order and prayed for the security and well-being of the Empire and its leaders. Galerius refers to another letter, now lost, which would instruct magistrates how to proceed in the light of the new edict. Thus, due to the failure of his persecution of the Church, the severity of his illness (which Lactantius says forced him to acknowledge God; *ANE* excerpt 246 note) and the pleas of his friend, Licinius, who could see personal political advantage in helping the Christians[1], Galerius conceded defeat. Within a few days he died of his illness on 5 May.

However, the end was not yet. At first Maximin consented to Galerius' policy of toleration, but then sought to acquire Galerius' Eastern provinces. Cities were invited to seek imperial authority to remove Christians or to require them to honour the gods (*ANE* excerpt 247 and note, relating to a rural town in Asia Minor in AD312). Maximin responded to such petitions by claiming that the gods rewarded a return to paganism with, for example, bountiful harvests. The Church in Egypt in particular, suffered terrible persecution. Peter, bishop of

---

[1] so Frend, WHC *The Early Church*, SCM: London, p121, 122

Alexandria, was martyred on 25 November AD311 along with many other bishops. Eusebius records his own eye-witness account of the persecution in Egypt at the time. Many were executed in one day; some were beheaded and others were burnt. Exhausted executioners had to relieve each other with breaks and voluntary martyrs joyfully offered themselves for execution (*Hist Eccl*, 8.9.4,5). Elsewhere, for example, Methodius, bishop of Olympus, Lycia, was executed in AD311, as was Lucian (a presbyter and theologian of Antioch), on 7 January AD312, in Nicomedia, home of Maximin's headquarters.

Developments in the West, however, brought the persecution of the early Church to an end. Constantine moved against Maxentius, son of Maximian, to acquire supremacy in the West. Maxentius himself had ended the persecution of the Church in Italy and North Africa after he acquired those regions in AD307. Maxentius was killed in October AD312 and Constantine attributed his victory to the God of the Christians (see next chapter). Maybe in an attempt to gain Christian support, in light of the renewed threat from the West, Maximin attempted to revert to Galerius' tolerance of Christianity. At the end of AD312 he instructed his Praetorian prefect, Sabinus, to suspend persecution. However, he did not specifically permit Christians to practise their faith and so they kept a low profile (Eusebius, *Hist Eccl* 9.9). In February AD313, Constantine and Licinius (the latter ruled the Balkans in the West) issued the historic **Edict of Milan**. It granted religious liberty to all citizens, not just to Christians, and the free and immediate restoration of properties formerly owned by Christians, individually or collectively (*ANE* excerpt 250). Letters were sent to provincial governors requiring them to implement the requirements of this edict by ensuring that property was restored to the Church (*ANE* excerpt 252: a letter from Constantine to the proconsul of Africa in AD313).

Two months later, Maximin was defeated in battle by Licinius and died in August AD313. An uneasy relationship developed between Constantine in the West and Licinius in the East, which led to conflict between the two in AD316 and AD324. With Constantine he had granted religious toleration to all in the Edict of Milan in February AD313 and in June of that year formally proclaimed the toleration for the Christians at Nicomedia. The Council of Arles, Gaul, met in the years AD314-319 and ruled, among other things, on what should be done with those, including clergy, who had lapsed in the Great Persecution. Various forms of discipline and penance were required, dependent on the circumstances of the lapse and bishops were to use their own discretion in individual cases (*ANE* excerpt 272). However, in about AD319 Licinius began to renew action against Christians in his own realm, believing that their loyalty lay with Constantine. Licinius removed Christians from his palace and demoted soldiers who refused to sacrifice to the gods. He acted against bishops too, forbidding them from holding synods, even manipulating the execution of some, who endured cruel deaths. Others went into hiding. Churches in

Pontus in Asia Minor, were demolished or closed down. Worship was not to take place indoors, nor with men and women together. Women were to be instructed only by other women. The details have been preserved by Eusebius (*ANE* excerpt 273 and note). Licinius apparently intended to widen the scope of his persecution of Christians but was defeated by Constantine in AD324. Constantine was now sole emperor and reaffirmed toleration for all in a letter to the Eastern provinces (*ANE* excerpt 275).

Tasks

a. Summarise the terms and impact of the five edicts of persecution and Maximin's revival of paganism.

b. Outline the reasons for and terms of Galerius' edict of toleration.

c. Comment on Maximin's treatment of the Church from the publication of Galerius' edict of toleration until his defeat by Licinius.

d. Give details of the origin and terms of the Edict of Milan.

e. Explain how and why Licinius departed from the Edict of Milan and how Constantine finally brought the persecution of the Church to an end.

The consequences

Just as the Decian persecution had resulted in schism over the treatment of those who had compromised or complied during the onslaught, so it was with the Great Persecution – and with more lasting consequences. The Melitian schism in Egypt and the Donatist schism in North Africa, were both unhappy legacies of the Empire's last assault on the Church.

Peter, bishop of Alexandria, went into hiding to avoid arrest, probably in AD304. In his absence, Melitius (or Meletius), bishop of Lycopolis in Upper Egypt, began conducting ordinations in Alexandria and beyond, without Peter's approval. Melitius was condemned by Peter and a schismatic Melitian church developed, including among its number, for a while, Arius, who was at the centre of a major doctrinal controversy of the fourth century. While this schism was about the authority of the patriarch of Alexandria over Egypt, it was later viewed by Epiphanius (*Panarion* 68. 1-3) as a controversy over the treatment of those who had lapsed during the persecution – Peter adopting a lenient attitude and Melitius a rigorous one. On the whole issue see *ANE* excerpts 242-244 for the initial controversy; excerpt 281 for Arius' connection with the Melitians; and excerpts 292 and 298 for the Council of Nicaea and Athanasius in relation to the Melitians.

The Donatist schism of North Africa also originated in the Great Persecution, concerning the issue of the status of those who had handed over Scriptures, or books perceived as Scriptures by the authorities. While in the East such action was not regarded as apostasy, in the West some regarded it as so. Mensurius, bishop of Carthage, had handed over books to the authorities. His archdeacon, Caecilian, succeeded him, but because one of those who consecrated Caecilian was regarded as a *traditor* (one who had surrendered books), Caecilian's appointment was rejected by some. Numidian bishops appointed a rival bishop of Carthage, Majorinus, whose successor, Donatus, became the leader of a schism that was investigated, persecuted and eventually tolerated by Constantine in AD321 (see *ANE* chapter 26; pp210. 211 of this book). While the persecution of the Church ended in AD324, its consequences were to remain for a long time to come.

Task

Describe the impact of the Great Persecution upon the Church.

Practice Essay Titles

1. *Outline your knowledge and understanding of the course of persecution during the third century. (30)*

   Explore the claim that the Church's response to persecution was of more significance than persecution itself (15)

2. *Describe the main events of the Great Persecution (30)*

   Comment on the view that this persecution was significantly different from those preceding it. (15)

A2 level   Constantine

Constantine's life and religious policy, including the Council of Nicaea.

(CCEA Specification)

Objective

In this chapter we shall gain a knowledge and understanding of the life, conversion and religious policy of Constantine, including the Council of Nicaea, and of their impact upon the Church.

LIFE

CONSTANTINE (THE GREAT) WAS born around AD272 in the town of Naissus – modern Nish, Serbia, south-eastern Yugoslavia. His father, Constantius, was a senior army officer and his mother, Helena, Constantius' concubine. To understand Constantine`s rise to power we must appreciate the changes that were made to the government of the Empire by the emperor Diocletian (reigned AD284-305). In AD285, Diocletian appointed Maximian (AD285-305) as his deputy. The government of the Empire was expanded further in AD293 with the introduction of a tetrarchy ('rule by four'). While Diocletian and Maximian remained the senior emperors, each known as an 'Augustus', Galerius was appointed as deputy to his father-in-law, Diocletian, and Constantius was appointed as Maximian's deputy, each known as a 'Caesar'. Constantius, because of age, was senior to Galerius. Over all was the unifying figure of Diocletian. Meanwhile, Constantine had entered the army, like his father, and served in turn under Galerius and Diocletian.

There were further changes at the top in May AD305 when the Augusti Diocletian and Maximian abdicated. Their positions were filled by their Caesars, Galerius and Constantius, the latter being the senior Augustus. Maximin (Maximinus Daia) and Severus, whose allegiance lay with Galerius, became their Caesars. However, according to contemporary historian Lactantius (*On the Deaths of the Persecutors* 18.8), there was an expectation that Constantine and Maxentius (son of Maximian) would become the new Caesars.

The resulting political landscape was that Constantius oversaw Britain, Gaul and Spain and Severus was responsible for Italy, North Africa and the Upper Danube. Galerius was in charge of the Balkan provinces and Asia Minor, and Maximin managed Syria, Egypt and Libya. Galerius granted Constantius' request that his son, Constantine, be sent west to accompany him.

Change occurred again when Constantius died in York on 25 July AD306. Constantine was proclaimed Augustus by his father's troops. Such an act was a challenge to Severus who, as Constantius' Caesar, was to be the next Augustus. To avoid conflict, Galerius recognised Severus as Augustus and Constantine as Caesar, a situation which Constantine settled for. Things became more complicated when, just four months after Constantius' death, Maximian's son, Maxentius, was proclaimed emperor in Rome. Severus sought to quash the coup d'etat but Maximian had come to the aid of his son, and Severus' troops, who had once served Maximian, deserted him. In AD307 Severus was captured and compelled to commit suicide. An attempt by Galerius to crush the revolt also failed.

Constantine married Maximian's daughter Fausta in AD307, having previously fathered a son, Crispus, to a concubine named Minervina. Maximian, back in imperial politics since his son's revolt, appointed Constantine as Augustus, just as he had done with his father two years before. As Severus' Caesar, Constantine had to take the place of the dead Augustus. However, Galerius did not recognise this appointment and, at an imperial conference in the city of Carnuntum in AD308, Galerius' friend, Licinius, was appointed Augustus in the West to replace Severus. In AD310, a revolt by Maximian against his son-in-law, Constantine, was put down by the latter, celebrated in a panegyric the same year (*ANE* excerpt 248).

Galerius' death in May AD311 left behind an empire divided between Maximin in the East (Asia Minor, Syria, Egypt), Licinius in the Balkans, Maxentius in Italy and North Africa and Constantine in Britain, Gaul and Spain. While Severus and Galerius had failed in their attempts to remove the usurper, Maxentius, Constantine marched into Italy in the summer of AD312. In the autumn he engaged his brother-in-law, Maxentius, at the Battle of the Milvian Bridge, some five miles north of Rome. Sensitive to criticism of his former policy of remaining behind the city walls, and inspired by the Sibylline books, Maxentius crossed the bridge. However, forced to retreat across the bridge, Maxentius was drowned in the Tiber, where thousands of his men also lost their lives. Constantine had taken Rome and his victory over Maxentius was marked by the Arch of Constantine, erected in Rome about AD315 (*ANE* excerpt AD251).

Constantine and Licinius met in Milan in AD313 and issued an edict of religious toleration for all their citizens. At the same time, Licinius married

Constantine's half-sister, Constantia. With the defeat of Maximin by Licinius at Adrianople (modern north-west Turkey) later in AD313, Licinius was now supreme in the East, as was Constantine in the West. However, tensions between the two rulers resulted in war in AD316 when Licinius lost most of the East to Constantine. In the following year, Constantine's eldest son, Crispus, was appointed Caesar, as were Constantine II (his son by Fausta) and Licinius II. As we have seen (p199), Licinius began to persecute the Church in the East in about AD319, because of its perceived loyalty to Constantine. Increasing persecution by Licinius led to a final conflict between the two emperors in AD324. Constantine emerged victorious and in the same year founded a new city as his capital – Constantinople or 'Constantine's City' (formerly Byzantium; now Istanbul, north-west Turkey). He remained sole emperor until his death in May AD337.

Task

Outline the key events in Constantine's life and rise to power.

CONVERSION

Constantine would have encountered Christians while in the East, particularly in the court of Diocletian, and may have had Christians in his own family. He had a half-sister, Anastasia, whose name may reflect Christian influence (*anastasis* is Greek for resurrection). However, his conversion to Christianity is linked with the Battle of the Milvian Bridge in AD312. Before his defeat of Maxentius at this battle, Constantine apparently had a vision or visions which caused him, subsequently, to attribute his victory to the God of the Christians. Two contemporary accounts of his conversion have come down to us.

The earliest account was written within five years of the battle by Lactantius (lived about AD250-320), a Christian Apologist who in his later years tutored Constantine's eldest son, Crispus. In his *On the Deaths of the Persecutors* (44.3-6; *ANE* excerpt 249), Lactantius records that on the night before the battle Constantine was told in a dream to mark his soldiers' shields with the heavenly sign of God. In obedience to this instruction he marked Christ on the shields by putting an X on them, the shape of the cross, with the top bent over. This would have been a form of the Chi-Rho symbol ie the first two Greek letters of the word Christ combined. By this sign, Constantine's army was victorious.

The other account is given by Eusebius, bishop of Caesarea, Palestine (about AD260-339; bishop from around 313), author of the famous *History of the Church* (or *Ecclesiastical History*). Soon after Constantine's death in AD337, he wrote his *Life of Constantine* in honour of the emperor. In this latter work (1.26-30; *ANE* excerpt 249), Eusebius reports that, some time before the Battle of the Milvian Bridge, Constantine realised that he would need divine assistance and deliberated about which god he should select as his patron. He decided to pray to the god of his monotheistic father. While he was praying, about midday, he (and his army) saw a trophy in the shape of a cross of light over the sun. Attached were the words "By this conquer". After wondering what this meant, he saw Christ in a dream with the sign he had seen in the sky, who then told him to make a copy of the sign and to use it as protection in all conflicts with his enemies. Then, Constantine instructed goldsmiths and jewellers to make a copy of the sign in gold and precious stones. Eusebius adds that he received his information from Constantine himself, on oath, a long time after his initial vision.

There are obvious differences between these two versions, such as when the significant dream occurred and the absence of any reference to the soldiers' shields in Eusebius. Even though Eusebius claims that his account came from the emperor himself, it was recounted to him a long time after the event and then recorded at the end of Eusebius' life. Further, Eusebius' objectivity is somewhat suspect, when we recall that his *Life of Constantine* is more hagiographical than biographical – he had an idealised view of Constantine as a model Christian. In the next century, the Church historian, Socrates, would complain that in his *Life of Constantine*, Eusebius was more concerned with praising the emperor than accurately reporting facts (*Hist Eccl* 1.1). However, there is clearly agreement on the core fact that before his defeat of Maxentius in AD312, Constantine had a dream in which he was told to enter battle with the sign of the cross. His compliance with this instruction represented his trust in the central event of the Christian faith.

However, the reality of Constantine's conversion to Christianity has been challenged by some[1], and defended by others[2]. The evidence is ambiguous. A panegyric delivered in honour of Constantine, two years before the Battle of the Milvian Bridge, records his vision of and reverence for the god Apollo (Sol Invictus:The Unconquered Sun), accompanied by the god Victory ('Nike'; *ANE* excerpt 248 and note). Constantine's coins reveal a continuing reverence for the Sun god after AD312 – for five years after this in the West and for twelve years after in the East. His coinage bore the words 'For the Unconquered Sun, his Companion'. The Arch of Constantine, erected in Rome by AD315, in honour of 'the liberator of the city' who defeated Maxentius, contains no

---

[1] eg Kee, Alistair *Constantine Versus Christ*, SCM: London, 1982

[2] eg Keresztes, Paul *Constantine: A Great Christian Monarch and Apostle*, JC Gieben: Amsterdam, 1981

reference to Christianity, but rather images of the Unconquered Sun (*ANE* excerpt 251). Further, Constantine and his successors, for some time, retained the pagan title *Pontifex Maximus* (Supreme Priest), signifying their leadership of traditional Roman worship. Again, as late as AD321, Constantine approved of consulting soothsayers (*Theodosian Code* 16.10.1). This evidence, as well as his killing of his son, Crispus, in AD326 and his wife, Fausta, shortly after, does not sit easily with the idea that Constantine made a genuine Christian commitment around AD312.

Thus, in the mid nineteenth century, Jacob Burckhardt represented Constantine as a man driven by personal ambition and political concerns[1]. Indeed, it has been argued that his adoption of and preference for Christianity was not a matter of religious conversion but rather a politically motivated policy due to its perceived potential for unifying all the citizens of the Empire. Hence, his personal involvement in seeking to resolve the Donatist schism and the Arian controversy (see below), was not due to a concern for ecclesiastical harmony or religious orthodoxy , but rather, for political unity throughout his Empire.

However, there is also evidence of a real Christian faith on Constantine's part which leads in less cynical directions, not least of which are the two contemporary accounts of Constantine's vision which affirm his Christian commitment. It is even possible that Constantine became a Christian as early as 306 when he was proclaimed Augustus by his troops and ended the persecution of the Church in his domain at that time. Certainly, from AD312 there is evidence of his personal preference for Christianity. The Edict of Milan, issued jointly with Licinius in AD312, reveals a particular concern for Christianity, while granting tolerance to all religions (see p199 and *ANE* excerpt 250). His correspondence from AD313, including the introduction of legislation and policies favouring the Church (see below and *ANE* excerpts 252-254, 274-279), certainly reveals his commitment to Christianity. Paul McKechnie states that any doubts about the reality of Constantine's Christian faith should be dispelled by the emperor's 'Speech to the Assembly of Saints', which he dates between 317 and 325[2]. Here, Constantine speaks approvingly of repentance and praise to the Saviour and of his wish that the Christian revelation had been given to him long ago.

The ambiguity of the evidence relating to Constantine's conversion can be explained to some degree by the fact that, though he was a Christian emperor, he initially presided over a largely pagan empire. Thus, the names of pagan gods were gradually replaced with general, rather than specifically Christian, terms for the deity. Hence also the gradual transition from pagan to Christian

---

[1] *The Age of Constantine the Great*, 1949; German original, 1853

[2] McKechnie, Paul *The First Christian Centuries*, Apollos/IVP: Leicester, 2001, p238

symbolism on coinage. The first Christian symbols appeared in AD315 and the last pagan ones in about AD323. Further, it appears that Constantine did not regard reverence for the Sun god as incompatible with Christianity. Henry Chadwick notes how the two were connected and even confused in early Christianity eg Clement of Alexandria's depiction of Christ as the Sun god, Christian worship on the day of the Sun and the early fourth century celebration of Christ's birth on the 25 December, the birthday of the Sun god[1]. Indeed, Norbert Brox goes as far as to claim that Constantine never abandoned the Sun god[2]; rather, the dramatic shift for Constantine was a change to a Christian form of worship. Further, to polarise the debate about the sincerity of Constantine's Christianity into a matter of either religious or political motivation, is to fail to appreciate that State and religion were inseparable in Roman thought.

Certainly, Constantine's eventual baptism at the end of his life (*ANE* excerpt 307) should not be seen as a late commitment to the Christian faith, but as a common practice due to the seriousness of post-baptismal sin, especially by rulers engaged in warfare.

Tasks

a. Outline the two contemporary accounts of Constantine's conversion, commenting on their historical reliability.

b. Discuss the ambiguity of the evidence regarding the genuineness of Constantine's conversion.

SUPPORT OF THE CHURCH

What is clear is that from the Edict of Milan in AD312, Constantine's religious policies generously favoured the Church. The Edict of Milan, of course, granted religious tolerance to all, of whatever religious persuasion. Constantine, though, did not establish Christianity as the State religion which all citizens must follow – the emperor Theodosius I would decree this in AD380, over forty years after Constantine's death. Jews and pagans were not forced, physically or legally, to abandon their faith and join the Church. We have seen, indeed, that pagan tradition and symbolism remained with Constantine for some time after AD312, as a matter of pragmatic courtesy to the old religion.

However, his role as a patron and benefactor of the Church became evident in a variety of ways. Thus, legislation was introduced from AD313 onwards

---

[1] Chadwick, Henry *The Early Church*, Penguin: London, 1993, p126, 127

[2] Brox, Norbert *A History of the Early Church*, SCM: London, 1994, p48, 49

which indicates imperial support of Christianity. Underpinning the Edict of Milan were imperial letters to provincial governors requiring the restoration of confiscated property to the Church (*ANE* excerpt 252: AD313). The Church's clergy were financially subsidised by the State and exempted from the pressures of public office to allow them to devote themselves to religious concerns (*ANE* excerpts 253 and 254: AD313). Indeed, because overburdened town councillors sought clerical positions in order to evade their workload, legislation was introduced to bar them from clerical office (*ANE* excerpt 277; about AD320). However, Jews who formerly had enjoyed exemption from town councils were now required to serve on them (*Theodosian Code* 16.8.3). Clergy also enjoyed tax exemptions (*Theodosian Code* 16.2.10). The social status of bishops,in particular, was enhanced by legislation – slaves could be formally released in the presence of bishops, who were also legally recognised as judges even of secular issues (*Theodosian Code* 4.7.1; 2.8.1; *Code of Justinian* 1.13.1; 1.27.1). Such legislation provided for the Church and its clergy a public and civic importance which was previously unknown.

Other legislation in favour of the Church includes recognition of Sunday as a day to be free from inappropriate labour (*ANE* excerpt 276: AD321, though possibly in honour of the Sun god), the suppression of soothsayers (*Theodosian Code* 9.16.1: AD319) and, according to Eusebius, the abolition,of pagan sacrifices (*Life of Constantine* 2.45). However, this claim by Eusebius has been debated since no legislation to this effect was implemented in Constantine's day, even if Christian officials would have avoided conducting public sacrifices. General legislation appeared to become more humane under Christian influence (*ANE* excerpt 274, especially relevant note). Constantine's promotion of Christianity was apparent in that most crucial institution of the State – the army. It has been asserted that, from the start, the army was an instrument of Constantine's religious policies and those of his successors. Prayers mandated for the troops before his historic defeat of Maxentius and during his conflict with Licinius meant that civil wars became holy wars[1]. A field chapel and military chaplains were provided for the troops. Sunday became their festal day and Christian officers were favoured in promotion (Eusebius, *Life of Constantine* 4.52).

A very tangible and enduring sign of Constantine's support of Christianity was his construction of impressive and expensive Church buildings, in addition to the restoration of property confiscated during the Great Persecution. Shortly after the Battle of the Milvian Bridge, Constantine gave Fausta's palace to the Church, which became the home of the bishops of Rome (St John Lateran). Also in Rome, St Peter's was erected at great cost and effort over , what was believed to be, the apostle's resting place. A large church was erected over the grave of St Lawrence in Rome,a famous martyr

---

[1] Leadbetter, Bill *The Early Christian World* Ed Philip Esler, Routledge: London, 2000, p271

during the reign of Valerian. In his new city, Constantinople, the emperor built not pagan temples but great churches, including one dedicated to Peace and another to the Apostles(where he intended to rest as the thirteenth apostle; *ANE* excerpt 307), and the beginnings of the Church of Holy Wisdom. Pagan temples were plundered to finance the construction of the new city and Constantine's generous patronage of the Church, a powerful symbol that the old religion was giving way to the new. In Palestine, the Church of the Holy Sepulchre was founded on the presumed site of Jesus' crucifixion and resurrection. Helena, the emperor's mother, had churches erected at Bethlehem and the Mount of Olives.

Constantine privileged the Church in another important way when he covered the cost of the production of new Bibles. Shortly after the dedication of Constantinople in AD330, the emperor instructed Eusebius of Caesarea to produce fifty Bibles (Old and New Testaments) for the new churches in his new city. The emperor would finance the project and the transport of the Bibles to Constantinople. Professional scribes prepared the magnificent and elaborately bound volumes (Eusebius, *Life of Constantine* 4.36, 37). Less than thirty years before, imperial policy had been the destruction rather than the production of the Church's Scriptures.

Overall, Constantine's religious policies amount to a gradual Christianisation of the Empire as he legally and financially privileged the Church. A Christian emperor over a Christian Empire was the idealised vision of Eusebius of Caesarea in his *Oration on the Tricennalia of Constantine* in AD336 – Constantine as earthly monarch represented God the heavenly monarch (*ANE* excerpt 306). While the clergy were bishops within the Church, Constantine saw himself as appointed by God to be bishop of those outside the Church, his pastoral care extending to all his citizens (*ANE* excerpt 305).

Task

List the various ways in which Constantine favoured the Church.

SCHISMATICS AND HERETICS

While Constantine granted religious freedom to all in the Edict of Milan (AD312) and reaffirmed this for the East after his defeat of Licinius (AD324), it is also clear from correspondence in AD326 that his religious policies would actively privilege and benefit only the 'Catholic' Church, as distinct from 'heretics and schismatics'. Not only would the latter fail to benefit from such favours but they would be subject to various public obligations (see *ANE* excerpt 278). However, in the same year, Constantine directed that the orthodox, yet schismatic, Novatianists (see p191) should be allowed to retain their own church buildings and cemeteries, yet without attempting to acquire property rightly belonging to the Catholic Church (*ANE* excerpt 279 and note). Constantine's energies, however, were directed primarily at dealing with two other enduring cases of dissent within the Church – Donatism and Arianism.

In the conclusion to the previous chapter we saw that the Donatist schism of North Africa originated in the Great Persecution. The appointment of Caecilian as bishop of Carthage was rejected by some as invalid because one of those who consecrated him had apostatised in the persecution, by handing over books to the authorities. A rival bishop of Carthage was appointed, Majorinus, whose successor, Donatus, became the leader of the schism (see chapter 26 of *ANE*: 'The Outbreak of the Donatist Schism, AD304-321').

In AD313 the Donatists (if we may call them such at this stage) appealed to Constantine through Anulinus, proconsul of Africa, concerning their opposition to Caecilian and asking that judges from Gaul should rule on the dispute.(*ANE* excerpts 260, 261 and note). Which group were the Catholic Church and, therefore, entitled to the imperial subsidies? Constantine referred the controversy to Miltiades, bishop of Rome who, along with bishops from Gaul, was to hear the two parties in Rome. The emperor's main concern was to avoid schism in the Church. Caecilian received a favourable verdict and the Donatists appealed a second time to Constantine, who called for and funded a council of bishops at Arles, Gaul in AD314 to give them a second hearing (*ANE* excerpts 262 and 263). Again, the verdict went against the Donatists (*ANE* excerpt 264; also excerpt 257, canon 14). After Constantine summoned to Rome a Donatist agent who had been exposed as a false-witness against Caecilian (*ANE* excerpts 265 and 266), the emperor finally ruled in favour of Caecilian in November AD316 (*ANE* excerpt 267). Imperial persecution of the Donatists followed (*ANE* excerpt 268) in early AD317 – an edict required the confiscation of Church property and the banishment of leaders. The persecution was abandoned in May AD321 by an emperor who lacked understanding of the strength of the Donatist convictions and who was anticipating war with Licinius (*ANE* excerpt 270). Less than ten years later, Constantine even tolerated the Donatist takeover of a Catholic building in Cirta, Numidia and paid for the relocation of the Catholic congregation (*ANE* excerpt 271).

Constantine's involvement in the Donatist controversy reveals his concern for ecclesiastical harmony and thus imperial unity. The emperor's intervention in Church affairs, albeit initiated by the Church itself, was a pattern to be followed by his successors, resulting in a loss of independence on the part of the Church. The fact that the Donatists initially appealed to the emperor and then, when the authorities turned against them, asked, 'What has the emperor to do with the Church?', reveals that imperial involvement in Church affairs could be a double-edged sword. Constantine, for his part, realised the futility of harsh measures in dealing with schism. Of greater consequence would be a dispute in the Egyptian church which would engulf the Empire and require imperial intervention, resulting in the first ecumenical Church council.

Task

Discuss Constantine's policy towards schismatics and heretics, with particular reference to the Donatists.

ARIANISM AND THE COUNCIL OF NICAEA

Arianism

In around AD320, Arius (about AD256-336), a presbyter in Alexandria, found himself in disagreement with his bishop, Alexander, at a meeting of clergy, during which Alexander was speaking about the doctrine of the Trinity (*ANE* excerpt 280). To Arius, it apparently appeared that Alexander's view of the relationship between the Father and the Son was like that of the heretic Sabellius who, a hundred years before, had taught that there was no essential distinction between the Father and the Son, the latter being the self-expression of the former. Arius' reasoning was, according to the fifth century historian Socrates, that if the Father begat the Son, then the Son must not have always existed and ,indeed, had his existence from non-existence (*ANE* excerpt 280; see excerpt 281 for a different account of the origins of the Arian dispute by another fifth century Church historian, Sozomen).

The exact sequence and dating of events in the controversy, as it developed between 320 and the Council of Nicaea in AD325, is unclear and subject to different analyses. Arius wrote to Alexander in AD320/21 claiming that his beliefs were consistent with tradition and Alexander's own teaching (*ANE* excerpt 284; see excerpts 286 and 295 for Arius' statements of his own beliefs). In this letter, Arius states that the Son, unlike the Father, is not eternal or unbegun; rather the Son was begotten by God's will before time, as God's perfect creature. As God's offspring, he was not of the same essence or substance (Greek: *homoousios*) as the Father, as if he were part or portion of God, since God's being cannot be divided or altered.

However, shortly after this letter, Arius wrote to Eusebius, bishop of

Nicomedia, the imperial capital in Asia Minor, complaining of Alexander's unjust persecution of him (ie Arius) and contrasting Alexander's beliefs with his own (*ANE* excerpt 283). Alexander's belief is that the Father and Son are co-eternal ie. the Son has always existed along with the Father. Arius, however, holds that the Son had a beginning, while the Father had not and that the Son is from nothing ie. he is not part of God or indeed of any substance. These teachings, says Arius, are the cause of his persecution ('driven out of the city'). Arius also refers to the condemnation of colleagues with similar beliefs, such as Eusebius of Caesarea. The letter concludes with a claim that Arius and Eusebius of Nicomedia are fellow-disciples of Lucian of Antioch (about AD240-312) – a claim which is generally regarded to be a spurious attempt to align himself with a prominent group within the Church.

Alexander, incensed at Eusebius of Nicomedia's support of Arius and his colleagues, wrote an encyclical letter to inform the Church at large that a synod of almost one hundred bishops from Egypt and Libya had condemned Arius for his teachings (*ANE* excerpt 282). In the letter, Alexander summarises the teachings of Arius and his colleagues, which he regards as contrary to Scripture and as their own invention: God has not always been a father; the Son has not always existed but was created by God out of nothing for the purpose of creating us; the Son is unlike the Father in essence and indeed alien to the essence of God; the Son does not perfectly know or comprehend the Father; the Son is mutable, capable of change, even of sin. While this letter is often dated around AD319, it seems unlikely that Arius would have written such a courteous letter to Alexander after it, in 320/21 (see above). Rowan Williams puts the letter much later, in AD325[1]. It may be that the letter was written just before the Council of Nicaea, in order to influence its outcome.

After Constantine defeated Licinius and gained supremacy of the East (AD324) he was faced with the Arian controversy in his newly acquired provinces, just as he had faced the Donatist controversy in the West. As in the latter dispute, his concern was for unity in the Church and thus, throughout the Empire. First, in AD324, he sent his theological adviser, Hosius (or Ossius), bishop of Cordoba in Spain, to negotiate peace between Alexander and Arius. Hosius brought them a letter from Constantine in which the emperor stressed his concern for unity and peace in the Church and beyond, and rebuked both Alexander and Arius for even discussing, let alone dividing over, 'small and very insignificant matters' which are not among the 'leading doctrines' of the faith. When intellectual subtleties are made public, it leads to blasphemy or schism, either because of lack of clear explanation by the speaker or accurate comprehension by the hearers. The two disputants should extend tolerance

---

[1] Williams, Rowan *Arius: Heresy and Tradition*, Darton Longman & Todd: London, 1987

and forgiveness to each other, otherwise the evil of division would continue to affect a large number of their people (*ANE* excerpt 287). The emperor's characterisation of the cause of the dispute as a trifling matter reveals his lack of theological awareness at the time, comparable to his lack of understanding of the strength of convictions in the Donatist controversy.

In sharp contrast to Constantine's view of the matter, early in AD325, a council of bishops at Antioch in Syria regarded the issue to be the most important of all, excelling all others, since it related to the whole mystery of the faith (*ANE* excerpt 288). The creed issued by the council stressed that the Son had always existed, that he was not a creature, but was begotten mysteriously, from the Father and not from nothing, and that he was immutable. In addition to these anti-Arian statements, the creed concluded with anti-Arian anathemas, condemning those who denied the teaching of the creed. Three of those present, including Eusebius of Caesarea, were provisionally excommunicated for refusing to affirm the creed and for allegedly holding the same views as Arius. These men had until the Council of Ancyra, to be held later in the year, to repent and recognise the truth. In the event, Constantine changed the venue of this episcopal synod to Nicaea to make it more convenient for European bishops, because of the good climate and so that the emperor himself might attend to observe and participate in the deliberations (*ANE* excerpt 289). Thus, the famous Council of Nicaea was summoned by imperial demand.

Tasks

a. *Outline the course of the Arian controversy until the Council of Nicaea.*

b. *Identify the specific teachings of Arius that were objectionable to Alexander.*

The Council of Nicaea

No minutes or details of the proceedings of this historic council have been preserved. However, information provided by Eusebius of Caesarea, two Church historians of the next century (Sozomen and Socrates) and in imperial letters, give us some idea of what occurred. The creed and some twenty canons of the council have also been preserved. Bishops from all over the Empire were summoned and the cost of transport and lodgings were met by the State. While Nicaea is regarded as the first ecumenical (world-wide) council of the Church, in reality, this was not the case. Though figures vary, it appears that nearly three hundred bishops attended. But it was not a comprehensive gathering. While the East was well represented, including from beyond the Empire, Armenia, Mesopotamia and Persia, only a few from the West were present, including Hosius of Cordoba, Caecilian of Carthage and two presbyters from Rome representing their bishop, Silvester.

The council was formally opened on 20 May AD325, in an imperial building in Nicaea. The bishops sat in facing rows and rose to receive Constantine, who entered in his richly ornamented imperial attire. The emperor occupied a lowly seat, instead of an imperial throne, between Alexander of Alexandria and Hosius of Cordoba. After a speech of welcome, given probably by Eustathius, bishop of Antioch, Constantine reminded them that the purpose of the council was to achieve unity and peace. To underline this, he then ,in the presence of the bishops, burnt letters of petition and complaint that they had sent to him. There were lively debates, chaired probably by Hosius, between three main groups – Arius, supported by Eusebius of Nicomedia and others; Alexander, supported by his deacon Athanasius(later to play a leading role in the defeat of Arianism) and others; and the largest group headed by Eusebius of Caesarea, representing a mediating approach. Not that the various positions were neatly defined. In the next century, Socrates reports that it was like fighting in the dark with hardly anyone knowing why they were attacking each other (*Hist Eccl*, 1.23).

After an initial examination of Arius (who chanted his beliefs), the proposal was made, probably by Hosius, that unity could be achieved by the production of a creed on which all could agree. The first creed was presented to the council by Eusebius of Nicomedia and his Arian colleagues, but was immediately rejected. Next, Eusebius of Caesarea presented the baptismal creed of his own church, possibly to rehabilitate himself in the light of his provisional excommunication at a recent council (see earlier). While this creed appeared acceptable to the Arians (its vague wording could bear an Arian interpretation), it did not please the anti-Arians who knew that it did not resolve the controversy. Eusebius claims that Constantine was pleased with his creed but suggested that the word *homoousios* ('same essence/substance') should be added to define the relationship between the Son and the Father (*ANE* excerpt 291, where Eusebius presents both his church's creed and the council's creed). The word was not popular, not only because it was not a biblical term, but also because of its use in the previous century by Sabellians and also by Paul of Samosata (*ANE* excerpts 225, 226, 230). The creed that the council eventually produced – the Creed of Nicaea – contained a number of clearly anti-Arian statements as well as adding anti-Arian anathemas (see p41-43).

The authority of the emperor and the threat of exile ensured that the vast majority of the bishops signed the creed. However, two Libyan bishops, Theonas and Secundus, refused and were excommunicated along with Arius.

Eusebius of Nicomedia and Theognius of Nicaea were exiled shortly after for refusing to sign the anti-Arian anathemas appended to the creed and for associating with Arian heretics banished by the emperor (*ANE* excerpts 294 and 296). Eusebius of Caesraea's embarrassment at signing the anti-Arian creed, and also at the fact that it could be interpreted in both Arian and anti-Arian ways, is clear from his letter to his own church written after the council (see *ANE* excerpt 291).

The 'great and holy Synod' also dealt with matters of Church discipline and clerical regulation in an attempt to standardise ecclesiastical practice throughout the Empire (see *ANE* excerpt 290). The emperor wanted unity in matters of organisation and discipline as well as theological agreement. Thus, clergy were to remain within their own cities and not seek appointment elsewhere; a bishop was to be appointed by all the bishops in his province or at least by three and with the consent of the others. The appointment, however, had to be ratified by the province's metropolitan bishop. The customary special authority of the bishops of Alexandria, Rome, Antioch and Jerusalem was confirmed, with the metropolitan rights of Caesarea being safeguarded in the last case. Episcopal synods were to be held twice a year, before Lent and in the autumn, to deal with matters of clerical discipline. Novatianist clergy were to be recognised if they conformed to Catholic teaching and practice. However, their bishops would be junior to Catholic bishops. Paulianists (followers of Paul of Samosata) should be baptised again and their clergy ordained by a Catholic bishop, if found to be suitable. Legislation was also passed on the role of deacons and the treatment of the lapsed.

A letter from the council to the Egyptian Church (*ANE* excerpt 292) reveals that other matters dealt with included the Melitian schism in Egypt (see previous chapter). Melitius' ordinations were to be recognised, though as inferior to Alexander's. Further, no new appointments could be suggested or made without Alexander's approval. A decision was reached, too, on standardising the date of Easter – all churches would now determine the date independently of the Jewish Passover and observe the traditional and majority custom.

The Council of Nicaea ended on 25 July with a great banquet attended by Constantine, celebrating the twentieth year of his reign. The emperor judged the council to have been a success and accorded divine authority to its rulings – the will of some three hundred bishops, being men of character guided by the indwelling Holy Spirit, must also be the will of God (*ANE* excerpt 293). However, the next almost sixty years would show that the Arian controversy was still very much alive, until its resolution at the Council of Constantinople in AD381.

a. *Summarise the proceedings and decisions of the Council of Nicaea.*

b. *Outline the contents of the Creed of Nicaea, noting specifically its anti-Arian statements and anathemas. (See pp41-43).*

CONCLUSION

The 'conversion' of Constantine, his patronage of the Church and the beginnings of the alliance of Church and State, have been interpreted variously as a blessing, a curse and a mixture of both. Certainly, as we have seen, the Church benefited legally and financially in various ways.

However, Tony Lane has noted three problems that arose from the link between Church and State which began with Constantine[1] First, many pagans embraced Christianity only superficially, which resulted in moral decline and the acceptance of pagan practices within the Church. Constantine's support of the Church made it socially attractive and Eusebius, reflecting on the emperor's life, complained that many had entered the Church insincerely to gain social benefits (*Life of Constantine* 4.54.2). We may note here too the growing influence on the Church of pagan notions of worship, particularly in its increasing emphasis on priesthood and sacrifice – justified from the Old rather than the New Testament. Second, the persecuted Church became a persecuting State Church. Despite Constantine's policy of religious freedom, action was taken against, for example, Donatists and Arians (see above). Later emperors (eg Justinian in the sixth century) would legislate against and oppress Judaism and pagan religion. Third, the Church's alliance with the Roman Empire resulted, inevitably to some degree, in Christianity becoming a largely European religion.

We may note, too, that the Church began to loose its independence as emperors increasingly intervened in matters of doctrine and discipline. Its religious freedom and moral integrity were compromised by State concern for political unity. The relationship between the religious authority of the Church and the political authority of the State was problematic. Bishops at the Council of Serdica (AD342-3) petitioned the emperor to prevent State officials interfering in Church affairs and to urge that they keep to political matters.

Whatever assessment one makes of Constantine's religious policies, there is

---

[1] *The Lion Concise Book of Christian Thought*, Lion Publishing: Tring, 1984, p11

no doubt that they changed the status and form of the Church from being the persecuted, independent minority of pre-Constantinian times into the powerful, culturally dominant institution of medieval times.

Task

Assess the impact of Constantine's religious policies upon the Church.

Practice Essay Titles

1. *Outline the life of Constantine until the Council of Nicaea. (30)*

   Discuss the motivations of his conversion to Christianity. (15)

2. *Describe Constantine's involvement in the Arian controversy, including the Council of Nicaea. (30)*

   Evaluate the impact of Constantine's conversion and religious policies upon the Church. (15)

The School of Alexandria

The School of Alexandria, with particular reference to the life and writings of Origen.

(CCEA Specification)

Objective

In this chapter we shall gain a knowledge and understanding of the Christian School established at Alexandria in Egypt, focusing especially on the life and writings of its most influential teacher, Origen.

THE CITY OF ALEXANDRIA in Egypt became an important centre of Christianity in the early Church. Founded by Alexander the Great about 331BC, it developed as a city of Greek culture and philosophy. The home of a large Jewish community, it was there that the Old Testament was translated into Greek from the third century BC. The resulting translation, the LXX/Septuagint, was much quoted by the writers of the New Testament. In this city the Jewish writer Philo (about 20BC – AD50) sought to harmonise Greek philosophy with the Old Testament by applying to the latter an allegorical (ie non-literal, metaphorical) method of interpretation.

It is unclear how Christianity first arrived in Alexandria, though Eusebius records an unverifiable tradition that Mark, the supposed author of the Gospel that bears his name, brought Christianity to the city in about AD40, where he was later martyred (*Hist Eccl* 2.16). Eusebius also refers to the existence of a Christian school in Alexandria, which he describes as 'a school of the faithful', 'a school of sacred studies' and a 'catechetical school' (*Hist Eccl* 5.10.1; 6.3.3; *ANE* excerpts 156 and 168), which suggests that there new converts and possibly children from Christian families were taught the fundamentals of the faith. A certain Pantaenus, a converted Sicilian Stoic, is named as head of the school in about AD180, but Eusebius knows that the school existed before that, as a matter of 'primitive custom'. It has been argued, however, that despite Eusebius' fourth century claims, there was no second century school in Alexandria, but only independent Christian teachers[1].

Clement of Alexandria, who succeeded Pantaenus in about AD190, regarded his predecessor as an able teacher who was faithful to apostolic tradition (see *ANE* excerpt 157 and note). Clement himself is often considered to be the first Christian scholar, but his successor, Origen, who took over in AD202/203, was arguably the most able (and controversial) scholar of the early Church.

The challenge facing both Clement and Origen was to present orthodox, apostolic Christianity in an intelligent, intellectually defensible way before educated, philosophically minded Alexandrians and as an alternative to the apparently intellectually superior versions of Christianity taught by Alexandrian Gnostics such as Basilides and Valentinus (see pp160-161). To pagans and Gnostics, the church in Alexandria seemed to have a simple, basic faith. Clement describes the perception of orthodox Christians as irrational animals doing good works without knowing what they are doing (*Stromateis* 1.45.6), while Origen speaks of an uneducated faith as intolerable (*Philocalia* 5.7; see *ANE* excerpt 191). Thus, the school of Alexandria strove to present a Christianity that was both philosophically tenable and apostolically faithful. Whether it succeeded or not has been a matter of some debate.

Give an account of the beginnings and purpose of the school of Alexandria.

CLEMENT OF ALEXANDRIA

Clement of Alexandria (not to be confused with the Apostolic Father known as Clement of Rome) was born into a pagan family in about AD150, probably in Athens. After his conversion to Christianity (the details of which are unknown) he was instructed by various Christian teachers, the last and best of whom was Pantaenus, head of the catechetical school in Alexandria (see above and *ANE* excerpt 157). When Pantaenus died in about AD190, Clement succeeded him as head of the school. He then left Alexandria due to the persecution under Septimius Severus in AD202/03 (see p186) and fled to Cappadocia in Asia Minor, where he died around AD215.

Three of Clement's writings have survived: *Protrepticus* ('Exhortation'), which exhorts pagans to become Christians; *Paedagogus* ('Tutor'), a sequel to

---

[1] van den Broek, Roelof *Studies in Gnosticism and Alexandrian Christianity*, Brill: Leiden, 1996

his first book which instructs new converts on Christian living; and *Stromateis* ('Carpets' or 'Miscellanies'), which is a collection of comments on various themes.

The *Protrepticus* is an apology, composed like a symphony, which criticises the perceived absurdities of pagan mythology and mystery religions (*ANE* excerpts 158-159). In *Paedagogus*, Christ is the *logos* (see p114) who trains and guides Christians. The first part of the book focuses on the importance of love, while in the remainder there is moral guidance on all kinds of issues. For instance, advice is given on the table manners of a guest – no gulping, spitting or wiping of the nose! The extremes of asceticism and materialism are to be avoided and the example of the *logos* must be followed (*ANE* excerpts 160-161). *Stromateis* is a complicated work of eight books. Like Justin before him, Clement states that just as the Law (ie the Old Testament) prepared the Jews for the coming of Christ, so philosophy had a similar role for the Greeks (*ANE* excerpt 162). In this book, Clement rejects the idea that sin is inherited from Adam and emphasises free will. Further, faith is but the foundation of the Christian life upon which knowledge (*gnosis*) is built. The move from paganism to faith must be followed by a change from faith to knowledge. Then the final stage is love (*ANE* excerpt 165). The spiritual Christian is a true Gnostic who does good, not out of fear or for reward, but out of love and for goodness' sake, and attains the highest degree of heavenly glory (*ANE* excerpts 163-164). In this work Clement also refers to the teaching of Basilides and Valentinus and argues that the rule of faith must be adhered to (*ANE* excerpts 59, 67 and 166).

Task

Outline the life and writings of Clement of Alexandria.

ORIGEN

Life

Eusebius is an important source of information for Origen's life (*ANE* excerpts 168-170, 172). While some of this information is based on oral tradition which may be unreliable hagiography, Eusebius also had access to over 100 of Origen's letters and refers at times to documentary evidence contemporary with Origen.

Origen was born in Alexandria around AD185 to parents who were Christians or who were soon to become so. However, the third century anti-Christian writer Porphyry, claims that Origen was born and bred as a pagan

(*ANE* excerpt 184). He died in Caesarea in Palestine by AD254 from injuries received in the Decian persecution (AD250/1). His father, Leonides, a centurion, who had encouraged him as a boy to memorise the Scriptures and read Greek classics, was martyred during the persecution of Septimius Severus in AD202/3. Origen, who was nearly seventeen, had written to him urging him to stand firm. A tradition reported by Eusebius, claims that as a teenager, Origen himself was saved from martyrdom when his mother hid his clothes to prevent him going outside! After his father's death the family was left in poverty. Origen, however, was supported by a wealthy lady who cared for him. This lady was an associate of an Antiochene heretic named Paul, with whom Origen would not pray. After his father's death, Origen applied himself to further study and teaching. According to Porphyry, Origen studied under Ammonius Saccas, a Platonist philosopher in Alexandria (*ANE* excerpt 184).

The persecution under Septimius Severus in AD202/3 not only claimed the life of Origen's father but also forced Clement away from Alexandria. His place as head of the catechetical school was filled by Origen, who was only eighteen; the appointment was made by the bishop Demetrius. He soon decided to teach Christianity exclusively and sold his library of pagan literature (but compare *ANE* excerpts 168 and 169). He lived an austere life of study and self-discipline with little sleep (he lay on the floor) or food or possessions, and spent some of his time visiting Christians in prison. Eusebius reports that at this early stage of his life Origen castrated himself so that he could more easily teach female catechumens. It is not certain if this is a reliable tradition, but at the end of his life Origen certainly criticises a literal interpretation of Jesus' words concerning those who make themselves eunuchs (Matthew 19: 12).

While in charge of the school at Alexandria, Origen also travelled to other parts to lecture and preach. He visited Rome in AD212, Arabia in AD215 and Caesarea, Palestine in AD216, where he delivered lectures in church at the request of the bishops. He had left Alexandria due to a massacre there under the emperor Caracalla. His bishop Demetrius ordered him back to Alexandria, protesting that it was not right for a layman to preach in the presence of bishops (*ANE* excerpt 170). To solve this problem, in about AD228 the bishops at Caesarea ordained Origen as a presbyter when he was on his way to deal with church problems in Greece (*ANE* excerpt 170). This created even more offence to Demetrius, especially since Origen had left without his permission. Further, as Origen's bishop, only he had the right to ordain him, and anyhow, the ordination of a eunuch was not permitted. It seems that Demetrius' actions were motivated somewhat by jealousy of Origen's ability and popularity. Once back home, synods, in turn, banished Origen and invalidated his ordination in AD231. Origen's excommunication was confirmed by Demetrius' successor and Origen then left for Caesarea (*ANE* excerpt 171). Around this time, such was his fame that he was invited by the mother of the emperor (Alexander Severus) to speak to her on Christian matters (*ANE* excerpt 172). In Caesarea he was invited to establish another catechetical school, where he taught for the remaining twenty years of his life.

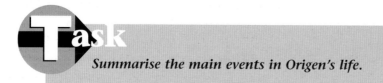

Summarise the main events in Origen's life.

Writings

Origen was a prolific writer from an early age. His impressive literary output was financed by Ambrose, a wealthy convert from Valentinian Gnosticism, who provided Origen with seven stenographers as well as copyists (*ANE* excerpts 169; 171 and note). However, only a minority of his many writings have survived. His apparent condemnation by the Second Council of Constantinople in 553 appears to have resulted in the destruction of much of his work. The situation is further complicated by the fact that little of what does survive has been preserved in the original Greek. Most of his existing work has come down to us in Latin translation. For example, of an original 574 homilies (sermons), 388 are lost, 166 are Latin translations and only 20 are in the original Greek. Further, Latin translations of his work were often paraphrastic rather than literal. His work was also edited to remove perceived heresy and to 'improve' its orthodoxy. Thus, when Rufinus translated Origen's *On First Principles* in the fifth century, Jerome made his own translation, accusing Rufinus of editing Origen's work in the interests of orthodoxy. However, lest we despair of having any accurate idea of what Origen himself actually wrote and taught, it appears from the Greek texts that do exist that we have a fairly clear picture of what the man himself believed.

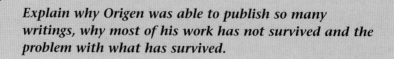

Explain why Origen was able to publish so many writings, why most of his work has not survived and the problem with what has survived.

We may classify his surviving writings into four broad categories for convenience.

i) Biblical writings

Origen was above all a biblical scholar who concentrated on the content and meaning of the biblical texts. His concern for having an accurate biblical text is evident in his massive *Hexapla* (Greek for 'sixfold') in which he set down six versions of the Old Testament in parallel columns for critical comparison. While only fragments of this work have survived it appears that the six columns were as follows. The first column contained the Hebrew text. Origen, unlike most early Fathers, made the effort to learn the original language of the Old Testament. This was followed by the Hebrew text in Greek letters (ie a transliteration), useful for those who did not know how to pronounce Hebrew and for churches who may have wanted the Old Testament read in Hebrew in their services, as in the synagogue. The remaining four columns were current Greek translations of the Old Testament: the first by Aquila in column three, Symmachus in column four, the Septuagint/LXX in column five and finally Theodotion's translation in column six. Origen's fifth column, the Septuagint, contains signs indicating differences from the original Hebrew text. In some books, especially the Psalms, other columns contained three further Greek versions. Origen also produced a similar work known as the *Tetrapla*, containing the four main Greek translations in the *Hexapla* (for Eusebius' comment on the *Hexapla* and *Tetrapla* see *ANE* excerpt 174; the note to this excerpt includes another view of the *Hexapla*'s content).

This work, unique in the early Church, reveals Origen as a pioneer of the textual criticism of the Bible, ie the comparison of copies and versions in an effort to establish the original text. Clearly Origen did not regard the Septuagint (often quoted in the New Testament) to be the sole, authoritative Old Testament Greek text. In his debates with Jewish rabbis Origen knew that there must be agreement on a common Old Testament text.

Origen also produced biblical *commentaries*, that is, detailed explanations of the content of biblical books. This for Origen was his main task – the exegesis or interpretation of the Bible. Unfortunately, many of his commentaries have not survived. Of 291 books of commentary only 16 remain, and no commentary has been entirely preserved. One of his earliest and largest commentaries was on John, though only 8 of its original 32 books remain (quoted in *ANE* excerpt 171). Origen considered John to be the best Gospel and tells us that while we begin by knowing Jesus as redeemer and physician we must go on to know him as John presents him – as life, light, truth and wisdom. His commentary on Romans (reduced from 15 to 10 books by Rufinus) referred extensively to the Old Testament to explain Jewish beliefs to his Gentile contemporaries. The commentary on Song of Songs, containing but four of the original ten books, is an example of the Alexandrian love for allegorical interpretation of the Bible (see above on Philo). Throughout the commentary the bridegroom and bride are viewed as Christ and the Church or as the logos and the soul of the individual Christian (see page 227 on Origen's allegorical interpretation of Scripture).

As well as the *Hexapla* and *commentaries*, Origen's many *homilies* or sermons may be included among his biblical writings. These sermons were preached mostly to churches in Caesarea, after his withdrawal from Alexandria. Though many have been lost, those that remain – such as his homilies on Genesis, Numbers, Joshua, Psalms, Jeremiah, Ezekiel and Luke – give us an insight into Origen's mystical and spiritual approach to the Bible, as well as his homiletical ability and pastoral sensitivity (*ANE* excerpts 80, 180, 183: note; 191). Finally, Origen also wrote *scholia* (brief exegetical notes) on various Bible passages in Exodus, Leviticus, Isaiah, Psalms 1-15, Ecclesiastes and John's Gospel (so Jerome, *Epistle* 33) but none has fully survived.

Tasks

a. Describe the four sub-categories of Origen's biblical writings, providing an example for each.

b. Outline the contents of the Hexapla *and comment on its significance among early Christian writings.*

ii) Theological writings

Origen's main theological writing (ie writing concerned with Christian teachings and doctrines) is his *On First Principles* (*De Principiis/Peri Archon*), which mostly survives in a paraphrastic translation by Rufinus and a few Greek fragments. It was written primarily against Gnosticism and is sometimes referred to as the first Christian 'systematic theology'. However, it is also regarded as an exploratory rather than a dogmatic work, in which Origen investigates theological issues in a sometimes open-ended way.

In four books, *On First Principles* deals broadly with God, the world, humanity and Scripture. Origen begins with the summary of apostolic teaching handed down in the tradition of the Church as the rule of faith. Only teachings which agree with this are to be believed. However, the spiritually gifted will explore and speculate concerning the grounds of these elementary teachings (*ANE* excerpt 175). As well as dealing with the being and character of God, the first book covers, among other things, the nature of angels, the resurrection body and the final judgement. The second book relates to the creation of the world and here Origen rejects Gnostic teaching concerning the inferiority of the Creator God as distinct from the Father of Jesus. Other themes explored include the Holy Spirit, the soul and last things. Book three deals with human freedom, biblical history and philosophy, among other topics. The fourth and final book of *On First Principles* focuses on the divine inspiration and meaning of the Scriptures.

We may also include among his theological works his *Dialogue with Heraclides*, discovered in Egypt in 1941, in which he deals with the doctrines of the Trinity and the soul. The work is an account of the minutes of a church council in which Origen was invited to refute the errors of Bishop Heraclides.

iii) Apologetic writing

Around AD248 Origen's patron Ambrose persuaded him to write a reply to a work entitled *The True Discourse* (its Greek title is variously translated) that had been written in the late AD170s by a Platonist anti-Christian called Celsus. The contents of this work are known to us only because Origen preserved most of it in his reply, *Against Celsus* (*Contra Celsum*). Fortunately, the eight books of *Against Celsus* have been preserved for us in the original Greek.

In the first two books Celsus objects to Christianity on various grounds claiming that it is an illegal, secret, irrational, demonic religion based on blind faith. As a literary device he expresses various objections using the persona of a Jew through whom he criticises Jesus and Jewish Christians. It is claimed that Jesus was born immorally, learned sorcery in Egypt, proclaimed himself as God and that his lowly life was unworthy of God. Jewish Christians (book 2) have been deceived by Jesus to leave the faith of their ancestors and have believed the tale of Jesus' resurrection, based on the unreliable testimony of a few people. Origen responds to Celsus' objections by, for example, noting that sorcerers do not call people to a moral life and that the reality of the resurrection is confirmed by the moral transformation of the apostles.

Book 3 includes Celsus' criticisms of Christianity as a religion divided into various sects, whose adherents are mostly people of low class and little intelligence, many of whom were formerly immoral. Origen replies that philosophy too is divided into different branches, that Christianity does seek to address the intelligent but must also meet the needs of the uneducated and that most Christians had been respectable people who wanted to improve, while others had been morally transformed.

In books 4 and 5 Celsus objects to the incarnation. If God came down then he left his own dwelling place. Also, why did he not come much sooner to save humans? Further, the Old Testament's account of God's acts are so embarrassing and incredible that Jews and Christians resort to allegorical interpretation of the Scriptures. Again, God's concern with the Jews rather than other nations demonstrates that Christianity is not a universal faith. Origen responds that the incarnation demonstrates the love of God in taking human nature to raise it to himself and that the Jews believe in one God to whom all have access.

Celsus' arguments that Christianity had borrowed from the superior culture and philosophy of the Greeks and that Christians are not loyal citizens of the Empire are dealt with in the remaining books of *Against Celsus*. Origen replies that the Scriptures are superior to the writings of the philosophers and that Christians are loyal citizens, but not to the point of compromising their faith (see *ANE* excerpts 110-117 for examples of Celsus' criticism of Christianity; excerpts 185-190 are also from *Against Celsus*).

iv) Devotional writings

On Prayer and *Exhortation to Martyrdom* were written in Caesarea after Origen's move from Alexandria. *On Prayer* is dedicated to his patron Ambrose and a certain Tatiana, who had asked for instruction on the subject. Origen deals with the necessity, benefits, types and manner of prayer, as well as providing a commentary on the Lord's Prayer. The book argues for the effectiveness of prayer against a fatalistic predeterminism which regarded prayer as pointless.

Exhortation to Martyrdom is addressed again to Ambrose but also to a certain Protoctetus, during the persecution under the reign of Maximin (AD235-238). Origen wrote as one whose own father had been martyred in AD202 and who would be martyred himself in the AD250s. He warns his readers against idolatry and apostasy and tells them that their conflict is observed by God, the angels and the demons, as well as by humans. They must stand firm, inspired by the example of previous martyrs, and as priests, offer themselves in sacrifice to God.

Task

Give examples of Origen's theological, apologetic and devotional writings, providing a brief account of each example.

Theology

We have seen that right at the beginning of his main theological writing, *On First Principles,* Origen outlines the main beliefs of the Church in its rule of faith. This apostolic tradition of the Church is the standard by which all beliefs must be judged. However, in Origen's view, these were but foundational teachings. While they might satisfy the simple and ordinary believer, the spiritually gifted and able Christian will advance beyond the elementary truths to investigate and explore further (*ANE* excerpt 175). This willingness to speculate beyond the rule of faith meant that Origen's teaching became controversial for many with a more conservative attitude to theology and resulted in his condemnation in later times.

i) Scripture

At the beginning of the fourth book of *On First Principles* Origen refers to "the divine Scriptures both of the Old Testament as they say, and of the New, as it is called". As well as accepting the authority of the Old Testament books recognised by the Jews (Eusebius, *Hist Eccl* 6.16.1-17.1), he also frequently made use of the Apocrypha (additional books in the Greek Old Testament). He referred to all the twenty-seven books that are now in the New Testament, twenty-one of which he says are undisputed but six of which are doubtful (Hebrews, 2 Peter, 2 and 3 John, James and Jude). His belief in the inspiration and authority of the Scriptures is apparent in his many 'biblical' writings – the *Hexapla*, commentaries, homilies and scholia.

We have seen too that Origen interpreted the Bible allegorically, regarding the literal, plain message of the text as also containing higher spiritual significance. In this he was following in the tradition of various writers who sought to make texts more acceptable by interpreting them metaphorically, such as the Stoics did with Homer and Philo of Alexandria with the Old Testament. Thus, for example, viewing the wars against the Canaanites in the book of Joshua as morally inconsistent with Christianity, Origen interpreted them allegorically as representing spiritual warfare (*ANE* excerpts 182,183 and notes). Origen in fact considered that biblical texts had three levels of meaning, corresponding to the three parts of the human constitution (*ANE* excerpt 181). The *body* of the text is its literal meaning for simple believers, the *soul* is its moral lesson for the more mature believer, and the *spirit* is its spiritual or mystical teaching for the spiritually perfect believer. However, JND Kelly observes that in practice Origen appears to have used another threefold scheme of interpretation – biblical texts have historical, typological and spiritual meanings. Thus, when the Psalmist says (Psalm 3: 4) that the Lord lifts up his head, the reference is , according to Origen, firstly to David, then to Christ (vindicated by God) and finally to the Christian who enjoys glory through being united with Christ[1].

Task

Discuss Origen's allegorical interpretation of the Bible, commenting on its origins and providing illustrative examples.

ii) The Trinity

Origen held that God is a single (ie not compounded), immaterial (ie not physical), incomprehensible (ie beyond understanding), intellectual being. As regards God's omnipotence and impassibility, Origen is ambiguous. Thus he refers both to God's unlimited and limited power (*On First Principles* 2.9.1; 4.4.8; *Against Celsus* 5.23), and he affirms both that in Scripture God has feelings (such as pity) and that such passages must be understood metaphorically, since the divine nature is free from affection and change (*Homilies on Ezekiel* 6.6 and *On Numbers* 33.2).

In his summary of the rule of faith Origen affirmed that the Son is also God and that the Spirit is united with the Father and the Son in honour and dignity. However, Origen also taught that the Son is lesser than the Father and that the Spirit is lesser than the Son (*ANE* excerpt 177). Thus for Origen there is a hierarchy within the Trinity. Though the Son has always existed along with the Father, eternally generated/begotten by him (*ANE* excerpt 180), he is subordinate to the Father. He is a secondary God (*ANE* excerpt 177) and not the only true God (*Commentary on John* 2.2.16; 2.10.75). Indeed, prayer should be addressed to the Father alone and not to the Son (*On Prayer* 15). The Spirit is lower in rank to the Son and, unlike the Son, has not always existed. Indeed, it was through the Son (the logos) that the Spirit came into being – "... there are really three persons, the Father, the Son and the Holy Spirit ... only the Father is unbegotten; ... all things came into being through the logos ... of all these things the Holy Spirit is the most honourable ..." (*Commentary on John* 2.10.75; *ANE* excerpt 175, note 4).

---

1 Kelly, JND *Early Christian Doctrines*, A&C Black: London, 1977, p73

Summarise Origen's teaching concerning God in general and the Trinity in particular.

iii) Creation

Origen reasoned that God has been eternally creative and did not begin to create when he made this physical world. God was ruling over an eternal realm of rational beings before he made our world. Just as there will be another world after the present one, so previous worlds have also existed (*On First Principles* 1.2.10; 3.5.3). The physical world and indeed all things were created by God through his logos.

iv) Humanity

In the pre-cosmic world rational beings freely chose to rebel against God at the instigation of the Devil. Depending on the extent of their sin, some became archangels, angels, humans or demons. The present world was created for those rebels who became humans, their pre-existing souls now bound to flesh as a punishment. Restored rational beings are freed from evil and from their bodies to return to their previous state. This cycle of fall and restoration continues due to the existence of previous and prospective worlds (*ANE* excerpts 176 and 178).

Such an understanding of the origin of human beings and of sin required Origen to allegorise the story of Adam's fall in Eden so that human rebellion occurred before the creation of this world. God's clothing of Adam and Eve with 'garments of skin' symbolises the bodies to which the fallen beings were joined, as a punishment for their revolt (*Against Celsus* 4.37-40). However, the body itself (contrary to Gnostic teaching) is not evil (*Against Celsus* 3.42). Yet, despite his allegorising of the Genesis passage, Origen, in his *Commentary on Romans*, seems to regard human sin as an inheritance from Adam (5.4f). Sin is due also to the misuse of free will and to demonic influence (*ANE* excerpt 175).

Briefly describe Origen's teaching on creation and the origin of evil.

229

v) Salvation

The salvation of the human race required the incarnation of God's Son, the logos (*Commentary on John* 1.20). The soul of Jesus pre-existed with all other souls and remained with the logos while the others fell away. United with the logos this soul was also united with real flesh in the virgin's womb by the Holy Spirit (*On First Principles* 2.6). Thus the divine logos, possessing both body and soul, came to save human nature in its entirety (*Dialogue with Heraclides* 7).

Fallen human beings are restored through fellowship with the logos, our model and pattern, into whose likeness we are changed and share in the divine being (*Against Celsus* 1.68; 8.17; *On First Principles* 4.4.4). The union of the divine and the human in Jesus results in human nature becoming divine not only in Jesus but also in those who believe in him and obey his commands (*Against Celsus* 3.28).

However, salvation depends not only on the incarnation but also on the crucifixion. For Origen, the death of Jesus, which did not affect the logos (*Against Celsus* 4.15; *On First Principles* 2.6.3), was the conquest of the Devil (*Against Celsus* 7.17). Indeed, Jesus' death was a ransom paid to the Devil for the release of human souls. However, neither the Devil nor death could keep hold of Jesus (*Comm on Matthew* 16.8; 12.28). Jesus' death is also a sacrifice for sin offered on behalf of all rational beings, by which God is propitiated (appeased) and favourably disposed to sinners (*Comm on Romans* 3.8; *Hom on Numbers* 24.1; *Comm on John* 1.40). Origen, however, held that the sacrifice of Christian martyrs also atoned for the sins of believers (*Hom on Numbers* 14.1; *Exhortation to Martyrdom* 30). Finally, we may note that, in Origen, God also restores fallen beings through the sanctifying work of the Spirit in moral renewal (*On First Principles* 1.3.7,8).

Tasks

a. Describe Origen's teaching on the incarnation.

b. In Origen's view, how are fallen beings restored to God?

vi) The Church

The Church as a visible, earthly community is 'the assembly of believers', 'the city of God' and 'the body of Christ', of which Christians are members (*Hom on Exodus* 9.3; *Hom on Jeremiah* 9.2; *Against Celsus* 6.48). While the members of this Church may not be real believers (*Hom on Jeremiah* 20.3;

Comm on Matthew 12.12), the saints belong to the true and heavenly Church which has existed since before the creation of the world (*On Prayer* 20.1; *Comm on the Song* of Songs 2). Outside of the visible Church there is no salvation (*Hom on Joshua* 3.5).

In the Church's sacrament of baptism there is forgiveness of sins, liberation from the Devil and admission to membership of the Church (*Exhortation to Martyrdom* 30; *Hom on Exodus* 5.5; *Comm on Romans* 8.5). In those not baptised as infants there must be repentance and faith (*Hom on Leviticus* 6.2; on *Luke* 21; on *Exodus* 10.4). The baptised participate in Christ's death and resurrection (*Hom on Jeremiah* 19.14) and also receive the Spirit in the sacrament (*On First Principles* 2.10.7). However, sometimes Origen locates the gift of the Spirit in a post-baptismal laying on of hands (*On First Principles* 1.3.7).

In the Eucharist the Christian receives Christ's body and blood and therefore the consecrated bread and wine must be treated with reverence (*Hom on Jeremiah* 19.13; *Exodus* 13.3). It is not the bread itself, though, which sanctifies but rather the word spoken over it, while its benefit depends on a pure mind and a clear conscience (*Comm on Matthew* 11.14). Beyond the elements, and more important, is the logos, the true nourishment of the Christian. The general view of the Eucharist is for simpler Christians, while the profound Christian is nourished by the logos and his teaching, symbolised in the bread and the wine (*Comm on John* 32.24; *On Prayer* 27.1-5). The Eucharist is also a sacrifice of propitiation in that it disposes God favourably towards those for whom it is offered (*Hom on Leviticus* 13.3). As for the discipline of the Church, penance is granted only once for serious post-baptismal sins, though sins such as idolatry and adultery are unforgivable (*Hom on Leviticus* 15; *On Prayer* 28; see also *ANE* excerpt 188).

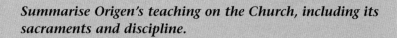

Task

Summarise Origen's teaching on the Church, including its sacraments and discipline.

vii) The Last Things

In his summary of the Church's rule of faith, Origen affirms that each soul will obtain eternal life or pass into eternal torment, depending on the deeds it has performed (*ANE* excerpt 175). The bodies of Christians will be resurrected as spiritual bodies, appropriate to the heavenly kingdom of God

(*Against Celsus* 7.32; *On First Principles* 3.6.6). There appears to be an intermediate state before the return of Christ and the final judgement, in which souls are prepared for their final destiny (*On First Principles* 2.11.6). Ultimately, there will be a final restoration of all things, even of the Devil himself, to God and to the original state. The restoration is viewed as a gradual process with endless rational beings in successive worlds progressing through purification at different stages (*On First Principles* 1.6.2,3; 3.6.3; *ANE* excerpt 179).

Task

What aspects of Origen's eschatology (teaching on the last things) would have proved controversial for the early Church?

Legacy

During and after his life-time, Origen was both praised and criticised for his theology. His belief that, while remaining faithful to the apostolic rule of faith, the mature Christian is free to speculate and explore beyond it, resulted in a mixture of orthodoxy and heresy in his own theology. Certainly, Origen regarded himself as true to the teaching of the Catholic Church (*Hom on: Joshua* 7.6; *Luke* 16.6). One of his students, Gregory Thaumaturgus, wrote in praise of him (*The Oration and Panegyric addressed to Origen*). In Caesarea, Pamphilus (AD240-309) copied most of his writings and wrote an *Apology* in his defence, as did his more famous pupil, Eusebius. In the fourth century, two Cappadocian fathers – Basil of Caesarea and Gregory of Nazianzus – produced a collection of Origen's sayings (the *Philocalia*).

However, Origen did have his opponents. In the third century, Methodius of Olympus criticised his speculations concerning pre-cosmic falls and also his allegorical interpretation of the Genesis account of Adam's fall. He also opposed what he viewed as Origen's denial of a real bodily resurrection. Opposition came also in the fourth century from Eustathius of Antioch and Epiphanius of Salamis. The latter contended that Origen had corrupted the Church's faith under the influence of Greek culture. Epiphanius, and later Jerome and the emperor Justinian, perceived Origen as a heretic who deliberately added orthodox teaching to his writings to make them acceptable. The difficulty that Origen's teachings presented may be seen in the bitter controversy between two fifth century translators of his *On First Principles*. Rufinus, as we have noted, was accused by Jerome of editing Origen's work to make it more theologically orthodox. Again, details of the life of the early Christian monk Pachomius (about AD292-346) have come down to us in a

Greek tradition in which Origen is condemned by the monk and in a primary Coptic tradition which has no such condemnation.

Certainly it appears that Origen's Platonist philosophy influenced certain aspects of his theology such as his (inconsistent) views on the impassibility of God and his understanding of salvation as deification (becoming divine), as well as his lack of interest in the historical character of Christianity. His speculations about pre-cosmic falls and the final restoration of all things (universalism) were problematic for more conservative Fathers. His subordinationist Christology was later developed further by Arius in Alexandria, who argued that the Son was not truly God (see previous chapter). While Origen's allegorical interpretation of the Bible was part of a wider Alexandrian tradition, it had its critics among fathers in the Antiochene tradition (such as Diodore of Tarsus and Theodore of Mopsuestia), who favoured a more literal interpretation of the Bible. Origen was finally condemned as heretical at the Second Council of Constantinople in AD553.

Yet, Origen was one of the first scholars and intellectuals in the Church. He sought to provide an intelligent orthodoxy before philosophically minded pagans and against Gnostic versions of Christianity. However, in this task he undoubtedly went beyond the boundaries of traditional orthodoxy as laid down in the rule of faith. There is no denying his immense contribution as a biblical scholar (the *Hexapla*), exegete (*Commentaries*, *Homilies*, *Scholia*), theologian (*On First Principles*, the first systematic theology) and Apologist (*Against Celsus*). His influence on the theology and spirituality of the Eastern Church would remain for centuries to come. Ultimately, Origen symbolises the challenge inherent in the task of Christian theology in every age, as it seeks to remain faithful to its apostolic heritage, while at the same time communicating its message meaningfully in contemporary thought forms.

Practice Essay Titles

1. *Describe the origins and purpose of the School of Alexandria. (30)*

   Evaluate the claim that it did not remain true to the Church's rule of faith. (15)

2. *Outline the life and writings of Origen. (30)*

   Assess his contribution to the development of the early Church. (15)

Cyprian, Bishop of Carthage

Andre Thevet *Les Vrais Portraits et Vies des Hommes Illustres*, 1584

A2 level Latin Christian Literature

The beginnings of Latin Christian literature.
Tertullian and Cyprian.

(CCEA Specification)

Objective

In this chapter we shall gain a knowledge and understanding of the first Latin Christian writings through a study of Tertullian and Cyprian.

LATIN CHRISTIANITY

THE EARLIEST EVIDENCE OF Latin Christianity appears in the late second century in Carthage (modern Tunis), North Africa, the home of Tertullian, the first important Latin Christian author. After its conquest by the Romans in 146 BC, Carthage became a Roman colony with a dominant Latin culture. Commercially and culturally the city maintained close links with Rome, directly northwards across the Mediterranean. Before Tertullian's writings at the end of the second century, the only Latin Christian literature is the Old Latin Bible and the account of the martyrs of Scilli, North Africa, in AD180 (*ANE* excerpt 24; see p86). But, Tertullian was 'the first to make Jesus Christ speak Latin'[1]. As we shall see, it was Tertullian who introduced Latin terms which became important in the eventual formulation of the doctrine of the Trinity – including the word 'trinity' itself!

Latin (Western) and Greek (Eastern) Christianity developed different theological traditions and perspectives due to their distinct linguistic, cultural and philosophical histories. In our previous chapter we observed that in Alexandria, further east along the coast from Carthage, writers like Clement

---

[1] David Wright in *The Early Christian World*, Vol 2 Ed Philip Esler, ch 33, Routledge: London, 2000, p1030

and Origen produced a speculative and mystical theology under the influence of Platonism. However, theologians in Carthage, such as Tertullian and Cyprian, produced a more conservative and pragmatic, even legalistic, theology under the influence of Stoicism. Faithfulness to the apostolic tradition of the Church was important and they were therefore critical of any speculative theologising which moved beyond this.

Tasks

a. Outline the evidence for the beginnings of Latin Christianity.

b. Describe the differences of perspective between Latin and Greek theology.

TERTULLIAN

Life

Despite his status as the first important Latin Christian writer and his impressive literary output, we know next to nothing with any certainty about the life of Quintus Septimius Florens Tertullianus. Outlines of his life are often based on risky inferences from his writings and on the scanty, unreliable information produced by Jerome (*On Famous Men*) nearly two centuries after his death. Thus it is unlikely, if not impossible, that he was the son of a centurion or a presbyter in the church at Carthage. Further, there is no firm evidence that he trained as a lawyer or went to Rome.

However, it is safe to deduce from his writings that he received a good education, including being trained in rhetoric – the skillful and persuasive use of classical literature, especially Plato. It is not clear how and when he became a Christian. He may have been impressed by Christian morality or by the courage of Christian martyrs such as the Scillians who were executed at Carthage in AD180. Whatever the cause, by the mid AD190s he was writing Christian literature and was married to a Christian.

Around AD206 (it is impossible to be specific) Tertullian became a supporter of the New Prophecy of Montanism, though it is uncertain if he parted company with the Catholic Church. The so-called 'Tertullianists' of Carthage, known to Augustine in the early fifth century, were probably adherents of Montanism rather than a schismatic sect formed by Tertullian himself. That his writings were preserved, including their Montanist sympathies, would suggest that there was no breach with the church in Carthage. Certainly writings from his Montanist period (see below) are increasingly critical of the Church, not least for its perceived moral laxity. Such a stance, as well as his Montanist leanings, no doubt accounts for the fact that he was never canonised. The year of his death (and indeed of his birth) is unknown, but he was still writing around AD212. It appears then that he was active as a Christian writer in the closing decade of the second century and in the opening decade or so of the third century.

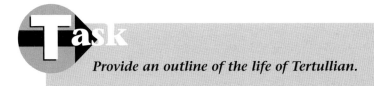

Task

Provide an outline of the life of Tertullian.

Writings

Readers of Tertullian have been impressed by his fresh, direct, rhetorical writing style as well as by his theological discussions. In the early fifth century Vincent of Lerins commented that the logic of his arguments was persuasive even when it failed to convince and added, 'Almost every word was an epigram and every statement a victory' (*Commonitorium* 18). His writings abound with memorable phrases and quotable statements. While his Greek writings have not survived, over thirty of his works have come down to us. It is possible to classify his works chronologically as pre-Montanist and Montanist, but it is more meaningful to categorise them according to their genre or literary type. Broadly, the works can be divided into three main groups: apologetic writings, anti-heretical or polemical writings, and moral writings.

i) Apologetic writings

Tertullian's *Apology* was one of his earliest works, written around AD197. It was addressed to provincial governors and specifically to the magistrates in Carthage. Continuing the work of earlier second century Apologists such as Justin (see chapter 8, p105), it sought to defend Christianity against imperial persecution and popular slander. Tertullian takes the role of an advocate, acting both as counsel for the defence of Christians and as counsel for the prosecution of pagans.

In the *Apology* Tertullian argues that it is unfair for Christianity to be condemned merely for the name 'Christian', when it has not been properly investigated. The innocence of Christians is seen in how their behaviour contrasts with criminals (*ANE* excerpt 133). Only the worst emperors, such as Nero and Domitian, have persecuted Christians, while good ones have been kind to them (*ANE* excerpt 135). Neither are Christians guilty of secret crimes alleged against them such as infanticide, cannibalism and incest (see pp74, 75). If pagans find such things repulsive why should not Christians also, since both share a common humanity? Further, Christians are not irreligious since they worship the true God. Pagan images are human creations which ironically suffer the same treatment in their manufacture as pagans inflict on Christians! The human soul itself bears witness to the living God (*ANE* excerpt 137). Tertullian, using the rhetorical device 'retorsio', turns this charge upon his opponents' heads – by rejecting the true God and worshipping deified humans it is the pagans who are irreligious. This is demonstrated too by their refusal to allow freedom of worship.

Tertullian also rejects the charge that Christians are disloyal citizens. Rather, Christians pray for the well-being of the emperor and of the Empire, which in effect is delaying the coming of God's judgement. In a new move in second century Christian apologetics, Tertullian states that Christians respect the emperor since God has put him in power – 'Caesar is more ours than yours, for it is our God who has appointed him ' (*ANE* excerpt 139). Indeed, if Christians wanted to rise up against the Empire their vast numbers would enable them to do so – 'We are but of yesterday and we have filled everything you have …' (*ANE* excerpt 140). Nor are Christian worship services immoral, since they are convened for worthy reasons (*ANE* excerpt 141). Tertullian protests too that Christians are blamed for natural disasters which occurred before Christians ever existed. On the occurrence of such events the pagan cry is heard, 'The Christians to the lion!' and Tertullian sarcastically adds, 'What, so many of them to one lion?' (*ANE* excerpt 135).

The inconsistency of the authorities is exposed in that while Christianity is treated as a philosophy it is not granted the freedom that philosophers enjoy. However, ironically, the cruel persecution of the Christians increases their numbers, since pagan onlookers are moved to enquire what motivates the steadfastness of its victims – 'The more you mow us down, the more we grow. The blood of Christians is seed.' (*Apology* 50.13).

Similar to the *Apology* is Tertullian's *To the Nations*, which, unlike the former, is addressed to the public in general. Possibly a first draft of the *Apology*, its first book protests that Christians are unfairly tried and falsely accused of crimes such as incest by those who are not aware of their beliefs (3: 'no name of a crime stands against us but only the crime of a name'). In its second book Tertullian ridicules pagan gods as merely deified human beings. *To Scapula*, possibly Tertullian's last surviving writing, was addressed to a persecuting governor in Africa in AD212, recalling God's judgement on former persecutors and informing the governor of the difficulties he might face because of Christian eagerness for martyrdom (*ANE* excerpt 136). Tertullian argues for religious liberty – 'it is assuredly no part of religion to compel religion.' (2). *On the Testimony of the Soul* is also an apologetic writing, developing a theme contained in the *Apology* that the soul is a natural witness to the God of Christian faith (see above).

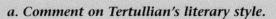

Tasks

> *a. Comment on Tertullian's literary style.*
>
> *b. Name his apologetic writings and give an account of his apologetic arguments.*

ii) Anti-heretical/polemical writings

Tertullian's *On the Prescription of Heretics*, written around AD200, is a general anti-heretical writing as distinct from his works written against specific heretics (see below). The word 'prescription' (Latin: *praescriptio*) in the title has been understood as a legal term in which a limit is placed on the debate before it begins, namely, the heretics can make no appeal to the Scriptures since, being Church writings, they have no right to them. Thus:

> *… not being Christians they have no right to the Christian Scriptures … Since you are none of mine, what are you doing on my property? Indeed, Marcion, what right have you to chop my wood? With whose permission, Valentinus, are you diverting my streams? By what power, Apelles, are you removing my landmarks? This is my property … I am the heir of the apostles.*

> (ANE *excerpt 147*).

Tertullian concludes the book with a reflection on his task by stating that heretics must be debarred from any discussion of the Scriptures.

In the *Prescription*, Tertullian argues that heresy originates from philosophy (despite his own indebtedness to Stoicism!) – 'What then has Athens to do with Jerusalem? What has the Academy to do with the Church? What have heretics to do with Christians?' (*ANE* excerpt 145). The Church must hold to its rule of faith and not go beyond it (*ANE* excerpt 143). The truth is found in the churches founded by the apostles, where their teaching has been faithfully preserved (*ANE* excerpts 142, 144). Indeed, the Church pre-dates the heretics (*ANE* excerpt 73). Tertullian also referred to the lack of proper church order and discipline among heretics (*ANE* excerpt 148).

Tertullian concluded his *Prescription* by promising to deal in the future with individual heresies and a number of such works have come down to us. His five-volume *Against Marcion* was his longest work (see chapter on Heresies for details of this book and *ANE* excerpts 74, 76, 77). *Against Hermogenes* was directed against a local Gnostic who held that matter was eternal, while *Against the Valentinians* dealt with the Egyptian Gnostic Valentinus and varieties of his teaching (see chapter on Heresies and *ANE* excerpt 61).

On the Flesh of Christ and *On the Resurrection of the Flesh* reject Gnostic denials of the reality of Jesus' human nature (docetism) and of the resurrection of the body. In his long work *On the Soul* Tertullian refutes philosophical and Gnostic ideas such as the pre-existence souls. He argues that the soul is inherited from one's parents (traducianism) and that it is material (*ANE* excerpt 153). In *Scorpiace* ('Antidote to the Scorpion's Sting') the scorpion is heresy and the antidote is biblical teaching summarised in the rule of faith. *On Baptism* was written in response to a Gnostic attack on the rite and rejects heretical baptism as well as infant baptism (see pp12-14 and *ANE* excerpt 151).

Finally, *Against Praxeas* is one of Tertullian's most important anti-heretical works, written about AD212 in his Montanist period. Praxeas is condemned for managing 'two pieces of the Devil's business' at Rome – 'he put to fight the Paraclete and crucified the Father' (*ANE* excerpt 146). That is, he rejected Montanist claims to be inspired by the Spirit (the Paraclete; see chapter on Heresies) and he also denied any real distinctions between the Father, the Son and the Holy Spirit, whom he regarded as temporary modes of the one God (later called 'modalism'). Tertullian replied by arguing that in God there is one divine nature (*substantia*) but also three distinct persons (*personae*), forming the trinity (*trinitas*). With the introduction of these terms Tertullian laid the foundations for later classical definitions of the doctrine of the Trinity. The polemical work *Against the Jews* defends Christian understanding of Old Testament prophecy. However, some scholars doubt that it is a genuine work of Tertullian.

Tasks

a. **Comment on the meaning of 'Prescription' in Tertullian's** On the Prescription of Heretics *and outline his arguments in this writing.*

b. **Provide a summary of** Against Marcion *(see chapter on Heresy, pp174, 176).*

c. **Discuss the origins and importance of** Against Praxeas.

d. **Provide brief notes on Tertullian's other anti-heretical writings.**

iii) Moral writings

Finally, a significant number of Tertullian's writings are concerned with moral behaviour and Church discipline. They are usually divided into pre-Montanist and Montanist writings, the latter works (from around AD206) displaying an intensification of the moral strictness of his pre-Montanist writings (see pp132-134).

Thus, while in *On Repentance* he permitted one opportunity for repentance from serious post-baptismal sins, in his Montanist *On Modesty* he criticised a bishop for permitting the same opportunity (*ANE* excerpts 152 and 154). Further, in the latter book he rejected the practice of martyrs bestowing forgiveness on fellow Christians, in contrast to his pre-Montanist *To the Martyrs* which encouraged steadfastness in persecution, and appears to favour the practice. Again, while in his pre-Montanist writings *To My Wife* (1.3.4) and *On Patience* (13.6) he approved of fleeing from persecution, in his Montanist *On Flight in Persecution* he forbids it, stating that Jesus' permission of it (Matthew 10: 23) was only for his original audience (6.2; 9.4). We may note too that while in *To My Wife* Tertullian permits his wife to remarry after his death (Bk.2), in his Montanist *On Monogamy* he regards the remarriage of widows as a sin amounting to bigamy (10; 15), basing his argument on Scripture but also on new revelation by the Holy Spirit (2.2; 3.9). The same opposition to second marriages is found in his Montanist *On the Exhortation to Chastity*.

In the Montanist *On the Veiling of Virgins* Tertullian discusses Paul's treatment of the issue (1 Corinthians 11: 1-16) and argues that all females (apart from young girls) should be veiled at all times, appealing again to the new standard of discipline introduced by the Paraclete (1.4,5,7). He deals with female attire in *On Women's Dress* and complains about the vanity of hair dye, cosmetics and jewellery. Rather, women should adorn themselves with the Christian cosmetics of simplicity and modesty – 'painting your eyes with shyness and your lips with silence, fixing in your ears the Word of God, putting on your neck the yoke of Christ ... Dress yourselves with the silk of honesty, the linen of holiness, the purple of modesty. Arrayed like this you will have God as your lover.' (2.13.7).

In relation to pagan society Tertullian condemns shows and games in the arena as unworthy of Christians – "... the world is God's, but the worldly is the Devil's" (*On Shows* 15). The greatest show will be the day of judgement. Participation in family celebrations is acceptable, unless pagan sacrifice is required. Christians may not be teachers or soldiers because of the pagan rituals involved in such professions. A similar theme is developed in *On the Crown* and in *On Idolatry*. In the latter he condemns other professions involving idolatry as unsuitable for Christians, such as astrology – "Some

241

astrologer you are if you didn't know that you would become a Christian!" (9.8). The mysterious work *On the Philosopher's Cloak* (*De pallio*) has been variously interpreted as a defence of the compatibility of philosophy and Christianity (a view which does not sit easily with statements in his *Prescription*; see above) and conversely, as a rejection of Roman vices. Finally, we may note *On Prayer*, which includes the earliest commentary on the Lord's Prayer and guidance on the practicalities of praying, and *On Fasting*, a Montanist defence of self-denial in contrast to the indulgent behaviour of Catholic Christians.

Task

Provide brief notes on Tertullian's moral writings, giving examples of how his Montanist writings are characterised by greater strictness.

Theology

i) The Trinity

Under the influence of Stoicism, Tertullian believed that, though God was spirit, he was also in some sense material and substantial (*Against Praxeas* 7). As we have noted, in *Against Praxeas* Tertullian rejected the view that the Father, Son and Spirit are not distinct persons but temporary manifestations of the one God (modalism). While there is a 'unity of substance' between the three persons, and the Son and Spirit 'share in the substance of the Father' (*Against Praxeas* 2, 3), still there are three distinct 'persons' who must not be confused (*Against Praxeas* 11, 12). Tertullian was the first to use the word 'trinity' (*trinitas*; eg *Against Praxeas* 3) and employed it to refer to three distinct persons (*personae*) in the one divine substance (*substantia*).

However, this threefold nature of God only became apparent at creation and in redemption (the 'dispensation' or 'economy'), when God's Son, who had existed with God as his Reason, came forth from him, and when the Spirit was sent by the Son from the Father. At that time the unity was distributed into a trinity of three persons (*Against Praxeas* 2, 5). Thus, the Father, Son and Spirit are respectively like the root, shoot and fruit of a tree, or the spring, river and canal, or the sun, ray and point of focus (*Against Praxeas* 8).

ii) Humanity

As we have seen, Tertullian held that the human soul is material, again due to the influence of Stoicism. As to the origin of the soul, it is derived from one's parents (*On the Soul* 27). And each soul has inherited sin from Adam, rendering it unclean (*Against Marcion* 1. 22; *On the Soul* 40).

iii) Salvation

To secure our salvation from sin, the Word became human, body and soul, in the womb of the virgin (*Against Praxeas* 26; *On the Flesh of Christ* 10-13). God lived on the human level that humans might live on the divine level (*Against Marcion* 2.27). Combining God and man in himself (*Against Marcion* 2.27), Jesus consisted of two 'substances' (*On the Flesh of Christ* 18), each with distinctive properties and functions. Thus, while his human nature suffered and died, his divine nature performed miracles (*Against Praxeas* 27).

While Christ's death is seen as a sacrifice for sin by Tertullian (*Against the Jews* 13; *Scorpiace* 7), he does not develop this teaching. Rather Christ is seen more as a teacher who enlightens humanity (*Apology* 21). 'Satisfaction' (ie reparation) is made not by Christ's death but by repentance and good deeds, which merit God's favour (*On Repentance* 5; *On Fasting* 3).

iv) The Church

In his pre-Montanist writings Tertullian appears to have held to the Catholic concept of the Church as a hierarchical institution, founded by the apostles and governed by their successors, the bishops (see page 239, under 'Anti-Heretical Writings'). The Church was the Mother of believers (*Against Marcion* 4.11) and outside of her there were no valid ministries or sacraments, no true Christianity (*On Baptism* 1.15). However, in his Montanist period he viewed the Church as a spiritual and charismatic community – the Church indeed is the Spirit and this 'Church of the Spirit', rather than the Church of the bishops, can remit sins (*On Modesty* 21). For Tertullian's views on the Church's sacraments and discipline see chapters 1, 2 and 9.

v) The Last Things

At death all human souls, apart from the martyrs, enter the underworld and experience punishment or comfort until Christ's coming, the resurrection of the body and the last judgement (*On the Soul* 55, 58; *On the Resurrection of the Flesh* 14). Before the final destruction of the world and the heavenly kingdom there will be a millennial kingdom on earth, during which saints will rise sooner or later according to merit (*Against Marcion* 2.24).

Outline Tertullian's teaching on the following:

a) **the Trinity**   b) **Humanity**   c) **Salvation**

d) **the Church**   e) **the Last Things**

Legacy

Tertullian's theological legacy has earned him the title 'father of orthodoxy' since, as we have noted, he invented theological terms that were used in later definitions of the Trinity. However, we have seen how his theology was shaped by Stoicism, particularly in his materialistic conceptions of the being of God and of the soul. But then, when has theology in any period of Church history remained unaffected by current ideologies? Yet, ironically, it could be argued that he was also hostile to the influence of pagan philosophy upon theological thinking (see page 239). He made an important contribution to apologetics, continuing the work of second century defenders of the faith in the face of imperial persecution and pagan hostility. In the area of Christian ethics he appears to have been morally hardline, even before the ethical rigorism of his Montanist period. By comparison with Eastern writers, such as Clement and Origen, he seems to have perceived both theological and moral issues in very black and white terms. His alliance with Montanism, and particularly with its teaching that the Paraclete had introduced a new and stricter Christian morality, proved problematic for later orthodoxy. However, his literary skill and theological influence have ensured for him a continuing readership throughout the history of the Church, which has received him with a mixture of anxiety and admiration.

Assess the contribution of Tertullian to the life and development of the early Church.

CYPRIAN

Life

The next major figure in Carthage after Tertullian is Thascius Caecilius Cyprianus or Cyprian. While Cyprian was clearly influenced by Tertullian, he does not seem to have known him personally. However, Jerome reports that Cyprian daily read his writings, saying, 'Give me the master'. Our information about his life comes from his own writings, especially his letters, from an account of his life written by his deacon Pontius shortly after Cyprian's death (*ANE* excerpt 219) and, less reliably, from some later writers such as Jerome (*On Famous Men*).

It appears that Cyprian was born into a wealthy pagan family in Carthage around AD200. He received a good education and was by profession a lawyer and a teacher of rhetoric. It is probable that a lot of his time was taken up with the administration of his family's estates. Converted under the influence of a presbyter called Caecilius, whose name he adopted, in AD246, he began to share some of his wealth with the needy. Shortly after his conversion he addressed a work to a fellow Christian called Donatus, in which he describes his release from the moral corruption, materialism and injustice of pagan life through the new birth of baptism.

Very soon after, he became a deacon and it was probably during this time that he sold some of his estate to help the poor. After a short time as a presbyter, and only some two years after his conversion, he was appointed bishop of Carthage around AD249. This appears to have been by popular request and was probably due to his good education, his social standing and his kindness to the poor. A minority, including five presbyters, were opposed to his swift promotion to the episcopate. He was not bishop of Carthage very long when the Decian persecution began in January AD250. Cyprian went into hiding and pastored his flock by means of his many letters. Returning around Easter AD251, after over fifteen months, Cyprian had to deal with various problems in the aftermath of the Decian persecution – the treatment of the lapsed, the schisms of Novatus (Carthage) and Novatian (Rome) and the controversy with Stephen, bishop of Rome, over heretical baptism (for the details on Cyprian, the Decian Persecution and its aftermath, see chapter 12). While Cyprian survived the Decian persecution he was tried in AD257 and martyred on 14 September AD258 under Valerian (*ANE* excerpt 258).

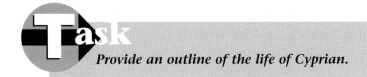

Task

Provide an outline of the life of Cyprian.

Writings

Cyprian was the first bishop in the West to produce Christian literature. The main themes of his writings – some 81 letters and a dozen treatises – were determined largely by the Decian persecution and the controversies that followed in its path. Thus penance, the unity of the Church and baptism are his principal concerns and account for much of his writing. His letters, in particular, provide us with details on the course of the persecution and the debates concerning the lapsed, the Novatianist schism and heretical baptism (see chapter 12, p185; *ANE* excerpts 196-204, 210-218, 221).

Cyprian's most important writing is his *On the Unity of the Catholic Church*, which he read to the bishops at the Council of Carthage, April-June AD251 (*ANE* excerpt 205). The book appears to have been a response to schisms following the Decian persecution, specifically the schism of Novatus and other presbyters at Carthage and more generally the schism of Novatian at Rome. Its importance lies in the fact that it is the first writing dealing with ecclesiology (the doctrine of the Church). In its opening chapters Cyprian states that schism is the work of Satan. The unity of the Church, however, stems from its original foundation on one man, the apostle Peter, though the other apostles were equal in power (ch 4; see pp145-147 and *ANE* excerpt 205: note, for manuscript differences here). The unity of the Church is demonstrated in the unity of its episcopate (bishops), since individual bishops fully share in the oneness of the episcopate. Though the Church is spread far and wide, she is still one like the sun with many rays yet one light, or a tree with many branches yet one rooted trunk, or many streams from one source. None of these (rays, branches, streams) can exist apart from its source. The Church is the one mother from whose womb Christians are born, by whose milk they are fed and by whose breath they live (ch 5). And only within the one Church is salvation possible: "He cannot have God for his father who has not the Church for his mother." If escape was possible outside Noah's ark then it is possible outside the Church (ch 6).

Cyprian goes on to say that the unity of the Church is illustrated by the seamless robe of Christ (ch 7). The peace symbolised by the Spirit in the form of a dove is contrasted with the obstinacy of those who set themselves up as bishops without any authority (chs 8, 9). Schism cannot be justified by Jesus' statement that he is present where two or three gather in his name, since the context gives priority to agreement (ch 12; Matthew 18: 19, 20). Thus the prayers, martyrdoms, prophecies and miracles of schismatics are of no consequence (chs 13-15). The prevalence of schism is a sign that the end is imminent (chs 15, 16). God's judgement is upon those who rebel against his leaders, as in the case of Korah (ch 18; Numbers 16). Schism is a greater sin than lapse from the faith and even confessors (those who remained faithful during persecution) are guilty of it. If Judas the apostle finally fell, so may confessors (chs 19-22).

In *On the Lapsed* Cyprian argues that there is the possibility of repentance and restoration for those who lapsed during the Decian persecution. The period of peace before the persecution had resulted in moral laxity and materialism and thus the persecution was a divine test and judgement of the Church (*ANE* excerpt 194). There is criticism of the swiftness with which many complied with the decree to sacrifice to the gods (*ANE* excerpt 195) rather than fleeing as Christ commanded (Matthew 10: 23). While the lapsed may be restored, their discipline must be determined by the bishops rather than the confessors (though the advice of the latter may be considered).

Other writings of Cyprian include *To Donatus* (see above) and *Testimonies to Quirinius*. The latter book was addressed to a layman who requested guidance on biblical texts that could be used in controversy with the Jews. In three books this writing presents the biblical texts under various headings – book 1 deals with the fulfilment and replacement of the Old Covenant in Christ and the Gentiles; book 2 presents texts relating to Jesus as God, Messiah and Saviour; and book 3 covers Christian morality. The many biblical quotations are an important witness to the text of the Old Latin Bible. *On the Dress of Virgins* is a work which praises the unmarried state, ranking virginity next to martyrdom. Virginity is viewed as having spiritual and moral advantages over the married state, yet some virgins in their dress and social activities were not fulfiling their calling as they should.

On the Lord's Prayer is similar to Tertullian's *On Prayer* and, as well as containing a commentary on the Lord's Prayer, provides practical guidance on prayer such as posture (standing) and timing (the third, sixth and ninth hours). *To Demetrian* is an apologetic work in which Cyprian replies to an opponent of Christianity who made the usual pagan charge that troubles such as war, plague and famine were due to the anger of the gods whom Christians had deserted (*ANE* excerpt 220). Rather, argues Cyprian, these calamities are divine judgements on the pagans because of their immorality and persecution of the Church. *On Mortality* appears to have been written in response to the plague which reached Carthage in AD252 (see *ANE* excerpt 219 for Pontius' description of its effects). Cyprian explains that such afflictions were predicted by Christ and are not to be feared because the Christian possesses immortality. Nor should Christians be surprised that they too are struck down along with pagans, since their faith is being tried.

Cyprian's *On Works and Almsgiving* stresses that faith must be demonstrated by works, that charitable acts cleanse post-baptismal sins and will receive a heavenly reward. The two works *On the Advantage of Patience* and *On Jealousy and Envy* were written in the mid AD250s when tempers were rising in the controversy with Stephen of Rome over heretical baptism. Patience and harmony among the clergy is advocated while jealousy and envy have their source in the Devil, and were forbidden by Christ and the apostles who commended love even for one's enemies. Finally, in his *Exhortation to Martyrdom* Cyprian underlines the seriousness of idolatry, insists that only God is to be worshipped, encourages perseverance in the face of persecution and refers to rewards for those who are faithful.

a. Discuss the main themes of Cyprian's writings.

b. Give details of the origin and content of his most important writing.

c. Provide brief notes on his other works.

Theology

The practical emphasis of Cyprian's theology is due, as with his writing generally, to the issues arising from the Decian persecution. Thus, themes such as the nature of the Church, episcopacy and baptism predominate, rather than more abstract matters such as the relationship between the persons of the Trinity or between Christ's human and divine natures.

i) Humanity

Like Tertullian, Cyprian held that human beings had been morally affected by Adam's sin. Even the newborn, though they have not committed sin, have contracted the disease of the ancient death, since they are born as Adam's descendants. At the infant's baptism it is the sins of another rather than his own that are forgiven (*Letter* 64.5). Thus, both these Latin fathers had a doctrine of original sin.

ii) Salvation

In his death Christ suffered for, indeed bore, human sin and destroyed death (*On the Lapsed* 17; *Letter* 55.22). In his life he was the teacher whose commands must be obeyed (*On Works and Almsgiving* 1, 7, 23). By this obedience immortality is attained (*On the Unity of the Catholic Church* 2). However, as Roger Olson states, Cyprian is significant in the history of Christian theology because of his novel association of the doctrine of salvation and the doctrine of the Church[1].

---

[1] Olson, Roger *The Story of Christian Theology*, IVP: Downers Grove, 1999, p114

iii) The Church

This close association between salvation and the Church is summed up in Cyprian's memorable assertions, 'There is no salvation outside the Church' (*Letter* 73.21) and 'He cannot have God for his father who has not the Church for his mother' (*On the Unity of the Catholic Church* 6). The title of his most famous writing indicates his conviction that the Church is one. This unbreakable unity is seen at the Church's beginning, founded as it was on one man, the apostle Peter. Yet, as the original apostles had equal dignity so the Church's bishops are a college who, individually and collectively, share in the totality of the episcopate. The bishops collectively are the 'glue' which holds the Church together (*Letters* 33.1; 66.8; see earlier outline of Cyprian's *On the Unity of the Catholic Church*).

Only in this one Church, in its ministers and ministries alone, is salvation administered (see chapters 1, 2 and 10 for Cyprian's view of the sacraments and Church government). It is through the Church's baptism alone that sins are forgiven (*Letter* 64.5). Thus, schismatic baptism is no baptism at all (*Letter* 71.1; see earlier details on Cyprian's debate with Stephen). The case is the same with the Eucharist – where the Spirit is not present there can be no valid consecration (*Letter* 65.4). Further, since the bishop is the focus of the Church's unity, Cyprian can write, 'The bishop is in the Church and the Church is in the bishop … if anyone is not with the bishop he is not in the Church' (*Letter* 66.7). Schismatics, such as Novatian, therefore, in breaking away from the Church and its bishops and sacraments are not Christians, regardless of their orthodox beliefs – '… he is not a Christian who is not in Christ's Church' (*Letter* 55.24).

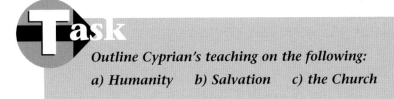

Task

Outline Cyprian's teaching on the following:

a) Humanity   b) Salvation   c) the Church

Legacy

Cyprian was more an ecclesiastical statesman than an insightful theologian. The pastoral urgencies of the Decian persecution and its aftermath made great demands on him, both as an inexperienced bishop and a recent convert. Yet it is his episcopal or pastoral role for which the bishop of Carthage is often remembered.

Theologically, Cyprian's most notable contribution to Christian thought is his teaching on the Church. His *On the Unity of the Catholic Church* was the first main writing on ecclesiology. His emphasis on the unity of the Church and his insistence that the Church with its ministers and ministries alone was the sole means of salvation, contributed to an institutional and hierarchical concept of the Church, as well as a sacramental and sacerdotal view of salvation. Thus, the Montanist Tertullian's Church of the Spirit and Cyprian's Church of the bishops represent contrasting ecclesiologies. Cyprian's understanding of the nature of the Church was shaped, of course, by the challenge posed by schism, following from the Decian persecution. His emphasis on the centrality of the bishops and the exclusive validity of the Church's sacraments continued the tradition of Ignatius (Cyprian has been called 'the Ignatius of the West') and was influential on the medieval Church's self-understanding. His teaching on the sacrificial nature of the Eucharist and the priestly function of the clergy (see chapters 2 and 10) was also influential in the same way.

Varying assessments have been made of Cyprian's ecclesiology. It may be seen as a necessary response to the threat posed by schism in order to prevent the sectarian fragmentation of the Church. However, his emphasis on bishops and the priesthood could be regarded as a clericalism which undermines the New Testament concept of the priesthood of all believers and the charismatic ministry of the laity. Coupled with this, the notion of the Christian minister as a priest offering the sacrifice of the Eucharist mediatorially on behalf of the laity does not sit easily with New Testament teaching on the sole mediation of Christ and the finality of his sacrifice on the cross.

Practice Essay Titles

1. Outline the life of Tertullian and provide a brief account of his writings. (30)

Evaluate the claim that Tertullian was the 'father of orthodoxy'. (15)

2. Summarise your knowledge and understanding of the career and writings of Cyprian. (30)

Assess his contribution to the development of the doctrine of the Church. (15)

Glossary

Abbot	monastic leader/father.
Allegorical	non-literal, metaphorical.
Anamnesis	commemoration.
Anchorites	another term for eremitic monks.
Apocalyptic	ideas and language similar to the book of Revelation (the Apocalypse) and often relating to the end of the world.
Apocryphal writings	writings of doubtful authorship or authority.
Apology	a book defending the Christian faith.
Apostolic/ episcopal succession	the idea that bishops are successors of the original apostles.
Arianism	teaching of Arius that the Son of God is not fully God nor eternal (after fourth century presbyter, Arius).
Asceticism	severe self-discipline and abstinence.
Bishop	a senior church leader.
Canon	rule, standard, list of authoritative writings eg the New Testament canon.
Catechumenate	the period of preparation for baptism.
Catechumens	those being prepared for baptism (related terms include catechesis, catehetical, catechumenate).
Catholic	universal, worldwide, distinct from schismatics and heretics.
Celibacy	the unmarried state.
Cenobites	communal monks.
Charismatic	relating to the gifts of the Spirit exercised by various church members.
Christology	the study of the person and work of Christ, particularly the former.
Deacon	a church official below the rank of presbyter; a 'servant' or assistant.
Docetism, docetic	the teaching that Jesus only seemed to be human and physical but was not in reality.
Dualism	two opposing powers or principles eg: darkness and light, good and evil.
Ecclesiology	teaching concerning the Church.
Ecumenical	worldwide, universal.
Egalitarianism	equality.
Episcopal	relating to bishops.
Eremites	solitary monks.
Eschatology	the last things, such as the return of Christ.
Essenes	Jewish Monks who lived near the Dead Sea before and during the beginning of Christianity.
Excommunication	removal from membership of the Church.
Exorcism	the expulsion of Satan or evil spirits.
Fathers	early Church writers and leaders.
Gentiles	non-Jews.

Hagiography	writing concerning the lives and legends of saints (holy people).
Hellenism, Hellenistic	Greek culture and influence.
Heresy, heretic	beliefs considered erroneous by the Church; a person who holds such beliefs.
Incarnation	the Son of God becoming flesh/human as Jesus Christ.
Judaizers	Christians who held that Jewish laws were still in force.
Kerygma	preaching, proclamation, the early Christian message.
Laity, lay	church members not holding office.
Liturgy	a set form of public worship.
Logos	the Word; the Son of God before his incarnation.
Modalism	denial that the Father, the Son and the Spirit are distinct persons, but rather three temporary modes of the one God; also known as 'modalistic monarchianism'.
Monarchical episcopacy/ monepiscopacy	government of one church by one bishop, first found in Ignatius' writings.
Monotheism	belief in the existence of one God.
Ordination	appointment to the Christian ministry.
Orthodoxy	correct belief, teaching of the Church.
Panegyric	extravagant praise in formal speech or writing.
Papacy, papal	relating to the office of the bishop of Rome, the Pope.
Paraclete	a term (parakletos) in John's Gospel for the Holy Spirit.
Passible	capable of or subject to suffering.
Polemic, polemical	contesting, disputing, opposing.
Polytheism	belief in the existence of many gods.
Presbyter	a church leader below the rank of bishop, also called an elder or priest.
Proselyte	a Gentile convert to Judaism.
Regeneration	being born again (rebirth) of the Holy Spirit.
Rite	religious ceremony or observance.
Sabellianism	denial of a clear distinction between the Father and the Son (after the early third century teacher, Sabellius).
Sacerdotal	priestly.
Sacrament	a Christian ceremony or rite eg: baptism, the Eucharist.
Schism, schismatic	breaking away from the Church.
See	an area of episcopal oversight.
Soothsayer	a person who foretells the future.
Syncretism	a mixture of beliefs from a variety of sources.
Synod	a council of bishops, sometimes with other clergy and also lay people.
Theology	religious teaching.
Trinity	one God in three persons: the Father, the Son and the Holy Spirit.
Typology	comparisons between people, events and institutions of the Old and the New Testaments.

Index

255